Mark Cullen's
Ontario Gardening

Also by Mark Cullen

The New Greener Thumb
Canadian Garden Design
The All Seasons Gardener
Real Dirt

Mark Cullen's
Ontario Gardening

How to get the most from your garden with
Canada's bestselling gardening expert

Mark Cullen

PENGUIN
CANADA

PENGUIN CANADA

Published by the Penguin Group

Penguin Books, a division of Pearson Canada, 10 Alcorn Avenue, Toronto, Ontario, Canada M4V 3B2

Penguin Books Ltd, 80 Strand, London WC2R 0RL, England

Penguin Putnam Inc., 375 Hudson Street, New York, New York 10014, U.S.A.

Penguin Books Australia Ltd, 250 Camberwell Road, Camberwell, Victoria 3124, Australia

Penguin Books India (P) Ltd, 11, Community Centre, Panchsheel Park, New Delhi – 110 017, India

Penguin Books (NZ) Ltd, cnr Rosedale and Airborne Roads, Albany, Auckland 1310, New Zealand

Penguin Books (South Africa) (Pty) Ltd, 24 Sturdee Avenue, Rosebank 2196, South Africa

Penguin Books Ltd, Registered Offices: 80 Strand, London WC2R 0RL, England

First published 2002

10 9 8 7 6 5 4 3 2 1

Manufactured in Canada.

NATIONAL LIBRARY OF CANADA CATALOGUING IN PUBLICATION DATA

Cullen, Mark, 1956–
    Mark Cullen's Ontario gardening / Mark Cullen.

ISBN 0-14-029700-6

    1. Gardening—Ontario. I. Title.

SB453.3.C2C845 2002   635.9'09713   C2002-901804-8

Visit Penguin Books' website at **www.penguin.ca**

To the good people at S.H.A.R.E. Agricultural Foundation

This Ontario-based, volunteer-driven organization provides a "hand up, not a handout" to marginalized farmers in Central and South America. S.H.A.R.E. makes a measurable difference to a lot of people; they can stretch a buck further than any organization I know, and they have fun doing it. Visit S.H.A.R.E. at www.shareagfoundation.org.

All of the royalties from the sale of this book are being donated to S.H.A.R.E.

Acknowledgements

With the greatest of thanks to a whole bunch of fine contributors:

Cynthia Good at Penguin Books, for opening my eyes to the wonderful Ontario gardens right at my feet.

Meg Masters, for her creative and thorough approach to writing and editing—I couldn't have done it without you!

Andrew Leyerle, for his beautiful photography, and Jack McMaster, for his wonderful illustrations.

Wendy Thomas, for her thoughtful and thorough editing of the manuscript.

Paula Barata, Janice Brett, Mary Opper, Catherine Dorton and Diane Turbide at Penguin Books, for guiding the book through the process and letting no detail go unchecked.

Brant Cowie, Dave Murphy, Leanne O'Brien, Barb Neri, Beth Johnston, Miriam Semple, Heather Brunton, Brian Taft, Donna Guilfoyle and Dana Lloyd at ArtPlus Group, for their terrific book design and production.

Dave Cornwell, my "horticultural editor" not just on this book, but also on CFRB Radio, and Robb Duncan, for assistance in putting the photographs together.

Mary, my wife, for her inspiration and patience, and the kids—Lynn, Heather, Emma and Ben—because they really do make our garden feel like home.

Contents

Introduction

Ontario. This is where I live. It's where my family has gardened for five generations, and it's where I spend most of my time travelling from garden to garden, shooting my TV show with my good friends at Home and Garden Television Canada (HGTV).

To a large extent, my days spent in Ontario gardens with HGTV have provided me with the inspiration and knowledge that have been poured into this book. Each year for the last four years I have visited at least 20 residential gardens for a minimum of one full day each. While there, I have had the time to explore just about every gardening idea, meet with the passionate gardening types who nurture these creations and talk about their gardens on air. It's great work, if you can call it that!

To title a gardening book "Ontario Gardening," however, is immediately to present yourself with a conundrum. Ontario is such a vast geographic expanse that what sounds like a tightly focused gardening approach instead needs to be written for gardeners from the tundra along the shores of James Bay to the balmy fertile land that hugs Lake Erie.

Growing conditions in Thunder Bay are closer to those in Winnipeg than those in Windsor. And certainly no book written with St. Catharines in mind is going to be particularly helpful to someone in Cochrane. What I have done, in light of those challenges, is combine basic information that can be of use to all gardeners, in this province as well as others, with information and ideas that touch on issues that are important to Ontario. I have included a chapter on northern gardening, which means in zones 3 and 4 rather than those usually referred to (especially in American gardening books) as "northern." I've included a chapter on native plants that includes only plants native to this province. And since this is a province that has a profound attachment to "the cottage" and "the lake," I have included some gardening ideas you can take up to your summer retreat.

While writing this book, I had to spend some time thinking about "gardening in Ontario." What occurred to me was that while the conditions in the province vary immensely, Ontario residents do have a shared past when it comes to gardening.

Since Canada is a young country, its gardening history is relatively short. But Ontario, covering as it does the former colony of Upper Canada and being home to much of the colony's early wealth, has more horticultural history than some regions of Canada. In the last few decades, a number of gardening historians have provided us with intriguing studies of this gardening past. Edwinna von Baeyer's *Rhetoric and Roses*, Eileen Woodhead's *Early Canadian Gardening: An 1827 Nursery Catalogue*, and most recently, Carol Martin's *A History of Canadian Gardening* all provide glimpses into Canada's early gardens.

As you might expect, early settlers did not have a lot of time for ornamental gardening, but most were devoted to kitchen gardens and larger-scale vegetable and fruit production for their own use and for the market. But by 1827 a wide variety of plant material was available (as William Custead's Toronto nursery catalogue of 1827 tells us), much of it imported from south of the border. Most of this would have been sold to the middle class or well-to-do, but the number of fruit trees and vegetables available suggests that those who gardened combined pleasure and food production.

By Victorian times, the practice of keeping ornamental gardening and vegetable gardening thoroughly separate had gained hold, and this standard was echoed in the new country of Canada. This rather formal approach set the stage for the civic improvement movement of the early century—beautification of home and public spaces was thought to lead to moral improvement and the discouragement of vice, sloth and spiritual decay. Ontario was the home of numerous civic improvement committees that initiated gardening projects in public places such as parks and schools, as well as homes. These beautification projects were meant to inspire civic-mindedness and good citizenship in those who lived among the gardens, and the actual physical labour of gardening (which was for a time part of the curriculum in many Ontario schools) was thought to combat a host of bad habits and antisocial behaviour. Gardening, then, was seen as intimately involved in the public good—it was a community effort and a social obligation.

The sentiments of the civic beautification movement may sound quaint, but I think they are not completely outdated. The rise in popularity of gardening in this province suggests that we appreciate the intangible benefits of working with a living canvas. We perhaps no longer feel that working in a garden, or having the benefit of green spaces around our homes and schools, will deter us from a life of crime or sloth (as the beautification movement wanted us to believe), but we understand the psychological benefits—the stress reduction and restorative gifts that come from bringing new life into the landscape. Long-term hospitals, in fact, often offer in-patient gardening programs, and many people see their gardens as the perfect place to work off some steam and leave the troubles of the day behind. In fact, "horticultural therapy" is immensely popular today.

My family has been part of this gardening renaissance for several generations. My father, Len Cullen, bought John Weall's landscape contracting business in north Toronto in 1947 for $2,200, money he saved from his paper route. Since then, the business has blossomed into an enterprise that is a source of pride for all of us connected to Weall & Cullen Nurseries Limited. Each year we provide service to over 300,000 Ontario gardeners—and that is a lot of gardening advice!

My aim in writing this book is to provide the kind of information that is both inspiring and useful at the most practical level. I hope you are stimulated by the contents of this book and that, through your gardening experience, you will discover the child within.

Keep your knees dirty,

Mark

PART I

The Ornamental Garden

In Sun and Shade

When it comes to sunshine, Ontario is a place of moderation—we don't have so many sun-filled days that our land is continually parched nor so few that our springs and summers are damp and overcast. But our province is so big that our attitudes to sun and shade may be quite different. For those in southern Ontario, "shade" can be quite a luxury during the heat of the summer; for those in northern Ontario, where the summers are shorter and the days cooler, shade in a backyard or garden may be most unwelcome. But for all of us who garden, the amount of sunshine that lingers over our property in any given day deserves our consideration when we plan our gardens.

Shade

Shopping for a new home recently, one of my friends was struck by how often vendors and real estate agents who found out she liked to garden used a house's "south-facing backyard" as a selling point. My friend lives in Toronto and was moving from a home with a shady, north-facing garden. Despite the supposed disadvantages of such a site, she had grown to love her cool green haven, especially during the blistering hot summers. The shade of her garden was filled with a lovely assortment of shrubs, flowers and foliage, and she could be outside comfortably reading in a chair or deadheading her flowers even in the heat of the mid-afternoon. She knows what many shade gardeners know—there are advantages to shade over full sun, despite some people's prejudices about it.

The majority of weeds favour full sun, so shade gardens often have fewer problems with noxious invaders. Many pests also avoid the shade. Without the heat of full sun, gardens lose less moisture to evaporation so their watering needs are reduced; likewise, slower rates of photosynthesis caused by the absence of sun mean that plants don't deplete soil nutrients as quickly—fertilizing can be reduced or even eliminated. And while some people assume that their plant choices are limited for a shade garden, experienced shade gardeners will tell you that there are all sorts of fabulous shade plants on the market. And native plants enthusiasts will point out that the shade garden is the perfect setting for a native woodlands garden.

Shade also protects you and your family from both the heat and the harmful UV radiation of the sun. In fact, the Weall & Cullen landscape designers have noticed more and more people asking for designs that provide shade in the garden by including structures such as pergolas.

Types of shade

It is important to keep in mind that "shade" is a relative term. It is different at different times of the day. Generally, afternoon shade is better for plants than morning shade. It provides a respite from the harshest, hottest sun and may protect plants rather than stress them. Conversely, a spot that is shady in the morning remains cool after the drop in temperature at night, and then is exposed to sun in the afternoon when it is most intense. For this reason the west side of a brick or stone wall can be a difficult place to grow plants. Areas of shade on the east side of fences or walls are more amenable to shade-loving plants. If the wall is stone or brick, however, it will retain the morning heat and this area of garden will stay warm or even hot.

Shade also changes according to what is providing the shade—buildings and walls generally cast the deepest shade. Evergreen trees provide shade year-round, even in the early spring when many shade-lovers benefit from the mild rays of the spring sun. Deciduous trees, however, allow lots of sunlight through their bare branches in the early spring and usually give filtered or dappled shade in the summer. Some trees with small open leaves and branches allow quite a lot of light through. Trees with dense canopies of leaves may, however, provide too much shade to plant under. And trees with shallow roots that lie close to the surface will consume much of the water and nutrient content of surrounding soil, creating dry planting conditions. (Maples have a notorious reputation for both their dense canopies and shallow roots.)

You may find definitions of the different types of shade contradictory and a bit baffling. Shade is usually divided into a number of categories, with the deepest shade referred to as dense or deep shade. After that there is a host of shade descriptions: dappled, light, open, semi, thin, partial, medium, half, full! Here is how I like to think of degrees of shade:

Partial shade: Partial shade generally refers to shade that does not last all day—it is found in locations that receive full sun for three to six hours a day. This is the easiest form of shade to work with, and in very warm areas of Ontario, having partial shade in the mid to late afternoon is a great benefit to many sun-loving plants that would be stressed by high temperatures and the intense sun of midday. Trees, vines, fences and other garden structures may also produce the equivalent of partial shade, as long as the shade that is cast is not total (there are plenty of open spots where the sun shines through) or lasts for the whole day.

Dappled shade: Sometimes referred to as open or light shade, dappled shade is created by the canopy of deciduous tree branches. There can be some light penetrating the leaves, but it is generally cool and dense during the summer. Areas with dappled shade may receive an hour or two of full sun a day, but when they are in shade there is still enough ambient light to support many types of plants. Because the shade is created by trees, however, it does not exist in the late fall, winter or early spring. It is the sort of shade that makes a lovely woodland garden *if* the soil is moist. Buildings that are some distance away and are not creating dense shade may also create some light shade, which has the same effect as dappled shade. This shade may change over the course of the year, depending on the angle of the sun.

Full shade: This type of shade describes an area that receives no direct sunlight, only diffuse light. Despite being in shadow for the full day there is enough reflected light for shade-tolerant plants to grow. You might find this type of shade on the north side of a wall or under very densely leaved trees, like mature maples and oaks.

Dense shade: Sometimes called deep or heavy shade, this is the most challenging shade for a gardener. It describes an area that receives very little or no light year-round. It is created by mature evergreen trees or by nearby buildings or is found at the floor of a mature woodland. Tall buildings can create a great expanse of dense shade, particularly on their north sides. This shade is also generally very dry as the buildings and/or the dense trees prevent rainfall from reaching the soil underneath. Very little can be grown in these conditions.

If you have to have a garden or areas of a garden in shade, the following ideas will make the most of your gardening efforts.

Strategies for the shade garden

❀ Because there are both annuals and perennials that are shade-lovers, you'll get the greatest variety of bloom time, colour and shape if you incorporate both into your garden design. Perennials and bulbs are particularly useful for early spring colour and mid-season foliage. Annuals can provide a lively splash of colour for the rest of the season.

❀ Many perennials that do well in the shade are low-growing types that have wonderful leaf colours and shapes but less spectacular flowers. They can be great for groundcovers and borders in the shade. Use groundcovers where grass is difficult to grow.

❀ Green is the dominant colour in a shade garden. Choose plants with a variety of leaf colours, shapes, sizes, heights and textures to add interest to the garden.

❀ Use light-coloured flowers as these are easier to see and make a greater impact in a shady garden than dark colours like red, purple or deep blue. White is especially effective in deeply shaded gardens where you are trying to attract attention.

❀ Glossy-leaved plants have more impact than matte or fuzzy leaves in the shade.

❀ Red-leaved plants contrast nicely with the green-leaved ones in shade: try coral bells 'Chocolate Ruffles' (*Heuchera* 'Coral Bells'), some of the rosy varieties of coleus, rose-coloured impatiens or *Ligularia* (leopard plant).

❀ Plant fewer varieties of flowers in greater numbers to create large swaths of colour in the shady garden. Subtle variations of colour and individual flowers tend to get lost in the shade.

❀ If the shade is created by trees, remember that their hungry, thirsty roots are depleting the soil of nutrients and drying it out. Supplemental fertilizing and watering is a good idea. Add organic matter annually to build up a layer of rich, humusy soil on top of tree roots. Remember that the vast majority of a tree's roots are in the top 1.2 m (4 feet) of soil, which means that your plants will be struggling to put down their own tender roots through a mass of fibrous tree roots.

❀ Shade reduces evaporation caused by sun and heat, and the resulting dampness (not to mention the more consistent air temperatures produced by shade) can lead to disease such as mould, mildew and rot. To avoid this, place plants a little farther apart in the shade to aid air circulation and always remove dead foliage as soon as you see it. Also keep an eye on organic mulches. If you suspect mould or fungus is growing in the mulch, turn the mulch over to allow the damper parts to dry out, or remove mulch altogether for a time (this may be a good idea, for example, during periods of continued precipitation).

❀ Lighten heavy soil with sharp sand or Profile (see p. 142) to improve drainage—since shady gardens don't experience as much evaporation, the ground can be boggy. About 10 kg per 1.1 square m (22 pounds per square foot) dug down 25 cm (10 inches) will quickly make a huge improvement.

❀ In dense shade, your best bet is not to try the impossible—devote this space to hard furnishings (benches, outdoor sculpture) and cover the ground with attractive mulches, paving stones or pebbles. If you want to have some colour here, use mobile containers with plants that can be moved from the dense shade to a sunny spot of the garden for at least several hours each day.

❀ Use plants that will naturalize in the setting (generally plants that are vigorous growers and sometimes aggressive). (See Native Plants and the Ontario Naturalized Garden, p.41.) Native plants that self-seed and travel will naturally find their optimum growing conditions in your garden.

- Avoid plants with fleshy, grey-green leaves—they tend to like full sun and dryness.

- White fences or walls reflect light. Consider painting walls, fences and hard furnishings in light colours. If you are using paving stones, bricks, gravel or chipped stones for paths, select those lightest in colour.

- Create some sunny spots or change full shade into dappled shade where possible. If you have large trees that cast full shade, hire an arborist or landscaping company to thin the trees so that a little light shines through the branches.

- Keep in mind that the nature of shade in your garden may change in time as trees in the area mature.

- Shade can be seasonal as the angle of sun changes over the year and the foliage develops on trees and other tall plants. If your garden is sunny in spring and shady in summer, plant plenty of spring-blossoming bulbs like daffodils, narcissus, tulips and hyacinth (crocuses do not work so well). Also consider native woodland plants and other spring-flowering perennials. If planted with shade-lovers like hostas, ferns, astilbes and lobelia, the latter will take over in summer and hide dying foliage of bulbs or other spent flowers.

- The farther north you go, the more likely that your sun-loving plants will not be able to tolerate shade, even the lightest kind. Take advantage of stone or brick walls that retain heat and plan your beds for areas of the garden that have the lightest shade.

- Since dry shade is generally more difficult to grow in than moist shade, look for shade- and drought-tolerant plants if faced with these conditions. You may also want to employ some sort of in-ground watering system, or use soaker and weeping hoses covered with mulch to provide frequent, adequate moisture. But if you opt for the in-ground watering system, keep the switch on "manual" and water only as required.

Lawns and shade

Many books and articles on shade gardening ignore the topic of lawns and shade; others recommend forgoing a lawn if you have a shade garden. I am an unapologetic fan of the lawn—I like the look of the even green carpet and I find it a wonderful transition between flower beds, trees and other garden elements. If you are a lawn fan too, by all means try establishing a shade lawn. But take into account the challenges a lawn presents for the shade gardener.

Turf grass does not enjoy shade. If you want a lawn, select grass seed mixes specifically recommended for shade. Creeping red fescues, chewings fescues, sheep fescues and hard fescues (there are a number of cultivars of each) are useful grasses for full or dense shade, but chewings fescue doesn't tolerate foot traffic well. Perennial ryegrass cultivars and tall fescues also have some shade tolerance. A few shade-tolerant cultivars of Kentucky bluegrass are now available. The key to finding an attractive and truly shade-tolerant grass seed is to buy a premium mix from a reputable garden centre—bargain seed mixes are likely to disappoint when put up against the challenges of shade. Remember, the ultimate quality of your lawn is determined by the quality of the seed, above all else.

Shade lawns need TLC—they have a more difficult time recovering from or tolerating stress than turf in full sun. Avoid heavy foot traffic on shade grass if possible and pay special attention to the shade lawn's watering, mowing and fertilizing needs. Because evaporation in the shade is reduced, and moulds and fungus flourish in the absence of sun, water your shade lawn as infrequently as possible, but water deeply (see Watering and Xeriscaping, p. 165 for more on watering). You may also need to treat the lawn periodically with organic sulphur if you notice moulds and fungus. When mowing, do not cut the grass shorter than 7.5 cm (3 inches), and avoid cutting more than one-third of the blade length, to encourage deep root development and to reduce stress. (A mulching mower can be helpful too—it produces a very thin layer of shredded grass blades that are a natural source of nitrogen and that protect grass roots from the drying effects of air movement and any sun that may reach your lawn.) Be cautious when fertilizing your shade lawn—because of reduced photosynthesis the grass needs less nitrogen than grass in full sun. Use a good-quality, slow-release nitrogen fertilizer for best results. But don't neglect the fertilizing—low soil fertility will lead to a weakened lawn, especially in the shade. Your lawn will benefit most from *late* fall fertilizing, when the tree roots are no longer competing for moisture and nutrients, and the absence of leaves means more sun is getting to the grass.

Shade lawns are often susceptible to broadleaf, shade-loving weeds and to moss. If you have been caring for the lawn as described above and you continue to experience these problems, there may simply be too little light for successful grass growing. Pruning trees and tall bushes may help to get more light to the grass. Moss can be discouraged by aerating the lawn (tools to do this can be rented from equipment rental companies and from some garden centres) and by improving drainage over the site (this can be a huge task, however). While adding limestone to the soil is sometimes recommended to combat moss, check your soil's pH before going this route. If your soil already has a high pH, adding limestone will not help and may very well hurt your lawn.

Sow lawn seed in the fall for hardier shade grass by next summer. Also make sure that fall leaves are promptly removed from the lawn so they don't impede growth of new grass.

If, however, you have full or dense shade, or have had no success with your shade lawn after following all the recommendations above, you may want to forgo grass altogether. Mulches, both organic and crushed stone, make nice coverings in dense shade. Shade-loving groundcovers like pachysandra, periwinkle, lamium and euonymus are good choices for full or partial shade.

SHADE ANNUALS

Begonias, tuberous and fibrous (*Begonia*)
Browallia (*Browallia speciosa*)
Caladium (*Caladium*)
Calla lily (*Zantedeschia*)
Coleus (*Coleus* × *hybridus*)
Dusty miller (*Senecio cineraria*)
Elephant's ear (*Colocasia esculenta*)
Forget-me-not (*Myosotis sylvatica*)
Fuchsia (*Fuchsia*)
Impatiens (*Impatiens*)
Lobelia, trailing varieties only (*Lobelia*)
Plectranthus (*Plectranthus*)
Wishbone flower (*Torenia fournieri*)

SHADE PERENNIALS FOR AVERAGE TO MOIST SITES

Anemone (*Anemone*)
Astilbe (*Astilbe*)
Bleeding heart (*Dicentra*)
Bloodroot (*Sanguinaria canadensis*)~
Bluebells (*Mertensia*)
Bottlebrush grass (*Hystrix patula*)
Canadian wild ginger (*Asarum canadense*)~
Climbing hydrangea (*Hydrangea petiolaris*)
Coral bell (*Heuchera*)
Creeping Jenny (*Lysimachia nummularia*)
Dead nettle (*Lamium*)
Epimedium (*Epimedium*)
False Solomon's seal (*Smilacina racemosa*)~
Fern—many varieties
Foamflower (*Tiarella cordifolia*)
Foxglove beardtongue (*Penstemon digitalis*)~
Gentian (*Gentiana*)
Globeflower (*Trollius*)
Hellebore (*Helleborus*)
Hosta or plaintain lily (*Hosta*)
Jack-in-the-pulpit (*Arisaema triphyllum*)~
Jacob's ladder (*Polemonium*)
Japanese spurge (*Pachysandra*)
Lady's mantle (*Alchemilla*) (can be invasive)
Meadowsweet (*Filipendula*)
Monkshood (*Aconitum*)
Ostrich fern (*Matteuccia*)
Sharp-lobed hepatica (*Hepatica acutiloba*)~
Snakeroot (*Cimicifuga racemosa*)~
Solomon's seal (*Polygonatum*)~
Sweet woodruff (*Galium odoratum*)
Trout lily (*Erythronium americanum*)~
Virginia creeper (*Parthenocissus vitacea*)~
Virgin's bower (*Clematis virginiana*)~
Wild creeping phlox (*Phlox stolonifera*)~
Wood poppy (*Stylophorum diphyllum*)~
Wood sorrel (*Oxalis oregana*)
Yellow archangel (*Lamiastrum*)

SHADE PERENNIALS FOR AVERAGE TO DRY SITES

Bottlebrush grass (*Hystrix patula*)
Dead nettle (*Lamium*)
False Solomon's seal (*Smilacina racemosa*) ~
Foxglove beardtongue (*Penstemon digitalis*) ~
Goatsbeard (*Tragopogon*)
Goutweed (*Aegopodium*)
Lily of the valley (*Convallaria*)
Lungwort (*Pulmonaria*)
Sharp-lobed hepatica (*Hepatica acutiloba*) ~
Shootingstar (*Dodecatheon*)

Silver lace vine (*Polygonum aubertii*)
Solomon's seal (*Polygonatum*) ~
Trout lily (*Erythronium americanum*) ~
Virginia creeper (*Parthenocissus vitacea*) ~
Virgin's bower (*Clematis virginiana*) ~
Wild columbine (*Aquilegia canadensis*) ~
Wild geranium (*Geranium maculatum*)
Wild lupine (*Lupinus perennis*) ~
Zig zag goldenrod (*Solidago flexicaulis*)

TREES AND SHRUBS THAT TOLERATE SHADE

Birch (*Betula*)
Dwarf deutzia (*Deutzia gracilis*)
Euonymus (*Euonymus*)
Hydrangea (*Hydrangea*)

Pea shrub (*Caragana*)
Serviceberry (*Amelanchier*)
Sugar maple (*Acer saccharum*)
Weeping mulberry (*Morus alba pendula*)

VEGETABLES AND HERBS FOR SHADE
Most of these will do nicely in partial shade.

Arugula	Coriander	Lovage	Spinach
Borage	Cress	Mint	Tarragon
Cabbage	Endive	Parsley	Thyme
Chervil	Garlic chives	Rhubarb	
Chives	Leaf lettuce	Sorrel	

~ a plant native to Ontario

Sunny gardens

Most gardeners feel blessed if they have a south-facing garden filled with day-long sun. And indeed, with these conditions you have the greatest number of plants to choose from and optimum growing conditions for many flowering plants, trees and shrubs. Rock gardens, meadow gardens and vegetable gardens also have the greatest success in sunny sites. Keep in mind, however, that full sun makes certain demands of the gardener. Many plants love the sun, but so do weeds. Plant densely to make it tough for weeds to establish themselves. Full sun also causes a great deal of moisture loss by the plants and by the soil. You should pay special attention to the watering methods you employ in a full-sun garden and opt for those that are most efficient and effective in their distribution. Consider using soaker and weeping hoses or installing in-ground watering systems to provide consistent and adequate moisture and to conserve water. Mulching with fine bark mulch is especially useful in the full-sun garden;

it's my favourite—preferred!—method of retaining valuable moisture, and it discourages sun-loving weeds.

When adding new plantings or making garden plans for your sunny garden, remember that the amount of sun your garden receives may change over time as plants mature. That lovely little silver birch might make a nice focal point to your backyard now, but will it be casting shade over the flower beds in five years? Many gardeners I know have admitted to inadvertently turning a sunny garden into a shady one. One person told me about planting a silver lace vine at the base of a chain link fence in the hopes that it would cover the half of the fence that was not hidden by the tall flowers in the bottom portion of her garden. It did just that and in the first year she was delighted by the result. The next year this vigorous grower had made its way, despite being aggressively pruned, to the bottom half of the fence. By the third summer, the plant that she and her neighbours had dubbed "the Stephen King vine" had thickly overgrown the whole fence, choking out all the morning light for the flower beds and seriously hampering the growth of the purple coneflowers, the obedient plants and black-eyed Susans. By the fourth year, the gardener was forced to dig it out to save her sun-lovers. (Sometimes the only practical solution to this kind of problem is to move house and get some good garden design advice next time!)

Also keep in mind that "full sun" may create quite different conditions depending on where you are in Ontario. On the one hand, some gardeners from northern Ontario have told me that because of their relatively cool summer days they have had success in full-sun gardens with plants recommended for partial shade. On the other hand, the full sun and the heat of some southern Ontario sites (particularly if they are some distance away from the moderating effects of the Great Lakes) can stress even sun-loving plants. In these conditions, many gardeners try to introduce a little afternoon shade to their gardens.

Creating shade

Before building or planting to create shade, determine where your tree, plants or structures must be located to provide shade in the afternoon. This is the most useful time of day to have your garden or part of your site in the shade. It provides a cool spot for both you and your plants during the hottest part of the summer day and it prevents your plants from having to endure the transition from a cool morning in the shade to a blazing afternoon in the full sun.

Awnings and umbrellas are sometimes used for shade, but increasingly people are opting for arbours and pergolas that can be planted with vines and shrubs such as euonymus or roses that throw up long flexible branches you can weave through the supports to create a green, living shelter. Shade trees are also a good choice and over time can cast a much bigger area into dappled or partial shade. Shade trees can also be positioned to keep houses, porches and patios cool in the summer.

Here are a few of my favourite shade trees

Columnar maple (*Acer platanoides* 'Columnare')
Green ash (*Fraxinus pennsylvanica*)
Japanese lilac 'Ivory Silk' (*Syringa reticulata* 'Ivory Silk')
Little-leaf linden (*Tilia cordata*)
Mountain ash (*Sorbus*)
Norway maple 'Crimson King' (*Acer platanoides* 'Crimson King')
Pin oak (*Quercus palustris*)
Pyramid English oak (*Quercus robur* 'Fastigiata')
Shademaster honey locust (*Gleditsia triacanthos* 'Shademaster')
Sunburst honey locust (*Gleditsia triacanthos* 'Sunburst')
White or canoe birch (*Betula papyrifera*)

Vines and climbing shrubs that will create shade (and can withstand heat and full sun)

Clematis (*Clematis*)
Climbing roses (*Rosa* spp.)
Honeysuckle (*Lonicera*)
Hops (*Humulus lupulus*)

BLOOM TIME
Whether working in sun or shade, when designing and planting your garden always take into account when those lovely flowers are going to bloom. A careful design can not only guarantee a garden full of blooms all summer but can also create a wonderfully fluid, ever-changing palette of colours in the landscape.

Bloom time—perennials

SUN	SHADE
Spring blooming	
Creeping phlox (*Phlox subulata*)	Barrenwort (*Epimedium grandiflorum*)
Cushion spurge (*Euphorbia polychroma*)	Bleeding heart (*Dicentra spectabilis*)
Daffodils and tulips (in fact, look over the entire spring-flowering bulbs selection in fall at your garden centre)	Blue corydalis (*Corydalis flexuosa*)
	Columbine (*Aquilegia*)
	Foamflower (*Tiarella cordifolia*)
False indigo (*Baptisia australis*)	Hellebore (*Helleborus orientalis*)
Globeflower (*Trollius* × *cultorum*)	Lungwort (*Pulmonaria* hybrids)
Heartleaf bergenia (*Bergenia cordifolia*)	Primrose (*Primula*)
Leopard's bane (*Doronicum caucasicum*)	Sweet violet (*Viola odorata*)
Marsh marigold (*Caltha palustris*)	Sweet woodruff (*Galium odoratum*)
Purple rock cress (*Aubrieta*)	Trillium (*Trillium*)
	Wood anemone (*Anemone nemorosa*)
Early summer blooming	
Balloon flower (*Platycodon grandiflorum*)	Coral bells (*Heuchera*)
Bee balm (*Monarda didyma*)	Foxglove (*Digitalis purpurea*)
Bellflower (*Campanula*)	Lady's mantle (*Alchemilla mollis*)
Butterfly flower (*Asclepias tuberosa*)	Woodland phlox (*Phlox divaricata*)
Common peony (*Paeonia lactiflora* hybrids)	
Cranesbill geranium (*Geranium*)	
Delphinium (*Delphinium* × *elatum*)	
Dwarf crested iris (*Iris cristata*)	
Lupine (*Lupinus* 'Russell Hybrid')	
Oriental poppy (*Papaver orientale*)	
Pinks (*Dianthus*)	
Siberian iris (*Iris sibirica*)	
Threadleaf coreopsis (*Coreopsis verticillata*)	
Variegated iris (*Iris pallida* 'Variegata')	
Midsummer blooming	
Blanket flower (*Gaillardia* × *grandiflora*)	Astilbe (*Astilbe* × *arendsii* hybrids)
Blazing star (*Liatris spicata*)	Goatsbeard (*Aruncus dioicus*)
Daylily (*Hemerocallis*)	Hosta (*Hosta*)
Globe thistle (*Echinops ritro*)	Japanese painted fern (*Athyrium niponicum*)
Hollyhock (*Alcea rosea*)	Lady fern (*Athyrium filix-femina*)
Joe Pye weed (*Eupatorium maculatum*) (formerly *Eupatorium purpureum*)	Maidenhair fern (*Adiantum pedatum*)
Queen-of-the-prairie (*Filipendula ulmaria*)	
Red valerian (*Centranthus ruber*)	
Sea holly (*Eryngium amethystinum*)	
Speedwell (*Veronica* hybrids)	
Tree mallow (*Lavatera thuringiaca*)	
Yarrow (*Achillea*)	

SUN	SHADE

Later summer/early fall blooming

Autumn Joy stonecrop (*Sedum* 'Autumn Joy')	Bigleaf golden ray (*Ligularia dentata*)
Black-eyed Susan (*Rudbeckia fulgida*)	Bugbane (*Cimicifuga racemosa*)
Blue star (*Amsonia tabernaemontana*)	Cardinal flower (*Lobelia cardinalis*)
Boltonia (*Boltonia asteroides*)	Japanese anemone (*Anemone* × *hybrida*)
False sunflower (*Heliopsis helianthoides scabra*)	Monkshood (*Aconitum*)
Goldenrod (*Solidago*)	Toad lily (*Tricyrtis hirta*)
Hardy aster (*Aster*)	
Helen's flower (*Helenium autumnale*)	
Hibiscus (rose mallow) (*Hibiscus moscheutos*)	
Obedient plant (*Physostegia virginiana*)	
Perennial sunflower (*Helianthus* × *multiflorus*)	
Plumbago (*Ceratostigma plumbaginoides*)	
Purple coneflower (*Echinacea purpurea*)	
Stonecrop (*Sedum spectabile*)	

Repeat/long season bloomers

Autumn Joy stonecrop (*Sedum* 'Autumn Joy')	Luxuriant bleeding heart (*Dicentra formosa* 'Luxurient')
'Ballerina' Cranesbill geranium (*Geranium cinereum* 'Ballerina')	Yellow corydalis (*Corydalis lutea*)
'Butterfly Blue' Pincushion flower (*Scabiosa columbaria* 'Butterfly Blue')	
Creeping baby's breath (*Gypsophila repens*)	
Gold yarrow (*Achillea millefolium* hybrids)	
Hollyhock (*Alcea rosea*)	
Hollyhock mallow (*Malva alcea*)	
Shasta daisy (*Leucanthemum* × *superbum*)	
Stella de Oro daylily (*Hemerocallis* 'Stella de Oro')	
Stoke's aster (*Stokesia laevis*)	

Bloom time—annuals

A great many of the annuals available to us have long, extended bloom times that start in late spring and carry on through the early fall; indeed, this is what makes annuals so popular with gardeners. For that reason, I have listed only those plants that bloom outside of the summer season.

SUN	SHADE
Spring or early blooming annuals	
Annual poppy (*Papaver* spp.)	Forget-me-not (*Myosotis sylvatica*)
Annual sweet pea (*Lathyrus odoratus*)	(a biennial)
Baby blue-eyes (*Nemophila menziesii*)	Pansy or viola (*Viola*)
California poppy (*Eschscholzia californica*)	Primrose (*Primula*)
Godetia (*Clarkia* hybrids)	
Pot marigold (*Calendula officinalis*)	
Flowers that continue to bloom nicely for the fall	
Canna lily (*Canna* × *generalis*)	Flowering tobacco (*Nicotiana* spp.)
Cape daisy (*Osteospermum*)	Lobelia (*Lobelia*)
Celosia (*Celosia* spp.)	Wax begonia
Cosmos (*Cosmos* spp.)	(*Begonia* × *semperflorens-cultorum*)
Dahlia (*Dahlia*)	
Flossflower (*Ageratum houstonianum*)	
Gazania (*Gazania rigens*)	
Geranium (*Pelargonium* × *hortorum*)	
Globe amaranth (*Gomphrena globosa*)	
Heliotrope (*Heliotropium arborescens*)	
Marigold (*Tagetes*)	
Melampodium (*Melampodium paludosum*)	
Million bells (*Calibrachoa* hybrid)	
Morning glory (*Ipomoea* spp.)	
Nasturtium (*Tropaeolum majus*)	
Ornamental cabbage and kale	
(*Brassica oleracea*)	
Pot marigold (*Calendula officinalis*)	
Salvia (*Salvia* spp.)	
Snapdragon (*Antirrhinum majus*)	
Statice (*Limonium sinuatum*)	
Strawflower (*Helichrysum bracteatum*)	
Sunflower (*Helianthus*)	
Sweet alyssum (*Lobularia maritima*)	
Zinnia (*Zinnia*)	

Of Gardens
Large and Small

Large or small, balcony or front yard, any garden should involve thoughtful planning. You can work with a landscape designer, or take a moment to research some of the ideas that guide garden design. For a much more thorough approach to garden design than I can give here, check out my book *Canadian Garden Design*. In *Mark Cullen's Ontario Gardening*, I address many of the most popular garden design ideas in Ontario. The number of garden enthusiasts in this province continues to rise, and as it does so too does the creativity of gardeners. People are finding all sorts of ways to garden, even without conventional gardens. The only consistent element in garden design trends is the increasing number of styles and approaches. Rooftops and balconies are being transformed into green, living spaces, and many people who have small sites that may have seemed inadequate for an extensive garden are revealing their potential with a host of inspiring small-space gardening approaches. Container gardening is also growing in popularity, even among those with plenty of space, as this technique can address many gardening challenges. And those with large sites are looking at new ways to create interest and intimacy in the garden.

The small garden

If you live in a brand-new development or have had the opportunity to tour any new neighbourhoods in this province recently, you'll notice one thing—houses are getting bigger but backyards certainly aren't! With the cost of housing rising steadily over the years, even the suburbs—areas that have always sold the idea of "space"—are featuring scaled-back versions of front and backyard (with the "saved" space being offered inside the house, I suppose). But as any urban gardener will tell you, limited space does not have to mean limited gardening. Working on a modest scale can produce striking results, but it takes some planning and some special considerations to turn a small area into a beautiful and efficient garden. Here are a few "rules of thumb" for small spaces:

❀ On a small site, everything is up-close and personal. If your pansies have become leggy and limp, you'll notice them immediately; if a shrub is too big or overgrown, it will stand out like a sore thumb; if you dislike the colour of the lilies you planted, they will catch your eye each time you enter the garden. Small gardens demand careful planning and attention as problems are harder to overlook than they might be in a large space.

❀ Hard furnishings and permanent structures will also be more noticeable in a small garden. If you are putting in a fence, for example, think carefully about what will be most attractive as well as practical for you. In small gardens, fences are usually visible from every vantage point. It may make sense to splurge a little on your fence, your garden shed or your garage to get just what you want.

❀ Also remember that solid fences around small gardens can restrict air flow and create shade over a great deal of the site. Opt for open-type fences— lattice work or even chain link—if they are surrounding a small space.

❀ Texture and foliage are especially important in the small garden as all plant material will be seen relatively close up. Choose annuals and perennials that have unusual and interesting leaves and flowers. Also opt for subtle colours, as very bright colours can be overpowering in a small space.

❀ Remember that all successful gardens have something happening in every season. For a small garden this means you need to squeeze variety into a small space by planting many different types of plants instead of wide swaths of the same plant, as you might in a large space.

- Gardening in small spaces often means shade. Choose shade-tolerant plants—check out In Sun and Shade, p. 3 for more shade gardening tips and ideas.

- Choose smaller spring-flowering bulbs (crocuses rather than tulips, for example) so that you can get more flowers and more colour into your small space.

- Today all sorts of herbaceous and woody perennials are available in dwarf varieties. Ask your local garden centre about these cultivars—choosing dwarf varieties of your favourite plants will allow you to use more plants in a small garden, giving your landscape increased interest.

- In a small garden, it may be a little more difficult to cover up (with other plantings) or overlook the spent foliage of spring bulbs. I suggest you plant your bulbs in portable containers that can be moved out of sight once the flowers are gone and the leaves are wilting.

- Create the illusion of more space by adding height to the garden. Trellises and arbours can support climbing plant varieties. Raised beds or terraces will also add height and create the feeling that there is more space than there is (especially useful if your garden features a slope). The walls of permanent structures and fences can also become part of the living garden (see Vertical Gardening, p. 28). Strong contrasts, as well as a variety of heights in the garden, reinforce that feeling of movement and space in the small garden.

- As many interior designers will tell you, sometimes by dividing space you can actually make it seem bigger. Don't be afraid to create a few little "rooms" or distinct areas of your small garden.

- Optical illusions, or *trompe l'oeil*, can work magic in a small garden. If you have two shrubs, one behind the other, you can create the illusion of greater distance between them (therefore greater space in the garden) by pruning the one behind so that it is smaller than the one in front. It will look smaller naturally because of the distance, but by making it smaller still, the eye will think it is even farther away. Another sort of *trompe l'oeil* could be a vine-covered arbour near the back of a garden that suggests a doorway leading to another significant part of the yard, even if it doesn't exist. A colourful door to nowhere can add whimsy to your garden. Anything that causes the visitor to pause and contemplate is worth consideration.

* Be creative with your use of space. Are there any areas of hidden space on your site? Perhaps a small pocket of soil at the base of the garage wall might be the spot for a vine-covered trellis. That ribbon of turf alongside the driveway might become home to a narrow flower bed. Is there enough light and good soil in the space between your house and your neighbour's to plant a luscious shade garden?

* Is your small yard primarily a children's playground or an open space for the dog? If so, you may want to limit your backyard gardening to a few hardy shrubs and some perimeter plantings. If the lawn at the front of the house, however, is not really being used, why not transform it into a front-yard garden? Not only will you create an attractive and inviting introduction to your property, but your front garden will be less likely to be trampled by small feet!

* Don't abandon large garden additions—just scale them back. Do you love the look of water features but don't have room for a pond? Why not put in a small fountain or an attractive bird bath with running water? Like the idea of a shady gazebo? Build a small pergola with a seating area underneath instead. If there isn't room for a bench, why not put a beautiful cast-iron garden chair in the spot?

* Some trees or shrubs are essential even in a small garden, but remember that they suck nutrients and water from the soil, making large demands on a small space. Use trees and shrubs judiciously and opt for small or dwarf varieties if available. Be prepared to amend the soil on a regular basis.

An arbour is a great alternative to a large gazebo if you have a small yard.

Balcony and roof gardening

From the CFRB building on Toronto's Yonge Street where I broadcast my weekly radio show, I have noticed a number of newly built condos and townhouses featuring both balcony and rooftop areas that seem to be landscaped almost as soon as the units are occupied. In fact, my publisher (who is in the same neighbourhood) was watching the construction of some townhouses across the street from her offices and asked one of the workers about what looked like an oddly designed roof. He explained that the "false" front that ran around the sides of the rooftop was actually a barrier wall so that residents would each have their own rooftop garden. There's no doubt about it—gardens are so important to people that builders of housing that was traditionally thought to be "gardenless," apartment buildings and condos in particular, have been encouraged to incorporate garden space in their plans. What's more, there are a number of organizations that are promoting rooftop and balcony gardening as an important part of urban environmental renewal. They point out that not only do these kinds of gardens maximize the use of urban space, they also provide a restorative green haven for city dwellers, additional oxygen to city air and even a potential source of fresh produce for the urban population!

If you have access to a rooftop or a balcony, I heartily encourage you to get growing. But before you do, familiarize yourself with the special needs of a balcony or a rooftop garden.

Microclimates

If you are gardening on high you are almost certainly gardening in a microclimate—you will have different growing conditions than the landscape at ground level around you and you need to assess those conditions before you begin. Which way does your balcony face? If it gets direct sunlight, at what time of day? Morning shade with afternoon sun presents challenges for the gardener as plants stay cool throughout the morning only to be exposed to the hottest hours of the sun in the afternoon. If, however, your balcony or rooftop gets morning sun and afternoon shade you have perfect growing conditions for plants that like partial shade.

Perhaps your outdoor space is overshadowed by other buildings or by balconies above you. Is there enough reflected or ambient light to support a shade garden? Or are you planning a garden on a rooftop that gets full sun all day? Remember that since balconies and rooftops are almost invariably bordered by brick or concrete walls and floor, they retain heat.

Although temperatures at ground level are perfectly comfortable, the growing conditions a few storeys up may be intolerably hot as the sun heats up the exposed walls and floors. But an advantage is that while your ground-floor neighbours are gardening in zone 4 conditions, your zone 5 plants are thriving in their warmer home.

Another important factor that you must take into account in balcony or rooftop gardening is the wind. The higher you live, the greater the effects of the wind will be. Your garden will dry out very quickly, so use bigger containers that can hold more lightweight soil, and water frequently. Also consider adding water-retaining polymer crystals to your pots and hanging baskets to reduce the need for watering. Avoid small hanging baskets (anything under 25 cm/10 inches in diameter) if you live higher than the second storey—they will dry out too quickly, and might even become airborne in a strong wind! When grown on balconies and rooftops, evergreen trees and shrubs must be sheltered and protected from wind damage. Even if you are not using evergreens, you might want to create some wind protection for your garden. Plexiglass sheets can be attached to open railings of balconies, or canvas runners can be threaded through the uprights of railings. Hardy vines can also be grown along the railings. For rooftops, you may want to construct some additional barriers, whether hardy shrubs, fencing or other structures, to serve as windbreaks. Even with these kinds of barriers, however, conditions on a balcony or rooftop can be tough, so choose hardy plant material.

Structural and safety considerations

If planning a garden on a rooftop or balcony, you will almost certainly be gardening in some kind of container (see Container Gardening, p. 31). Keep in mind, however, that unlike the backyard gardener who might opt to use cast-iron planters around the site, you must be cautious about the weight of the containers you use. Not only do you not want to heave a 50 pound planter up a flight of stairs to the rooftop, you also don't want that planter, further weighted down by soil and water, to come crashing through your roof! Before planning your garden, check with your landlord or builder about weight restrictions for your balcony or rooftop. Use lightweight soil mixes or soil-less mixes (vermiculite and peat moss, for example). Choose lightweight containers—remember, if the soil is kept moist and

Rooftop gardens can use a variety of container sizes, as well as planting boxes and trellises to add a vertical dimension.

gravel or stone chips are used to add drainage at the bottom of the container, even poly-resin containers should be heavy enough to be stable and wind-resistant. Alternatively, some balcony gardeners use heavier pots, like clay or metal ones, but use lightweight drainage material, like Styrofoam packing pieces, at the bottom rather than stones or gravel.

Many rooftop gardens use containers that are very big—essentially they are raised beds or boxes constructed with lumber, sometimes quite handsomely finished. These work very well on rooftops as they can be planted more densely than smaller containers and do not dry out as quickly. For perennials, the additional soil also provides insulation over the winter. The planters themselves, depending on how they are constructed, may include some insulating material (like Styrofoam sheets) in their sides or walls. I recommend 2.5- to 5-cm (1- to 2-inch) thick Styrofoam sheets. Large planting boxes can also give a more traditional garden look to a rooftop, particularly if

HARDY AND WIND-RESISTANT PLANTS FOR BALCONY OR ROOFTOP
Vegetables: beans, cucumbers, eggplant, peppers, squash, tomatoes.
Vines: silver lace vine, Virginia creeper, morning glories, clematis, bittersweet.
Annuals: nasturtiums, lantana, zinnias, begonias, mandevilla, abutilon, helichrysum, geraniums, South African daisies, dusty miller, dwarf marigolds, straw flower, most herbs.
Shrubs: euonymus, boxwood, dwarf spirea, shrub roses (Explorer series).
Perennials: lady's mantle, dwarf daylily 'Stella d'Oro', sedums or stonecrops.

they are kept quite low. But again, gardeners have to make sure that the rooftop can bear the load before they construct these beds, and they must be careful to use lightweight soil mixes. If your rooftop garden plans are very extensive or ambitious, you may have to talk with a contractor about additional waterproofing and insulation for your roof.

Also be cautious if you're placing window boxes that hang outside of the railing over the street. When watering, you will have to make sure that the water, watering can and plants themselves don't end up on the ground (or passersby) below. If you place window boxes inside the railing, you will get a better view of them, and watering and weeding will be easier as well.

Other balcony and rooftop ideas:

* Many balcony and rooftop gardeners like to add a small water feature with running water to their site—a fountain or water-circulating bird bath. The sound of the running water helps to muffle noise from the street below.

* Since rooftops are often in full sunlight for most of the day, some rooftop gardeners install retractable awnings against walls or high railings so that they can shade their plantings during the hottest parts of the day. Garden centres and landscaping companies can recommend designs and fabrics that filter UV radiation and repel rain (useful during very wet periods or during particularly heavy downpours).

* Water, water, water. The chief challenge for rooftop gardeners is keeping their plants adequately hydrated. You may find you have to water your containers every day. Mulch; use moisture-absorbent polymers, vermiculite or peat moss in the soil; and protect plants from wind to reduce evaporation. Arranging containers in close groups, using larger boxes and containers, and planting densely will also help prevent moisture loss.

* See the Vertical, Container and Small Garden sections in this chapter for more ideas that you can use on your balcony or rooftop.

Large sites

When you browse the bookstore shelves or dig through the gardening section of your local library, you'll come across plenty of reading material about working with a small garden. There is even a good variety of books on the "no garden" garden—container, rooftop, balcony gardens and so on. Rarely, however, do you see a book on the sole subject of the "big garden." I suppose it could be argued that this is because all general gardening books can be used when you are working with a big garden—after all, there are no big challenges to overcome, no great restrictions, right? Certainly *I* see plenty of space as a wonderful opportunity, but then I have been gardening on a large suburban lot for years, and I also happen to know many very talented landscape designers! But the Weall & Cullen landscape designers tell me that they meet a lot of customers who are overwhelmed by their sites. This is particularly true of people moving from apartments or small urban lots to country or suburban lots. A visit to a reputable landscape designer is an excellent way to embark on a garden plan for a large lot (or a small lot for that matter). Here are a few other ideas to keep in mind if you have the gift of space.

❋ Plant in wide swaths. With a large lot, you have the luxury of creating dramatic sweeps of colour by planting a large number of the same flower. What's more, planting only one or two of a certain type of flower leaves that flower looking a little lost on the big canvas. If you do want a more subtle look than large groupings of plants provide, consider a meadow-type garden with a select number of flowers mixed together over a wide area to give a variegated look.

❋ Use rhythm and repetition to unify a large space. Repeating shapes and colours within a garden to create a pattern or a "rhythm" is sound design practice no matter what size your garden is, but it is an especially helpful technique if you are trying to draw together a large space. You can repeat large elements, like clusters of shrubs or groups of trees, and small elements, like mounding border plantings of campanula or alyssum. I've seen gardens where a particular shape was repeated to great effect—for example, spheres of allium or globe cedars. Some gardeners like to choose a particular colour that will echo throughout their garden. For example, grey-green foliage or white blossoms of a variety of plants can act as an accent tying a host of other colours together throughout the garden. Or you can choose a single colour or colour combination to repeat as the dominant pattern in the garden—blues and yellows, for example, or blazing shades of red and orange.

❋ If planned and planted thoughtfully, garden borders can give your large backyard a more "homey" feeling. By planting generous borders on all sides of the yard—what I call framing—you'll create a feeling of intimacy that many large yards lack. In smaller gardens, the depth or length of borders may be dictated by the size of your lot. But in a larger garden, you can frame your whole yard with the garden border. Begin

Residence

Fruit Trees

Rock Garden

Lower Patio
(Flagstone)

Stone Steps

Rock Garden

Upper Walkway
(Pea Stone)

Shade Garden

Arbour

Water Garden

Herb Garden

Stone Bench

Yew Hedge

Arbour

Rose Garden

Stone Bench

Yew Hedge

Cedar Hedge

Yew Hedge

Yew Hedge

A large lot (this one is 4.7 m × 3.3 m/15 × 10 feet) can accommodate a variety of garden rooms to add interest to the site. A small lot might use fewer divisions but still feature rooms or separate garden areas to give the illusion of space.

your designing process from the outer edges of your yard and work in. When determining the depth and width of garden you wish to have, keep the borders proportional to the size of the yard. Place small shade or flowering trees in the remaining lawn area, being careful to provide them with room to grow and to not block attractive views from the various vantage points in your home. Keep in mind that curved edges along the border are more pleasing to look at than straight lines. And remember, the deeper the garden border, the more likely you will want to add paths, stepping stones or other methods of allowing you to move into the borders to weed, cultivate or carry out other maintenance.

❁ Divide your garden into "rooms" or a series of smaller gardens with pathways, hard furnishings, fences (willow fences, log fences, cast and wrought iron) or trellises. Arbours can act as doorways (living doorways when planted with vines). Berms, groundcovers and garden borders can also mark divisions from one area of the garden to another. As mentioned in the discussion of small gardens, dividing an outdoor space into rooms does not make it seem smaller—it usually makes it seem bigger! Garden rooms on a big site add interest, variety and even intimacy to the space.

❁ Consider making some areas of your yard xeriscaped, naturalized or planned for low maintenance (see Native Plants and the Ontario Naturalized Garden, p. 41, and Watering and Xeriscaping, p. 165). By grouping plants with similar needs, you cut down on the maintenance required. For example, if you devote a portion of your garden to plants that are tolerant of dry conditions, you won't need to spend time watering that area as frequently. If the plants are a mixture of those that are drought-tolerant and those that aren't, you still have to water that area often. In addition, when plants' needs are matched by your conditions, they will thrive, either self-seeding or producing many offshoots. Anyone with a large garden is going to appreciate plants that require little watering, fertilizing or other upkeep!

❁ Use lawn to cover high-use areas and to make pleasant visual breaks between beds and garden areas. If water conservation is a concern, choose hardy drought-tolerant grasses. Don't worry if the lawn goes brown and dormant during dry spells; it inevitably bounces back when rain and cool temperatures return.

❁ Create an area of your site that can be the "work room" of the garden. This might be a holding area for plants you remove but want to relocate later; a place to try out plants to see if you would like them in other areas of the garden; or a place to grow transplants and seedlings for later use. You can also use this area to build or place compost bins (use more than one—I have three always on the go) or plant a vegetable patch. Your work room can be an area "out of sight" of the rest of the garden if you choose.

❀ If you have natural slopes on your site, install terraces or distinct levels—this can be a way of dealing with the grade of your site, or a way of adding visual interest and breaking up a large lot. Raised beds in various spots can also give visual variety and breaks.

❀ When you have a large site you have the luxury of installing large garden features like ponds, large fountains and even mini-waterfalls.

❀ You can also opt for larger sizes and more varieties of hard furnishings than those with a small site—benches, tables, chairs, umbrellas. When choosing trellises, arbours, pergolas, gazebos, fountains and statuary don't skimp on size if you are placing them in an open space. While it is still possible to go too large and overpowering in a large garden, you don't want hard furnishings to "disappear" or looked dwarfed by a big site.

❀ If you have a big site that is largely in full sun, consider creating some areas of shade. These spots can be used as a summer seating area or a woodland shade garden. See In Sun and Shade, p. 3 for more information about creating shade.

Vertical gardening

A friend recently told me about her neighbour's beautiful urban garden, a garden with an interesting addition. Years ago, the municipal hydro company disconnected the wires from one of the tall poles that lined the alley behind this gardener's house. The pole sat flush against her back fence and she was relieved that the unsightly thing was no longer necessary, until she realized that the hydro company was not removing the pole along with the wires. When she called to find out when the pole might be coming down, she got the run-around, and as the months passed she realized that it was going to be left there for the residents to worry about. She couldn't afford to pay for its removal herself, so out of desperation she planted some Boston ivy around the base of the pole. Now, years later, at the foot of her garden, rising behind her lattice-work fence and complemented by surrounding trees of various heights, is a wonderfully whimsical green tower that climbs 8 m (25 feet) into the sky before the leaves and stems come cascading down again like water off a living fountain.

Vertical gardening refers to the practice of using plants that can either be coaxed to grow up instead of out or that do so naturally. Its great advantage is that it uses very little horizontal garden space to create a large area of growth. It is a wonderful technique to employ where garden space is limited—in a small yard, a balcony or a rooftop. It is also a handy way to cover up or disguise unsightly fences, dull walls or unattractive structures like garages and fences. It can create shade where needed, and it also can provide privacy in a refreshing, unobtrusive way.

With vertical gardening, fruit, vegetables, flowers and foliage stay off the ground—keeping them away from soil-hugging pests like slugs and reducing soil-borne diseases such as mould and fungus. It improves air circulation around the plant, which also helps combat mould and fungus.

Vertical vegetable gardening is an ideal technique for those who have difficulty bending and stooping—it is much easier to harvest your pole beans as you stand than bending to gather bush beans. Pruning is also easier when standing!

Vertical gardening tips

❋ Remember that vertical gardening creates shade. Before planting any vines, fruits or tall-growing shrubs, check out where the shade will be cast and if this will work for you. Remember that the amount of shade cast will change as the plants grow taller and fuller.

❋ Choose vines with care—they have different ways of growing. Clinging vines hold on by tiny rootlets that grow from the stem (English ivy and Virginia creeper, for example). These rootlets can leave permanent markings on brick and siding, so you may consider growing these types of vines on a trellis that is at least 15 cm (6 inches) from any wall. Grasping vines (like sweet pea) use tendrils that wrap around slender supports and work best with a trellis, narrow poles or wire and string supports. Twining vines (pole beans, moonflower vine, trumpet vine, silver lace vine) grow around wider supports and can be used with thick uprights such as posts and tree trunks.

❋ Climbing or twining plants can be made to grow up trellises, fences, guy wires, vertical strings (you can use heavy-gauge fishing line for invisible supports), balcony railings or anchored fish net. You can also use wooden "tepees" made from three or four poles tied together, commercially available cages, arbours, pergolas and obelisks.

❁ Some vines and plants will need to be coaxed up a support until they are well established. You can do this by gently tying the growing tendrils to the stakes, lines or other supports using strips of cloth, yarn or soft twine in a figure 8 pattern. Avoid wire ties or twist ties as they may cut into the stems as the plant grows.

❁ If growing vegetables vertically, make sure you choose the right varieties. Most tomatoes can be grown in a cage or a tepee, but bush beans will not grow vertically although there are many varieties of pole beans that do. Likewise, if choosing cucumbers, choose a vining variety rather than a bush type.

❁ Some gardeners even plant melons and large squash along trellises. If you are growing something that will produce heavy fruit, you may need to support that fruit as it gets larger. A sling made from soft cloth, tied to the trellis or the supports, will keep the fruit from snapping off the vine.

❁ Remember that while fruit and vegetable yield per plant can sometimes be slightly less for twining varieties compared to their bush counterparts, their yield per square metre of garden space is great indeed!

❁ While growing vertically often means that rot and fungal diseases can be avoided (particularly with fruit and vegetables), it also means that shallow-rooted plants and vegetables may need more watering than bush types as they are losing moisture in their exposed setting. Pay special attention to the water requirements of your vertically grown plants, and mulch around the root zone to conserve moisture and cut down on the frequency of watering.

❁ If you are planting vines and shrubs for privacy, you may want to choose evergreens. Tall-growing euonymus, supported by a trellis or fence, makes a wonderful year-round privacy screen to zone 5. Some ivies are evergreen in certain zones—check out Baltic ivy, for example.

❁ Don't overlook the opportunity to "double up" when gardening vertically— vines can be planted along with shrubs and trees so the vines can grow over, up or through the trees. Mature tree trunks look splendid covered with Virginia creeper. I also like the look of Baltic or English ivy growing up a mature oak or locust.

❁ Some vines, such as clematis, like the sun, but need their roots kept cool or shaded. Plant early-blooming perennials around the base of the vine so that the roots are shaded even at the very beginning of the growing season.

Container gardening

At Weall & Cullen we have experienced an upswing in the demand for containers. I'm convinced that this is not only because there is now such a wonderful selection of containers on the market, but also because gardeners have discovered how very helpful and attractive container gardening can be.

Terracing containers on steps is an attractive addition to an entranceway and also makes the containers themselves less visible.

Containers can address all sorts of gardening challenges. They are the perfect solution for gardens with poor soil— plants that won't thrive in your poor soil conditions can do very well in pots. Likewise, if you have very alkaline soil, but want a few plants that like neutral or slightly acidic soil, you can plant them in containers with appropriate soil. As a matter of fact, think about using containers whenever your heart is set on something that has different requirements (soil, fertility, watering, sunlight) than the rest of your garden.

Containers also have the advantage of being mobile. Many folks with shade gardens will use containers for plants that need more sun than the beds get. Pots can be placed in a sunny area for several hours each day and then moved to the shade garden to provide a spot of colour where it is needed. Other gardeners who have sites that enjoy a great deal of sun may use containers for tender plants that struggle during the mid-afternoon— they can be moved to the shade during the hottest hours of the day. Some gardeners just love the ability to rearrange their potted garden at will— containers provide a great way to redesign your garden (without the shovel!).

Many cooks like to plant herbs and vegetables in pots that can be left outdoors but within easy reach of the kitchen. Many bring their potted herbs indoors for a winter window-sill herb garden. Likewise, a great number of gardeners use containers for favourite plants that are not really hardy in their zone. Plants stay out in summer and come indoors to a sunny spot in the house for the winter. I find that this is becoming an especially popular practice in many northern Ontario communities.

Container gardening also makes balcony and rooftop gardening possible.

And to top it off, container gardening cuts back on weeding! Even if a weed does sneak into the pot, containers, being raised off the ground and generally featuring loose, well-drained potting soil, are very easy to weed.

Tips for container gardening

❀ Containers should be big enough to accommodate plant, roots and sufficient soil. The opening must be wide enough to allow for easy watering, and the container must have drainage holes so that the soil does not stay waterlogged. If the container you have your heart set on does not have drainage holes, put the plants in a slightly smaller plastic pot with holes and set this on top of crushed gravel or small stones inside the pot.

❀ Make sure that the container has adequate drainage (even if it has drainage holes) by placing 5 to 7.5 cm (2 to 3 inches) of gravel, crushed stone or even broken terracotta pieces in the bottom of it before adding the soil mix.

❀ Containers are not really low maintenance. They tend to dry out quickly, so must be kept adequately watered. Larger containers dry out less quickly (some people recommend using containers that are no smaller than 30 cm/12 inches in diameter for this reason). The need for frequent watering is often offset by the fact that the water is going where it is needed and is not draining off to the surrounding lawn or pavement or being sucked up by a tree! You can also group potted plants together to help them conserve moisture and to reduce evaporation.

❀ Insert your finger into the soil to a depth of about 2.5 cm (1 inch) to check dryness. Add water until you see some of it flowing through the drainage holes—this means all the soil is thoroughly soaked. Never, however, let the pots stand in water. If using trays or saucers, dump out any overflow.

❀ Use a top-quality potting soil in containers. Most commercial mixes are actually a mixture of peat, finished compost, vermiculite and/or perlite—in other words, there is no "soil" (garden soil is generally too dense for containers and can introduce pathogens and weeds that can be difficult to manage). These mixes have the advantages of being more moisture retentive than garden soil and having no soil-borne insects, diseases or weeds.

❀ Potting soil generally does not contain much or any organic matter, and the limited amount of space at the root zone increases a plant's need for additional nutrients in the soil. Therefore, I recommend that your containers be given an application of slow-release fertilizer after being planted. A good-quality slow-release fertilizer will last up to three months, releasing nutrients every time you water. Perennials will need another application every spring after that. If you'd rather, you can fertilize every two weeks with other water-soluble fertilizers. Since annuals are hungry beasts (blooming all the time the way they do) I recommend a bi-weekly application of 20-20-20. You can also work in a bit of compost to the potting soil if you desire.

❀ Both polymer crystals and a new product called Profile (see p. 142) absorb moisture, and when they are added to potting soil they will keep it from drying out so quickly. They are permanent, never requiring replacement as long as the soil is viable, and they're available at most garden centres.

❀ A stone, brick or concrete patio will absorb heat during the day if it's in a sunny location. This can dry out and even scorch the roots of plants that are in containers (which heat up quickly even without the help of the hot patio). To insulate the containers somewhat, make sure they are raised above the surface of the patio— some planter boxes are available with legs, or for small containers, invert a saucer underneath the pot. Water diligently.

❀ Put heavy containers that are resting on flat surfaces on castors for ease of moving. Many garden centres now carry small platforms with castors for this purpose. (They have the added advantage of keeping the container off hot stone or patio blocks.) Or choose lightweight poly-resin containers that mimic stone or terracotta to make moving your plants much easier.

❀ You can combine annuals in the same pot, but I recommend that you combine tall-growing annuals with trailing ones—nothing is prettier than ivy cascading down a pot full of brilliant dwarf marigolds or the new, ever-blooming petunias.

CHOOSING CONTAINERS

When creating a container garden, use your imagination! All sorts of things can be used as containers—washtubs, wine barrels, galvanized steel pails. I have even seen funky chrome chairs à la 50s with seats removed and mesh baskets hung in their place!

Make sure, however, that you've got appropriate plants for your container and that your container is appropriate to your plants. If your container is an elaborate design or an unusual shape, choose a plant that complements it. In this case, simplicity in the planting is more appropriate— a lush fern or trailing ivy may be all that's needed if you want the container rather than the plants to be the focus. Likewise, choose containers and plants so that their colours complement each other.

If you'd rather have no attention drawn to the containers, you can make them "disappear" by terracing them—using pots of increasing size or placing similarly sized pots on ladders, steps or other platforms so that flowers and foliage from lower plants hide the pots above them. Another gorgeous look is to use plants whose flowers and foliage will cascade down the fronts of the pots, like English ivy, alyssum and trailing lobelia ('Cascade'), geraniums and sweet potato vine. If terraced, these container plants will create a colourful living green waterfall!

- Don't overlook dwarf trees and shrubs for container plantings. Like trees and shrubs in the garden they can be the "bones" of your container garden. If you use evergreens, they will also provide winter colour. Korean boxwood, dwarf Alberta spruce and dwarf white spruce are good choices for container gardening.

- Slugs like the undersides of pots. Inspect your containers for these visitors. If you find any, drop them in a pail of 1 part vinegar and 20 parts water.

Potted perennials and containers over the winter

Just like perennials in standard garden beds, perennials in pots will generally overwinter if hardy one zone above yours. Just keep in mind that they have less soil to insulate them from the harsh temperatures so may need some extra help withstanding winter weather. Consider using resin and poly-resin containers for perennials. They flex with the expansion of frozen soil and are less likely to break or crack. Another option is to use largish container boxes that can be lined with Styrofoam to insulate perennials for overwintering. If you are using clay, stone or metal pots, for winter safety you can place them inside a Styrofoam cooler or bucket lined with a blanket or other insulating material. Cover pots with a winter mulch, just as you would your garden beds. Shrubs or small trees that would be protected from wind and the weight of snow (see Planting tips, p. 147) in the garden should get the same treatment if they are planted in pots. If you can move container plants into a section of the garden where they are less exposed, do so.

Your containers may also need protection in winter. Keep in mind that when the soil freezes, moisture in it will cause it to expand. Therefore containers should be the sort where the top opening is wider than the rest of the pot. As the soil freezes it will be able to raise slightly through the opening. If, however, you use a container that is round or with a narrower opening than middle, the pressure of the expanding soil and water is likely to crack the pot. And in my experience, clay and terracotta pots are at high risk of breaking in Ontario's winter weather.

Because expanding soil can damage containers, many people remove all soil from containers that have been home to annuals after the season is over. If you take precautions as mentioned above, this added fall task is not necessary, especially for big containers. Cover the containers so that they don't

PLANTS FOR PATIO CONTAINERS
Sedge 'Frosty Curls'
  (*Carex Comans*)
Daylily 'Happy Returns'
  (*Hemerocallis* 'Happy Returns')
Purple leaf bugbane
  (*Cimicifuga ramosa* 'Atropurpurea')
Wormwood 'Silver Brocade'
  (*Artemisia stelleriana*
  'Silver Brocade')
Coral bells 'Amber Waves'
  (*Heuchera* 'Amber Waves')

absorb any additional moisture and top them up with fresh potting soil next spring. If you prefer to change your soil each season, use the old potting soil as mulch or add it to your composter.

If you are bringing a potted plant indoors for the winter, put it in "quarantine" for at least two weeks so that you can check for insects (a breezeway or a patio where you can inspect the plant daily is ideal). If you notice ants, aphids or any other crawling things, treat with an organic, ready-to-use spray like Aim and make sure all insects are gone before introducing the plant to your home.

For all potted perennials, whether they have spent the winter indoors or out, top up the potting soil each spring, and repot only when the roots have reached the sides of the container and have begun to grow out of the drainage holes at the bottom of the pot. Always go up only one size when you're repotting any plants.

Plant height and scale

Using a variety of plant heights in your garden is a wise design approach—whether you are maximizing space in a small site or adding visual interest to a large one. The following chart will give you some help in choosing plants of differing heights.

ANNUALS

Under 30 cm (1 foot)

Dahlberg daisy (*Thymophylla tenuiloba*) 10 cm (4")
Edging lobelia (*Lobelia erinus*) 10 cm (4")
Ice plant (*Mesembryanthemum*) 10 cm (4")
Sweet alyssum (*Lobularia maritima*) 10 cm (4")
Creeping zinnia (*Sanvitalia procumbens*) 15 cm (6")
Monkey flower (*Mimulus* × *hybridus*) 15 cm (6")
Moss rose (*Portulaca grandiflora*) 15 cm (6")
Pansy (*Viola* × *wittrockkiana*) 15 cm (6")
Sweet potato vine (*Ipomoea batatas*) 15 cm (6")
Viola (*Viola*) 15 cm (6")
Annual phlox (*Phlox drummondii*) 20 cm (8")
China pink (*Dianthus chinensis*) 20 cm (8")

Fibrous begonia (*Begonia* × *semperflorens*) 20 cm (8")
Flossflower, dwarf (*Ageratum houstonianum*) 20 cm (8")
Million bells (*Calibrachoa* hybrid) 20 cm (8")
Verbena (*Verbena* × *hybrida*) 20 cm (8")
Impatiens (*Impatiens*) 20–30 cm (8–12")
Nemesia (*Nemesia strumosa*) 22.5 cm (9")
Snapdragon, dwarf (*Antirrhinum majus*) 22.5 cm (9")
Swan River daisy (*Brachycome iberidifolia*) 22.5 cm (9")
Browallia (*Browallia*) 25 cm (10")
Dusty miller (*Senecio cineraria*) 25 cm (10")
Fan flower (*Scaevola*) 25 cm (10")
Gazania (*Gazania rigens*) 25 cm (10")

Under 60 cm (2 feet)

African daisy (*Dimorphotheca sinuata*)
30 cm (12")

Flowering tobacco (*Nicotiana* hybrid)
30 cm (12")

French marigold (*Tagetes patula*) 30 cm (12")

Globe candytuft (*Iberis crenata*) 30 cm (12")

Nasturtium (*Tropaeolum majus*) 30 cm (12")

Ornamental cabbage (*Brassica olaracea*,
Acephala group) 30 cm (12")

Ornamental kale (*Brassica olaracea*,
Acephala group) 30 cm (12")

Petunia (*Petunia* × *hybrida*) 30 cm (12")

Plume celosia (*Celosia plumosa*) 30 cm (12")

Toadflax (*Linaria maroccana*) 30 cm (12")

Tuberous begonia (*Begonia tuberhybrida*)
30 cm (12")

Vinca (*Catharanthus roseus*) 30 cm (12")

Zinnia (*Zinnia angustifolia*) 30 cm (12")

Cockscomb (*Celosia cristata*) 37.5 cm (15")

Dahlia hybrids, low-growing types (*Dahlia*)
37.5 cm (15")

Dwarf morning glory (*Convolvulus tricolour*)
37.5 cm (15")

Love-in-a-mist (*Nigella damascena*)
37.5 cm (15")

Scarlet sage (*Salvia splendens*) 37.5 cm (15")

Annual baby's breath (*Gypsophila elegans*)
45 cm (18")

Bachelor's button (*Centaurea cyanus*)
45 cm (18")

Bidens (*Bidens*) 45 cm (18")

Blue Victoria salvia (*Salvia farinacea*)
45 cm (18")

Geranium (*Pelargonium* × *hortorum*)
45 cm (18")

Globe amaranth (*Gomphrena globosa*)
45 cm (18")

Lisianthus (*Lisianthus*) 45 cm (18")

Rex begonia (*Begonia, Rex cultorum*
hybrids) 45 cm (18")

Snapdragon, medium (*Antirrhinum majus*)
45 cm (18")

Stock (*Matthiola incana*) 45 cm (18")

Sweet William (*Dianthus barbatus*) 45 cm (18")

African daisy (*Arctotis stoechadifolia* var.
grandis) 50 cm (20")

Pot marigold (*Calendula officinalis*)
50 cm (20")

Yellow cosmos (*Cosmos sulphureus*)
50 cm (20")

Heliotrope (*Heliotropium arborescens*)
55 cm (22")

60 to 90 cm (2 to 3 feet)

African marigold (*Tagetes erecta*) 60 cm (24")

Four-o'clock (*Mirabilis jalapa*) 60 cm (24")

Gloriosa daisy (*Rudbeckia hirta pulcherrima*)
60 cm (24")

Zinnia (*Zinnia elegans*) 60 cm (24")

Sunflower, dwarf (*Helianthus*) 60–90 cm (2–3')

Larkspur (*Consolida ambigua*) 75 cm (30")

Snapdragon, tall varieties (*Antirrhinum
majus*) 75 cm (30")

Annual fountain grass (*Pennisetum
setaceum*) 90 cm (3')

Calla lily (*Zantedeschia aethiopica*) 90 cm (3')

Canna (*Canna* × *generalis*) 90 cm (3')

Cosmos (*Cosmos bipinnatus*) 90 cm (3')

Flowering tobacco (*Nicotiana alata*) 90 cm (3')

Wheat celosia (*Celosia spicata*) 90 cm (3')

120 cm (4 feet) and over

Dahlia, giant-flowered varieties (*Dahlia*)
120 cm (4')

Datura (*Datura meteloides*) 120 cm (4')

Flowering tobacco (*Nicotiana sylvestris*)
120 cm (4')

Spider flower (*Cleome hassleriana*) 120 cm (4')

Annual sweet pea (*Lathyrus odoratus*)
1.2–1.8 m (4–6')

Sunflower, medium height varieties
(*Helianthus*) 1.2–1.8 m (4–6')

Elephant's ear (*Colocasia esculenta*) 1.5 m (5')

Mexican sunflower (*Tithonia rotundifolia*)
1.5 m (5')

Canary creeper (*Tropaeolum peregrinum*)
1.8–3 m (6–10')

Morning glory (*Ipomoea tricolor*) 2.7 m (9')

Hyacinth bean (*Dolichos lablab*) 3–6 m (10–20')

60 cm (2 feet) and under

Creeping phlox (*Phlox subulata*) 7.5–15 cm (3–6")

Kamschatka stonecrop (*Sedum kamtschaticum*) 10–22.5 cm (4–9")

Dwarf crested iris (*Iris cristata*) 15 cm (6")

English primrose (*Primula vulgaris*) 15–22.5 cm (6–9")

Foamflower (*Tiarella cordifolia*) 15–30 cm (6–12")

Sweet violet (*Viola odorata*) 20 cm (8")

Barrenwort (*Epimedium × rubrum*) 20–30 cm (8–12")

Fringed bleeding heart (*Dicentra eximia*) 22.5–30 cm (9–12")

Basket-of-gold (*Aurinia saxatilis*) 30 cm (12")

Bergenia (*Bergenia cordifolia*) 30 cm (12")

Dwarf blue fescue (*Festuca glauca*) 30 cm (12")

'Georgia Blue' speedwell (*Veronica peduncularis* 'Georgia Blue') 30 cm (12")

Japanese painted fern (*Athyrium nipponicum* 'Pictum') 30 cm (12")

Lamb's ear (*Stachys byzantina*) 30 cm (12")

Lungwort (*Pulmonaria saccharata*) 30 cm (12")

Pink (*Dianthus*) 30 cm (12")

Yellow corydalis (*Corydalis lutea*) 30 cm (12")

Vial's primrose (*Primula vialii*) 30–37.5 cm (12–15")

Japanese blood grass (*Imperata cylindrica* 'Red Baron') 30–45 cm (12–18")

Variegated Japanese sedge (*Carex morrowii* 'Variegata') 30–45 cm (12–18")

Maidenhair fern (*Adiantum pedatum*) 30–50 cm (12–20")

Columbine (*Aquilegia*) 30–60 cm (12–24")

Coral bells (*Heuchera* hybrids) 30–60 cm (12–24")

Golden grass (*Hakonechloa macra* 'Aureola') 30–60 cm (12–24")

Hardy geranium (*Geranium*) 30–60 cm (12–24")

Spiked speedwell (*Veronica spicata*) 30–60 cm (12–24")

Stoke's aster (*Stokesia laevis*) 30–60 cm (12–24")

Geum (*Geum*) 45 cm (18")

Lady's mantle (*Alchemilla mollis*) 45 cm (18")

Threadleaf coreopsis (*Coreopsis verticillata*) 45 cm (18")

Catmint (*Nepeta × faassenii*) 45–60 cm (18–24")

Leopard's bane (*Doronicum orientale*) 45–60 cm (18–24")

Pincushion flower (*Scabiosa caucasica*) 45–60 cm (18–24")

Christmas fern (*Polystichum acrostichoides*) 60 cm (2')

Crimson pincushion (*Knautia macedonica*) 60 cm (2')

Japanese primrose (*Primula japonica*) 60 cm (2')

Sea holly (*Eryngium amethystinum*) 60 cm (2')

Shasta daisy (*Leucanthemum × superbum*) 60 cm (2')

Stonecrop (*Sedum spectabile*) 60 cm (2')

Wormwood (*Artemisia ludoviciana*) 60 cm (2')

120 cm (4 feet) and under

Daylily (*Hemerocallis*) 30–90 cm (1–3')

Hardy chrysanthemum (*Chrysanthemum/ Dendranthema* hybrids) 30–90 cm (1–3')

Baby's breath (*Gypsophila paniculata*) 60–90 cm (2–3')

Balloon flower (*Platycodon grandiflorus*) 60–90 cm (2–3')

Beardtongue (*Penstemon*) 60–90 cm (2–3')

Bee balm (*Monarda didyma*) 60–90 cm (2–3')

Black-eyed Susan (*Rudbeckia fulgida*) 60–90 cm (2–3')

Blanket flower (*Gaillardia × grandiflora*) 60–90 cm (2–3')

Bleeding heart (*Dicentra spectabilis*) 60–90 cm (2–3')

Fern-leaf yarrow (*Achillea filipendulina*) 60–90 cm (2–3')

Gooseneck lysimachia (*Lysimachia clethroides*) 60–90 cm (2–3')

Hybrid sage (*Salvia nemorosa* hybrids) 60–90 cm (2–3')

Japanese iris (*Iris ensata*) 60–90 cm (2–3')

Masterwort (*Astrantia major*) 60–90 cm (2–3')

Peachleaf bellflower (*Campanula persicifolia*) 60–90 cm (2–3')

Red valerian (*Centranthus ruber*) 60–90 cm (2–3')

Toad lily (*Tricyrtis hirta*) 60–90 cm (2–3')

Variegated Solomon's seal (*Polygonatum odoratum* 'Variegatum') 60–90 cm (2–3')

Arendsii hybrid astilbe (*Astilbe* × *arendsii*) 60–120 cm (2–4')

Bearded iris (*Iris siberica*) 60–120 cm (2–4')

Garden phlox (*Phlox paniculata*) 60–120 cm (2–4')

Hardy aster (*Aster*) 60–120 cm (2–4')

Japanese anemone (*Anemone* × *hybrida*) 60–120 cm (2–4')

Male woodfern (*Dryopteris filix-mas*) 60–120 cm (2–4')

Obedient plant (*Physostegia virginiana*) 60–120 cm (2–4')

Purple coneflower (*Echinacea purpurea*) 60–120 cm (2–4')

Purple moor grass (*Molinia caerulea* 'Variegata') 60–120 cm (2–4')

Goldenrod (*Solidago* hybrids) 60–150 cm (2–5')

Northern sea oats (*Chasmanthium latifolium*) 75 cm (30")

Anise hyssop (*Agastache foeniculum*) 90 cm (3')

Blazing star (*Liatris spicata*) 90 cm (3')

Blue oat grass (*Helictotrichon sempervirens*) 90 cm (3')

Butterfly weed (*Asclepias tuberosa*) 90 cm (3')

Cinnamon fern (*Osmunda cinnamomea*) 90 cm (3')

Frances Williams hosta (*Hosta sieboldiana* 'Frances Williams') 90 cm (3')

Lupine (*Lupinus* 'Russell Hybrid') 90 cm (3')

Mullein (*Verbascum* hybrids) 90 cm (3')

Peony (*Paeonia* hybrids) 90 cm (3')

Boltonia (*Boltonia asteroides*) 90–120 cm (3–4')

Cardinal flower (*Lobelia cardinalis*) 90–120 cm (3–4')

False indigo (*Baptisia australis*) 90–120 cm (3–4')

False sunflower (*Heliopsis helianthoides*) 90–120 cm (3–4')

Globe thistle (*Echinops ritro*) 90–120 cm (3–4')

Hollyhock (*Alcea rosea* 'Powder Puff Mix') 90–120 cm (3–4')

Joe Pye weed (*Eupatorium maculatum*) 90–120 cm (3–4')

Ligularia (*Ligularia*) 90–120 cm (3–4')

Perennial fountain grass (*Pennisetum alopecuroides*) 90–120 cm (3–4')

Ostrich fern (*Matteuccia struthiopteris*) 120 cm (4')

Torch lily (*Kniphofia uvaria*) 120 cm (4')

Under 180 cm (6 feet)

Foxglove (*Digitalis purpurea*) 60–150 cm (2–5')

Meadow rue (*Thalictrum*) 60–180 cm (2–6')

Cushion spurge (*Euphorbia characias*) 90–150 cm (3–5')

Helen's flower (*Helenium autumnale*) 90–150 cm (3–5')

Monkshood (*Aconitum*) 90–180 cm (3–6')

Feather reed grass (*Calamagrostis* × *acutifolia* 'Stricta') 120–150 cm (4–5')

Tree mallow (*Lavatera* hybrids) 120–150 cm (4–5')

Bugbane (*Cimicifuga*) 120–180 cm (4–6')

Dephinium (*Dephinium elatum*) 120–180 cm (4–6')

Goatsbeard (*Aruncus dioicus*) 120–180 cm (4–6')

Perennial sunflower (*Helianthus* × *multiflorus*) 120–180 cm (4–6')

Queen-of-the-prairie (*Filipendula ulmaria*) 120–180 cm (4–6')

Giant feather grass (*Stipa gigantea*) 150 cm (5')

Rose mallow (*Hibiscus moscheutos*) 150 cm (5')

Switch grass (*Panicum virgatum*) 150 cm (5')

Under 240 cm (8 feet)

Yucca (*Yucca filamentosa*) 60–360 cm (2–12′)

Hollyhock (*Alcea rosea*) 120–240 cm (4–8′)

Pampas grass (*Cortaderia selloana*)
150–360 cm (5–12′)

Maiden grass (*Miscanthus sinensis*)
240 cm (8′)

Plume poppy (*Macleaya cordata*)
240 cm (8′)

Over 240 cm (8 feet)

Gunnera (*Gunnera*) 180–300 cm (6–10′)

Ornamental rhubarb (*Rheum palmatum*)
180–300 cm (6–10′)

New Zealand flax (*Phormium tenax*)
240–300 cm (8–10′)

Native Plants and the Ontario Naturalized Garden

I have always liked that scene in *The Wizard of Oz* in which Dorothy says, "If I ever go looking for my heart's desire again, I won't look further than my own backyard." That thought captures the truth about so much in life—including gardening. For years, Canadian gardeners have looked far afield seeking "new," exotic, exciting plant material, not realizing that the wildflowers that cropped up along the roadsides, in empty lots and among the cottage trees have been considered exotic, desirable imports to European gardeners since the "discovery" of the Americas. No doubt many Canadian travellers have admired certain flowers in foreign countries, completely unaware that they were originally Canadian native plants!

Native plants and naturalized gardening are becoming increasingly popular for a number of reasons. Some gardeners are indeed looking for something "new" and are bypassing recent cultivars of popular ornamentals for the "native" introductions to the nursery trade. Some want a completely different look for their gardens—a natural-looking meadow, for example, rather than formally designed flower beds. Others are taking an interest in native plants as an aspect of our natural heritage. Indeed, anyone interested in Canadian history should be interested in the land that Canadians have inhabited and called their own. Native plants also offer a host of practical advantages for the Canadian gardener.

The topic of native plants and naturalized gardens is, however, one that can be confusing. Are native plants simply ones that grow wild? Is a "naturalized" garden one of only native plants? Are wildflowers and native plants the same thing?

Generally speaking, native plant gardeners and environmentalists use the term "native" to refer to species that existed in North America prior to European contact. And native is, of course, a relative term: what is indigenous to one area of the United States or Canada is not necessarily indigenous to another. "Wildflowers" are those that grow without cultivation but they are not necessarily native. Many European imports have found Canadian soil is habitable and have spread far and wide on their own. Dandelions, Queen Anne's lace and field daisies are just a few of these newcomers. (According to the Ontario Federation of Naturalists, of the 2,600 vascular plants that grow wild in Ontario, 700—about 30 per cent—are exotics or aliens.)

Today many people are talking about "naturalized" gardens, but often these people are not talking about the same thing. Native plant enthusiasts and environmentalists are most often referring to an approach that attempts to return a local landscape to its pre-agricultural, pre-settler state: in other words, an area is being planted exclusively with species native to that region or microregion, creating a balanced ecosystem. When you see civic "naturalization" projects in parks, school yards and empty lots, this is generally what is being done. You may, however, be most familiar with "naturalized" gardens when used in reference to things like, say, crocus bulbs. In this sense, "naturalized" is referring to a plant behaviour—after being planted in a random "natural" way, plants are allowed to multiply and spread of their own accord. Wildflowers then are plants that have naturalized in the local landscape. To some gardeners and gardening writers the "naturalized garden" is similar to what I like to call the "low-maintenance" garden. It involves planting only what thrives in your garden conditions (no extraordinary measures, no fertilizing, little if any watering and so on). But it also involves using plant material that spreads and allowing those plants to find their own space in your garden, competing with other species until a balance is struck and a stable ecosystem is established. Because the plants do spread and shift, this means that the garden style is natural and unscripted in appearance. Borders and distinct groupings of plants give way to a fluid and everchanging landscape. In this gardening approach, native and hardy perennials are preferred over annuals, but native plants need not be used exclusively.

There are, however, plenty of good reasons to use native plant material in your garden wherever you can. Native plants have adapted to the local insect populations and are often very resistant to pests. They are also a wonderful habitat and food source for local wildlife. Native plants also provide a connection to surrounding natural areas—by planting native plants you are supporting local biodiversity and you are not introducing alien species that might compete with native plants in your area. Native plants are often touted as being low maintenance—as they are adapted to local environmental conditions they require less or no supplemental watering or soil amendments. This is true if they are chosen appropriately. As a matter of fact, I've noticed that certain native plants, like purple coneflower, black-eyed Susans and nursery-grown trilliums, have become increasingly popular in Ontario in the last few years.

While native plants have adapted to their native environment, many "alien" plants have also adapted (very quickly) to our environment, and since some of these invasive introductions have no natural predators here they can out-compete the natives. What this means is that if you do have aggressive exotic plants in your garden, you'll have to make sure they don't overtake the native plants. You will also have to weed your garden well until the native plants become established, which can take three to five years.

What's more, some native gardening proponents do acknowledge that while there are many native plants that nurseries and gardeners have known and loved for years, there are many other Canadian native plants that have never been grown by gardeners, so we simply don't know much about cultivating them. And while it is true that these native plants have adapted themselves to the conditions they now inhabit in the wild, we have no idea how adaptable they may be to the conditions in our gardens, even if we are attempting to restore our sites to their native state. For example, most woodland plants need not only shade but also a good supply of decaying leaves, bark and wood chips to recreate the humusy forest soil. A few are also dependent on fungal growth that flourishes on the forest floor but not often in our gardens. Some native plants, like meadow flowers, however, are adapted to nutrient-poor soil, and our well-amended loam—and our automatic sprinkler systems!—will have them growing out of control so that they become leggy or need to be staked. If you are gardening in an urban area, not all native plants will be able to cope with the air pollution and acid rain. The key, therefore, to using native plants successfully is to know your region, understand the growing conditions of your own site and match these conditions to the native plants that best suit them.

But how do you determine what is native to your area? Ontario is an enormous geographical expanse that spans four major regions. The most temperate is the Carolinian or Deciduous Forest region that hugs the lower Great Lakes from Grand Bend on Lake Huron across to Toronto. To the north of the Carolinian zone is the Great Lakes–St. Lawrence Forest region that runs along Lake Ontario and the northern portions of Lake Huron and spreads across the very top of Lake Superior. The vast expanse of thinly populated woodlands to the north of that is the Boreal Forest region. And in a tiny strip running along the base of Hudson Bay is subarctic Taiga and Tundra. All these regions produce plants that are unique to them and many others that are grown in other places as well.

The three predominant areas contain many smaller regions and microregions that include woodlands, savannah and tall-grass prairie. Before widespread farming and development of the land, savannahs and prairies existed in pockets primarily around the lower Great Lakes.

If you live in one of Ontario's northern reaches you may be able to look out your backdoor for evidence of what native growth looks like in your area! But if you live in the heavily populated "Golden Horseshoe" of southern Ontario, you may have trouble identifying your ecological zone by strolling through your neighbourhood. According to my good friend and naturalist Lorraine Johnson, 90 percent of Carolinian native vegetation has disappeared and three-quarters of Ontario's wetlands have already been destroyed. To discover what your area might have been like before it was cleared for agriculture or housing, check the following resources:

1. The Federation of Ontario Naturalists (www.ontarionature.org) has information and can also put you in touch with local naturalist groups in your area. Local conservation areas and societies may also have information.

2. The North American Native Plant Society may also be able to give you specific information about native plants in your area. Their Web site is www.nanps.org.

3. Wildflower books or field guides of your local area will list what plants are native to a particular area. I particularly recommend Lorraine Johnson's *The Ontario Naturalized Garden*. The Federation of Ontario Naturalists also offers a guide titled *Ontario Trees and Some Woodland Plants*.

4. Your local garden centre may also be able to help. If they carry native plants you can ask which bioregion they came from.

5. My Web site, www.markcullen.com, also has information on native plants and links to other sites and organizations that may be of help.

But keep in mind that you must also make a judgment of what native plants will work in your garden or what bioregion your property mimics. Perhaps at one point your backyard would have been part of an Ontario savannah. But now it is filled with succulent vegetation and shade trees. The soil may have been amended every year that you can remember and efficient watering systems are in place. Would returning it to a grasslands-like garden or a native meadow garden work or seem appropriate? Maybe not. Perhaps native woodland plants are a better choice. On the other hand, you may be in a newer neighbourhood that was once a wooded area but has been cleared for housing. Much of its topsoil may have been removed during development, so a meadow-like garden with native plants that thrive in full sun, poor soil and open conditions may be just the right solution. You may also have a number of different gardening conditions on your site, requiring different sorts of native plants. Remember that in the natural landscape there are dry and wet meadows, and dry or wet woodlands. There should be native plant choices for just about any garden condition you have!

The other important factor to remember if you are thinking about native plant gardening is that you don't have to create a garden of exclusively native plants. While some gardeners are interested in creating a wholly native ecosystem on their property, in my

RULE OF THUMB
Consider native plants rather than invasive or spreading non-natives if you live near a nature preserve, natural park or other natural areas that might become home to anything you plant on your site. If you do live in these circumstances, the nature reserve or park may well have information on local native plant species that you can use. And the Federation of Ontario Naturalists Web site (www.ontarionature.org) has lists and photos of invasive alien species to avoid.

experience, most gardeners like to make natives an addition to existing plantings, and often combine the native plants with others to create traditional or formal garden designs. Even from an environmental standpoint, your use of native plants does not have to be an all-or-nothing decision. "The Benefits of Growing Native Plants," a helpful pamphlet published by the Toronto Parks and Recreation department and the High Park Citizen's Advisory committee, notes that "if each gardener replaces just two invasive alien species with native plants, the results will be significant."

Native woodlands plants and gardens

Whether creating an entire "woodland" garden or using woodland native plants, you must have similar conditions to the natural homes of these flowers and shrubs.

WHAT WOODLAND PLANTS NEED

Shade

While many woodland plants receive sun or dappled sun in the early spring before the leaves are out on the trees, they spend most of the rest of the growing season in shade. The majority of woodland plants flower in the spring when they do get sun, but they won't thrive or survive in full summer sun.

Fertile soil

Woodland plants enjoy the rich, friable, humusy soil that is created by decomposing leaves. Even if you are starting with good soil, you will want to mimic nature and add a layer of organic matter at least once a year (this is a good gardening practice with non-native plants too!). A spring application of compost, well-rotted manure or leaf mould and the use of chopped leaves as a winter mulch are ideal. Many native woodland plants like slightly acidic soil.

Remember that the most pervasive colour in the woods is green—the colours of many woodland flowers are delicate and subtle, and a number of woodland plants feature wonderfully textured and shaped foliage rather than vibrant flowers. Wild Canadian ginger, for example, has a lovely deep-green heart-shaped leaf that more than makes up for its rather quiet rusty-brown flower. A number of woodland plants are spring "ephemerals," which means that after their early burst of colourful flowering they go dormant for the rest of the season (Dutchman's breeches or *Dicentra cucullaria* is an example of this). By all means, include some of these lovely plants in your garden, but make sure you have other summer plants that will grow to disguise the bare spots that spring ephemerals will leave in the garden.

SOME WONDERFUL WOODLAND PLANTS

Bee balm (*Monarda didyma*)
Black snakeroot (*Cimicifuga racemosa*)
Bloodroot (*Sanguinaria canadensis*)
Canada anemone (*Anemone canadensis*)
Canada lily (*Lilium canadense*)
Cut-leaved toothwort (*Dentaria laciniata*)

Dutchman's breeches (*Dicentra cucullaria*)
False Solomon's seal (*Smilacina racemosa*)
Foamflower (*Tiarella cordifolia*)
Jack-in-the-pulpit (*Arisaema triphyllum*)
Jewelweed or spotted touch-me-not
  (*Impatiens capensis*)

Mayapple (*Podophyllum peltatum*)
Sharp-lobed hepatica (*Hepatica acutiloba*)
Solomon's seal (*Polygonatum biflorum*)
Spring beauty (*Claytonia virginica*)
Trillium (*Trillium grandiflorum*)
Trout lily (*Erythronium americanum*)

Violet (*Viola canadensis*)
Virginia bluebells (*Mertensia virginica*)
Wild Canadian ginger (*Asarum canadense*)
Wild geranium (*Geranium maculatum*)
Wood poppy (*Stylophorum diphyllum*)
Woodland sunflower (*Helianthus divaricatus*)

ONTARIO NATIVE TREES AND SHRUBS

Alternate-leaved dogwood
  (*Cornus alternifolia*)
Canadian serviceberry (*Amelanchier
  canadensis*)
Chokecherry (*Prunus virginiana*)
Common grey birch (*Betula populifolia*)
Common juniper (*Juniperus communis*)
Creeping juniper (*Juniperus horizontalis*)
Downy serviceberry (*Amelanchier arborea*)

Large cranberry (*Vaccinium macrocarpon*)
Nannyberry (*Viburnum lentago*)
New Jersey tea (*Ceanothus americanus*)
Pin cherry (*Prunus pensylvanica*)
Red osier dogwood (*Cornus sericea*)
Redbud (*Cercis canadensis*)
Saskatoon berry (*Amelanchier alnifolia*)
Staghorn sumac (*Rhus typhina*)

ONTARIO NATIVE TREES AND SHRUBS BY REGION

Zones 5, 6 and 7: Carolinian trees and shrubs
Black walnut (*Juglans nigra*)
Chestnut oak (*Quercus prinus*)
Eastern wahoo (*Euonymus atropurpureus*)
Flowering dogwood (*Cornus florida*)
Pawpaw (*Asimina triloba*)
Sassafras (*Sassafras albidum*)

Shrubby St. Johnswort (*Hypericum prolificum*)
Spicebush (*Lindera benzoin*)
Sycamore (*Platanus occidentalis*)
White oak (*Quercus alba*)
Wild crabapple (*Malus coronaria*)

Zones 3, 4 and 5: Great Lakes–St. Lawrence Forest Region
American basswood (*Tilia americana*)
American mountain ash (*Sorbus americana*)
Balsam fir (*Abies balsamea*)
Balsam poplar (*Populus balsamifera*)
Black spruce (*Picea mariana*)
Eastern arborvitae or white cedar
  (*Thuja occidentalis*)
Eastern or Canadian hemlock (*Tsuga
  canadensis*)
Eastern white pine (*Pinus strobus*)
Elderberry (*Sambucus canadensis*)
Jack pine (*Pinus banksiana*)

Quaking aspen (*Populus tremuloides*)
Red maple (*Acer rubrum*)
Red oak (*Quercus rubra*)
Red pine (*Pinus resinosa*)
Striped maple (*Acer pensylvanicum*)
Sugar maple (*Acer saccharum*)
White ash (*Fraxinus americana*)
White (or paper or canoe) birch
  (*Betula papyrifera*)
White spruce (*Picea glauca*)
Yellow birch (*Betula alleghaniensis*)

Zones 2, 3: Boreal Forest Region
American mountain ash (*Sorbus americana*)
Balsam fir (*Abies balsamea*)
Balsam poplar (*Populus balsamifera*)
Black ash (*Fraxinus nigra*)
Black spruce (*Picea mariana*)
Black willow (*Salix nigra*)
Jack pine (*Pinus banksiana*)

Speckled alder (*Alnus rugosa*)
Tamarack (*Larix laricina*)
Trembling aspen (*Populus tremuloides*)
White (or canoe or paper) birch
  (*Betula papyrifera*)
White elm (*Ulmus americana*)
White spruce (*Picea glauca*)

Prairie and meadow gardens

While you might think of prairies as a landscape emblematic of the Midwest, tall-grass prairies (as opposed to mixed-grass and shortgrass prairies that exist in drier climes farther west in the continent) are native to areas of this province. They existed (and in some very tiny remnants still exist) around Windsor, Chatham, Leamington and Toronto; and farther inland, around London, St. Thomas, Brantford, Cambridge, Rice Lake and Peterborough. Other grassland landscapes, like oak savannahs, that often bordered the prairies and the plains of the Midwest were also found in Ontario. (For a wonderful example of the remaining oak savannah landscape in Ontario, check out The Pinery provincial park on Lake Huron's south shore. You can also see remnants of this landscape in Toronto in the century-old neighbourhood just north of Casa Loma, and in High Park and its surrounding area.) But even if you live in an area that was formerly the home of grasslands, re-establishing a prairie in your backyard is not likely to be an option, unless you have a vast tract of open land and a great deal of time at your disposal (a prairie habitat would take several years to establish). In fact, what most people are attracted to as gardeners is the idea of a meadow.

Meadows are a transitional ecosystem rather than a stable, self-perpetuating landscape like a prairie. They develop in areas where tree cover has been disturbed or removed, providing a sunny site, often surrounded by the original woodlands. Here grasses, forbs (herbs other than grasses) and wildflowers thrive until the shrubs and trees succeed them to cover the land.

True meadows are not, as you might assume, low-maintenance gardens, at least not initially. Many of the plants are slow to establish and are easy prey to weeds that will choke them out. What's more, meadow plants thrive in the same conditions as many weeds or invasive non-natives—disturbed, loose soil and full sun. In order to allow meadow plants to gain a foothold, the site must be prepared well to kill existing weed seeds in the soil. This means rototilling the earth before planting for at least one full season, using black plastic to cover the soil and kill weed seeds or applying herbicides on the soil. I have used a product called Wipe Out for this purpose with great success. It is low in toxicity,

Are you ready for a big change? When you look at your yard, are you tempted to rip out the whole thing, lawn and all, and start again with something unconventional? If so, a wild-flower meadow may be for you!

Here is a garden that is about as "unconventional" as it gets. While a meadow garden requires planning, the planting of carefully selected plant material (a meadow is not created by simply letting your site self-seed and "grow wild") and diligent weeding for the short term, a meadow is a great low-maintenance garden in the long term. And the subtle colours and tall, waving flowers and grasses make a gorgeous vista.

so it causes no soil contamination. And it works faster than plastic! (See my *The New Greener Thumb* for more details on eliminating weed seeds from soil.)

Once the soil is prepared, the meadow must be weeded aggressively for the first two years. What's more, to create a true meadow and help it thrive, you must use a mix of native grasses (at least 50 per cent) as well as native flowering plants. The grasses not only provide structural support for the flowers, but as they grow, they also cover the surface of the soil, leaving less space for weeds to get a foothold. In addition, because most wildflowers have deep roots, there's considerable space near the surface of the soil for weeds to establish their roots; however, the grasses can out-compete any weed seeds by establishing their own roots in the area just below the surface. Once meadows are established, they need little attention, other than mowing. Meadows need to be shorn to a height of 10 to 15 cm (4 to 6 inches) once a year. This shearing replicates the fires or grazing and trampling by animals that keep native grasses and flowers strong while reducing weeds and woody growth that would overcome them. And after your meadow garden is established, you must keep in mind that it is still a transitional ecosystem—plants are likely to spread themselves about and naturalize, changing the appearance of the garden over time.

True meadows are a delightful landscape—delicate and subtle in colourings, and ever-shifting in pattern and texture. If a meadow is appropriate to your site, the initial labour may well be worth it. Before embarking, however, read about meadow gardening further (Lorraine Johnson's *The Ontario Naturalized Garden* is an excellent resource) or consult a meadow gardening specialist such as Wildflower Farm outside of Schomberg, Ontario (www.wildflowerfarm.com), or Sweet Grass Gardens near Brantford (www.sweetgrassgardens.com). I also have meadow gardening information featured on my Web site.

There is no reason, however, not to use native plants to create a "meadow garden" that conforms more easily to the space, time and practices of an urban or suburban gardener than a true meadow might. As a matter of fact, I have noticed that over the last few years, many native meadow or prairie flowers have

WHAT MEADOW AND PRAIRIE PLANTS NEED
Heat and sun
Five or six hours of full sun.
Average soil
Most meadow plants do well in poor soil. As a matter of fact, high organic content and fertilizers can cause flowers to produce more leaves and fewer flowers. Leggy plants may need to be staked. Meadow and prairie plants do, however, need well-drained soil.

RULE OF THUMB
Many meadow plants can take up to three years to bloom from seed. If you are not planting an enormous area, buying transplants from a nursery or garden centre will give you delightful blossoms in the first year.

become increasingly popular at the Weall & Cullen garden centres—sun-lovers like black-eyed Susans, purple coneflowers, obedient plants and butterfly weed are being embraced for their drought-tolerance, hardiness and pest-resistance as well as their gorgeous petals.

Excellent native meadow plants

Black-eyed Susan (*Rudbeckia fulgida*)
Bottle gentian (*Gentiana andrewsii*)
Butterfly weed (*Asclepias tuberosa*)
Canada anemone (*Anemone canadensis*)
Canada lily (*Lilium canadense*)
Cardinal flower (*Lobelia cardinalis*)
Culver's root (*Veronicastrum virginicum*)
Dense blazing star (*Liatris spicata*)
Goldenrod (*Solidago*)
Ironweed (*Vernonia fasciculata*)
Joe Pye weed (*Eupatorium maculatum*)
New England aster (*Aster novae-angliae*)
Nodding wild onion (*Allium cernuum*)
Prairie smoke (*Geum triflorum*)
Purple coneflower (*Echinacea purpurea*)
Wild bergamot (*Monarda fistulosa*)
Wild lupine (*Lupinus perennis*)

Grasses

Big bluestem (*Andropogon gerardii*)
Indian grass (*Sorghastrum nutans*)
Little bluestem (*Andropogon scoparius*)

Interested in discovering what "native" ecosystems of Ontario looked like? The Federation of Ontario Naturalists Web site has a list of nature preserves and a guide to finding examples of the various ecological regions under the tab "Nature Networks". Many of Ontario's provincial parks also have wonderful examples of the native ecosystems of the area. At the Ontario Provincial Parks Web site, www.ontarioparks.com, parks are listed in a variety of ways, such as according to "heritage values," which include ecosystems. The site recommends the Rondeau, Short Hill, Wheatley, Turkey Point, Trillium Woods and Ojibway Prairie as great places to see examples of the Carolinian Forest. Many parks are good examples of the Great Lakes–St. Lawrence Forest in this province, especially in the north and northwest; examples in southern Ontario include MacGregor Point, Mono Cliffs, Frontenac and Bon Echo. There are also parks in the Boreal Forest and even one that is in the Tundra–Polar Bear Park on Hudson Bay.

The
Northern
Garden

This chapter is not about "northern" gardening as those in Florida might consider it. For Ontarians, the "north" is well above the 49th parallel, in other words, zones 2, 3 and 4. While the southern areas of our province offer some of the most fertile land and temperature climates in the country, a much larger geographic portion of Ontario calls the bedrock of the Canadian Shield home. This northern land offers some stunning beauty, but for gardeners, poor or rocky soil and a short growing season can be challenging. I have, however, visited wonderful gardens all across this province and have seen how a little ingenuity, experimentation and know-how can make gorgeous gardens possible in the most unexpected places. In the next chapter—Gardening at the Cottage—you will find some practical tips on addressing soil and landscape problems. Here are a few other ideas to consider when gardening in the northern zones.

Consider your rainfall

Is your area relatively dry? Many areas of northern Ontario are. Amend soil to improve water retention, mulch and consider putting a little money into improved watering methods—in-ground systems, soaker, drip hoses—and/or choose plant material with low water needs. Xeriscaping (see Watering and Xeriscaping, p. 165) may also address a number of your gardening challenges.

Consider your soil

If you are already working with a short growing season, it is important to keep in mind things that might shorten it further—things like the composition of your soil. Sandy soil heats up faster in the spring and holds heat longer, but clay soils work in quite the opposite way. Because clay soil is so dense, it takes a very long time for it to warm up in the spring, meaning that your friend with sandy loam may be seeing his perennials peek through the ground many weeks before your clay-filled soil shows any evidence of life. If you do have clay soil and want to see your flowers earlier or give your vegetables enough time to ripen before the first frosts roll around, consider undertaking large-scale soil amendments or replacement (see Digging, p. 161). Dig in plenty of compost, manure and sharp sand to create a loam that will warm up more quickly. Recently introduced "clay-breaking" soil amendments are helpful and *permanent*. I have used a product called Profile with success, and I recommend it if you choose not to remove the clay from your yard. Or you may want to consider creating raised beds.

Use raised beds

Raised beds have many benefits, such as improving drainage and making it easier to introduce soil amendments or replace soil without heavy digging or needing to remove existing earth. But in northern gardens they have the added benefit of warming up more quickly in the spring than beds at ground level. If they are placed against south-facing walls or built with a southerly exposure they warm up faster and stay warmer longer. Just keep in mind that raised beds also dry out quickly and will need more watering than ground-level beds. Because they drain well, they are prone to moisture loss, so don't fill them with sandy soil unless heavily amended with generous quantities of organic material—say, four parts compost and soil to one part sand.

Create and use microclimates

Spend some time in your garden identifying areas that may have different growing conditions than the rest of the garden or the rest of your area (see Microclimates, p. 54). Use pockets of warmer, more sheltered land to try plants that are only borderline hardy for your zone, or ones that have failed elsewhere in your garden. You can create a spot that will warm up early in the spring by building a brick or stone wall to enclose a south-facing area. If you identify cool spots in your garden, you can redesign the area around them to reduce this colder microclimate, or you may want to choose plant materials that are hardy to one zone below your own. Consider planting some tall trees around your garden to serve as windbreaks that will force the blowing air up, over and past your garden, but keep in mind that the trees will create more shade and root zone competition in your northern garden and may reduce your plant choices. You will likely want to consider windbreaks only if your property is very windy and exposed. Tall evergreens can also cut home heating costs by deflecting cold north winds. Creating and using microclimates is a useful gardening approach with a long history. In fact, the Victorian practice of building walled gardens was not just an attempt at gaining privacy; it was also an effective method of producing a variety of microclimates within a single garden.

Try alpine plants

Alpine plants are not considered especially easy ones to grow for most of the country, but depending on where you live in northern Ontario, you might have conditions that suit them. Alpine plants are native species of the Arctic tundra and of high mountain altitudes—often above the timberline. Most are small perennials that grow low and compact to withstand the weight of winter snow cover and protect them from strong winds that assail them the rest of the year. Growing close to the ground also ensures that they remain where it is warmest—next to the soil (or rocks) that will absorb and reflect the sun's heat. Many of these plants are also evergreen (they have adapted so they don't have to grow an entirely new set of leaves in each short growing season), so they will remain attractive long after the petunias and impatiens have drooped. Alpine plants also depend on your short summers with their long, relatively cool days.

Microclimates

In any growing zone (see zone map, p. 224), there will be many small areas where the climate is quite different from that of the surrounding terrain. These spots are called microclimates, and they are really just little zones within a zone. They are, however, seldom if ever identified—after all, they can be as small as a few square feet or as big as a few square miles. Yet identifying any existing microclimates in your yard and garden is a very useful exercise. You may find hotspots where you can try plants that are recommended for a zone or two higher than yours or are simply borderline for your zone. You may identify arid, windy or harsh areas that will challenge plants that grow successfully in other parts of your garden or neighbourhood. And you may notice cool areas in your garden—frost pockets—that will damage plants recommended as hardy in your zone. Identifying microclimates in your garden also may solve some of your enduring gardening puzzles—why do my neighbour's roses flourish, while mine seem to be barely clinging to life? Why did the hibiscus, which was doing so well by the side of the garage where no one could see it, give up the ghost when I moved it to a prime spot in the middle of the garden?

Microclimates are created by differences in the local topography. Rocks, stone and paved areas retain heat and may create a warmer climate in their area. Cities can be significantly warmer than the area around them because they have such a high concentration of concrete, pavement and buildings that all retain and release heat. What's more, a city's smog can trap heat and keep the warmer air close to the ground. Sizable bodies of water moderate temperatures, making the area surrounding them cooler in the summer and warmer in the winter. (Look at the differences between the landscape bordering any of Ontario's Great Lakes with regions farther inland for excellent evidence of this.) Even a small dip in the land can create a pocket of cooler temperatures as the cold air flows down to fill it. The southern exposure of houses or slopes will be sunnier and warmer, the northern exposure shadier and therefore cooler. A tour of areas south of the Niagara Escarpment, with their vineyards and orchards, quickly shows the warming effects of a southerly exposure on a large scale.

If you want to identify the potential microclimates in your yard, it may take a year or two of close observation during which you observe light levels, keep track of frost differences and make note of what thrives and what fails in various areas. Pay particular attention to identical plants located in different parts of your yard. They offer excellent indicators about differing microclimates. Take note of the first and last plants to bloom or to poke their way through the soil. Also, keep your eyes open for the following conditions:

Frost pockets and cool microclimates
Dips in the terrain and low-lying areas of your property are potential cooler microclimates. The north side of walls or dense hedges may also be areas that are significantly cooler than the rest of your property.

Wind tunnels and exposures
Windy exposures are always more challenging for plants and for gardeners. They may be significantly cooler than the rest of the garden, and they will certainly lose more moisture due to evaporation. Wind tunnels are places where the wind is forced through a narrow space, therefore picking up pressure and speed. This may happen between houses, structures, fences or trees. Any area of your garden that is raised and not protected by hedges, tall shrubs, trees or fences may suffer from wind that blows across it unimpeded.

Heat traps and protected areas
If in a sunny location (particularly a southern exposure), rocks, stones, pavement and brick walls will all absorb heat and release it to raise the surrounding temperature, creating a warmer microclimate. Light-coloured walls of any composition will also reflect the sun and heat and raise temperatures. Walls can also block the wind and therefore reduce wind chill. Similarly protected areas are those where snow collects and insulates the ground in the winter months.

Arid spots

There may be areas of your garden that are significantly drier than others. If you have areas of high ground, the leeside will be drier (the windward side is likely to get more rain). Also, the eaves of your house, garage or shed may prevent rain from reaching the ground, creating an often overlooked dry area in your otherwise well-watered garden.

> All the oxygen we breathe comes from the green living world around us. The plants in your yard—including your lawn—reduce air-borne and soil-borne pollutants and produce "fresh air." A lawn covering one average-size Ontario residential property provides the equivalent of *all* the oxygen required by one adult.

Air pollution

High levels of carbon dioxide can raise air temperatures slightly by absorbing UV radiation, but don't mistake these warmer areas for good growing conditions. Because the carbon dioxide has trapped the UV radiation, the amount of sunlight your plants get for photosynthesis is reduced. And smog and acid rain may cause damage to foliage. Some trees and shrubs tolerant of these adverse conditions include acanthopanax, caragana, Russian olive, little-leaf linden, skyline locust, euonymus, lilac, honeysuckle, alpine currant and privet.

Addressing microclimates

Identifying your microclimates may help you in choosing what plants you place where. But you may also decide to treat areas of your garden differently, according to the microclimate of each.

- Use plenty of mulch in frost pockets to protect your plants and avoid freeze/thaw cycles. Straw and shredded bark work well as winter mulches.

- Use hardy, deep-rooted plants that have less chance of being damaged by freeze/thaw cycles in frost pockets.

- Thin hedges if their density is creating a frost pocket on one side.

- Amend soil with compost or leaf mould (partially decomposed leaves) to help retain moisture under eaves, in heat traps, and other areas prone to dryness.

- Use heat traps as areas for vegetables and other annuals that will thrive in the extra warmth. Early spring–flowering bulbs are great choices for heat traps too—they will bloom even earlier.

- If you have the opportunity to design your garden and structures, try to avoid creating or maintaining areas where the wind is channelled through narrow passages. You may also want to break up areas where the wind blows unimpeded by installing a windbreak in the form of a fence, a line or grouping of trees or a hedge. Keep in mind that very dense hedges, and solid walls or fences, will not solve your problems—they force wind up, creating air turbulence and downdrafts that buffet plants on the other side (see illustration, p. 56). Planting a windbreak at the bottom of a slope will only impede the downward flow of wind and keep the cooler air over your garden.

- If you have a hilly property, take advantage of those warmer south-facing slopes by using them for early plantings of "hot crop" vegetables or flowering plants.

- Microclimates can also be created to cool down areas. Plant small trees and shrubs around the garden to create some partial shade and cooler air and soil for those plants that don't fare well in full sun and extreme heat.

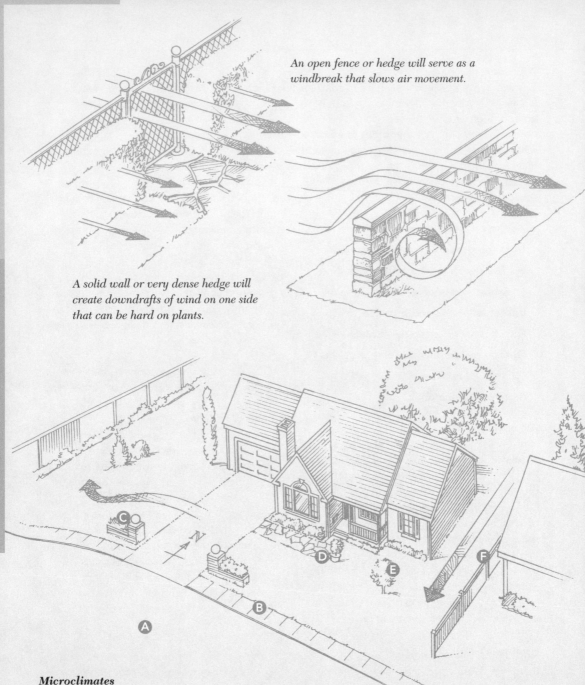

An open fence or hedge will serve as a windbreak that slows air movement.

A solid wall or very dense hedge will create downdrafts of wind on one side that can be hard on plants.

Microclimates

Ⓐ Areas near roads may have higher temperatures because of air pollution.

Ⓑ Brick or stone walls will be shady (and therefore cooler) on the north side and sunny and warm on the south side.

Ⓒ Areas where the ground is lower may trap cool air, making them "frost pockets."

Ⓓ South-facing walls, especially light-coloured ones, will create warmer areas.

Ⓔ Areas directly beneath rain gutters and eaves will be drier than surrounding areas.

Ⓕ Narrow passages between two structures may become wind tunnels.

Since these plants are small and compact and need good drainage, a rock garden or a rocky slope are ideal settings for them (see The Rock Garden, p. 70). But you may also want to try them in containers or raised beds, as long as you prepare the appropriate soil. They can also be planted in the gaps of retaining walls or along stone or gravel paths.

If planted at the bottom of a sloping rock garden or between paving stones, the effect is often referred to as an "alpine lawn." Fragrant alpine plants are often chosen for these locations so they will release their scent if walked on. Creeping or woolly thyme is popular for this use.

Alpine plants are adapted to porous, rocky, well-drained soil. If your soil has a great deal of clay, you will not be successful with these plants. In rich soils, you will have to dig in some sharp sand, grit or cinders to lighten the soil. Alpine plants also tend to favour neutral or slightly acidic soils. If you have cold winters but your snow cover is inconsistent, these plants must be insulated with a loose winter mulch.

Be careful when purchasing alpine plants, however. All alpine plants are ideal for rock gardens (see p. 71) but not all plants sold as rock garden plants are alpines—they may simply be small plants that are suitable for rock gardens. Ask your local garden centre if in doubt and check the zone requirements of each plant. If you are unable to find alpine plants in your garden centre, you may have to propagate plants from seed.

Use your long days

You may have fewer frost-free days than the Niagara region, but you will also have more hours of daylight in the summer in northern Ontario. When the sun doesn't set until 10 o'clock in July, plants are able to engage in photosynthesis and growth for much longer each day without having to withstand scorching temperatures. Choose plant material that likes plenty of sun, and plan your beds where they will get the most unbroken light. If you live along the northern shore of Lake Superior with its temperate effect on temperatures, you may find that some plants recommended for partial shade or partial sun can thrive in full sunlight.

Choose hardy perennials to be the backbone of your garden

Consider using more perennials. True, your zone may limit your choices somewhat, but hardy perennials, particularly ones with interesting foliage and shapes, will allow you to extend the season at both ends. You may want to

MARK'S TEN FAVOURITE HARDY PERENNIALS,
BULBS, TREES AND SHRUBS

Birch varieties, esp. dwarf Arctic birch (*Betula nana*)
Cotoneaster, Peking (*Cotoneaster acutifolius*)
Downy serviceberry (*Amelanchier arborea*)
Ninebark (*Physocarpus opulifolius*, esp. 'Dart's Gold')
Roseroot (*Sedum rosea*, syn. *Rhodiola rosea*)
Saskatoon berry (*Amelanchier alnifolia*)
Scilla and grape hyacinths (*Muscari*)
Siberian peashrub (*Caragana arborescens*)
Tatarian dogwood (*Cornus alba*)
White cedar (*Thuja occidentalis*)

include plenty of hardy trees and shrubs in your garden designs—white (paper or canoe) birch (zone 2), Siberian dogwood (zone 2), bearberry cotoneaster (zone 3) and Saskatoon berry (zone 2) maintain their beauty even as the seasons change, giving brilliant fall leaf colours and lovely branch structures for the winter garden. Planting plenty of early spring bulbs among your perennials will also add greenery and colour while your perennials are just beginning to peek through the soil.

Plant early

Lois Hole, my good friend and Edmonton's much admired gardening expert, loves to tell her many fans to "plant early." It's a great piece of advice. If you want to get the colour (or the vegetables) started early in your northern garden, by all means plant your annuals early. In most parts of northern or northwestern Ontario that means super-hardy annuals like pansies and violas can be planted in April or early May. Peas, carrots, onions, garlic and lettuce can be sown then too. In fact, rather than wait until all risk of frost is gone, get *all* your cold-tolerant annuals in the ground by your average last frost date (see the chart on p. 227). Half-hardy annuals and shade-loving plants can follow in the next few weeks. If you have a sudden cold snap, cover your plants with snow (for your hardy plants) or burlap (for the half-hardy annuals). You may lose a few, but the extra weeks of blooms are surely well worth the risk.

Include hardy bedding plants for no-fail gardening

Including plenty of hardy annuals allows you to fill your beds with colour a few weeks early—a bonus when you're facing a too-short summer! There are a number of beautiful bedding plants that can survive freezing temperatures quite handily. If they do get a little frost damage to their new growth, pinch it off—you may encourage fuller growth in the long run.

Baby's breath (*Gypsophila elegans*)
Bachelor's button (*Centaurea cyanus*)
California poppy (*Eschscholzia californica*)
Common stock (*Matthiola incana*)
Evening primrose (*Oenothera*)
Flanders poppy (*Papaver commutatum*)
Geraniums (*Pelargonium hortorum*)
Godetia (*Godetia amoena*)
Lavatera (*Lavatera trimestris*)
Nemophila (*Nemophila*)
Nigella (*Nigella*)
Opium poppy (*Papaver somniferum*)
Ornamental kale and cabbage (*Brassica oleracea*)
Phlox (*Phlox drummondii*)
Pink (*Dianthus chinensis* and *D. caryophyllus*)
Pot marigold (*Calendula officinalis*)
Salvia (*Salvia splendens*)
Snapdragon (*Antirrhinum majus*)
Sweet alyssum (*Lobularia maritima*)
Sweet pea (*Lathyrus*)
Sweet William (*Dianthus barbatus*)
Violas and pansies (*Viola* spp.)
Virginia stock (*Malcomia maritima*)

Keep in mind that all "early" planted annuals should be hardened off for ten days to two weeks before planting. Hardening off prepares the young plants for their transition from the consistent growing conditions of a greenhouse to the rise and fall of temperatures and moisture levels outside. On the first day of the process, put your seedlings or purchased annuals in a shaded spot outside for a couple of hours, then return them indoors. With each following day, leave them out for a little longer. Protect them from the wind and other harsh elements. After a minimum of ten days, they are ready to put in the ground.

Pansies and violas are popular choices for northern gardens as they are very frost hardy. They can be planted in early spring, but it is increasingly popular to plant pansies in the fall to liven up an autumn landscape. The new Second Season types have (what I call) natural anti-freeze built in. They bloom very early in the spring and are perfect for fall planting as well.

Experiment and consider treating some perennials as annuals

As I discuss in the section on microclimates (see p. 54), you may be surprised at what you can grow in certain areas of your garden where you have a zone within a zone. What's more, you may find that some plants not considered especially hardy can survive your northern climate surprisingly well. Remember that deep, consistent snow cover insulates your plants over the winter and prevents that bane of many more southerly gardeners: the freeze/thaw cycle. Warm winters can mean that rain soaks the soil, only to freeze solid the very next day and encase plant crowns in ice. All that wet winter weather can rot roots. Hot, humid summers can also be tough on some perennials. So cooler summers and deep-freeze winters might actually work in your favour with some perennials (this is why gardening is sometimes an easier endeavour in northerly Edmonton, in comparison to frequently balmy Calgary). If you like a perennial that is rated as a zone higher than your own, why not try it in a protected, southerly exposure in your garden? You may lose it over the winter, but you might also be pleasantly surprised.

If you can afford to lose a few "perennials" every year, you can give yourself a little more variety in your garden. One southern Ontario gardener I know told me she was passionate about hellebores, but finds they are a hit-and-miss choice for her garden. A few years ago she decided to consider them "annuals" for her garden. Each spring she checks to see what has survived and then replaces the plants that didn't make it. Given that many species come in a variety of new colours and shades, this approach also gives you the opportunity to play with colour as you keep the shape of your beds relatively consistent.

Try container gardening

Have you got your heart set on a perennial that you fear won't make it through your long cold winter? Why not plant it in a container that can be brought indoors and placed in a sunny window for the winter? A number of gardeners I know in southern Ontario do this with Chinese hibiscus and oleander, and while most perennials do need a cold or dormant period, there's no reason you can't try it with tropical plants or others that are hardy only in much warmer zones. See Of Gardens Large and Small, p.17 for more information about container gardening.

Use a cold frame

If you want to use plants that are difficult to keep going in your zone, and you don't want to replace them each year, you can also build yourself a cold frame where you can move these half-hardy plants to overwinter. My book *The All Seasons Gardener* gives detailed instructions for building a simple and effective cold frame. Prefabricated, small collapsible cold frames are also now available at many garden centres. You may also want to try cloches and other frost-protection devices like the "wall of water" and floating row covers at the beginning of the growing season.

Use your snow!

Snow really can be a lifesaver for perennials. When winter snows settle on my zone 5 garden, I like to gather it off my paths and driveway to cover my more tender perennials. This is an especially useful technique if you live in any area where snow actually stays frozen in the winter months! Snow acts as the perfect winter protection, keeping the ground insulated, allowing for air circulation and eventually providing moisture to your beds.

If you have a stretch of unseasonably warm weather in late winter or early spring, I recommend that you move the remaining snow in your yard onto your perennial beds to slow down the early emergence of plants and keep the ground from thawing and then perhaps freezing again. (You can also cover your plants with burlap, old blankets or straw if the snow has disappeared. Don't use plastic, however. It provides very poor insulation and traps moisture.)

Protect your tender or less hardy plants
Fall/winter

In any area that experiences a frosty winter, gardeners will find that many evergreens, including broad-leaved evergreens, such as rhododendrons and roses, benefit from protection. This is of course especially true for gardeners who wait out long, harsh winters. Sunny and windy winter days can dry out the needles of evergreens. Snow and ice accumulation on branches can cause damage and breakage. (And in areas with milder or inconsistent winters, the freeze-thaw-freeze cycle can heave small plants right out of the ground.) To give plants the best possible chance to make it through these cold days, winter protection is well worth a little extra time and effort in the fall.

Evergreens

❀ Loosely wrap burlap around the plant or build a small screen with posts and burlap to protect the plant. If wrapping the plant itself, leave the top and bottom open about 30 cm (1 foot) to allow air circulation. If using posts to build a screen, dry leaves can be used between the burlap and the plant as insulation. This is especially useful with small or recently transplanted evergreens.

❀ Wrap small upright evergreens with strong twine or cord to prevent the branches from being bent or weighted down by snow and ice, particularly if they are foundation plantings, which are vulnerable to ice and snow

You can protect small trees and shrubs over the winter in a variety of ways:
Ⓐ *Make a cage with four stakes and burlap. This can be filled with chopped leaves.*
Ⓑ *Loosely wrap burlap around the plant, securing with twine and leaving the top and bottom open.*
Ⓒ *Bind small upright evergreens with heavy twine.*

that falls off the roof. You can also put up shelters for them—an inverted, V-shaped structure can be made from two large boards; or small, table-shaped coverings can be placed over the plantings. Stretchy nylon mesh called Vexar is available at most garden centres. Stretched over your upright cedars and junipers in the fall, it is another excellent and easy way to protect shrubs and trees from ice and snow.

❀ Broad-leaved evergreens such as rhododendrons and hollies should be shielded from the wind and partly shaded with burlap screens to prevent moisture loss over the winter. Another excellent way to protect them is with an application of an antidesiccant—a product that help plants retain water. I recommend Wiltpruf for both broad-leaved evergreens like rhododendrons and boxwood, as well as for other evergreens, like dwarf Alberta spruce—it's a cheap insurance policy!

Roses

❀ Prune rose bushes to about half their height. Then mound soil around the base of each plant to between 30 and 40 cm (12 and 16 inches) deep. If necessary, bring soil from another part of the garden or use triple mix (compost, soil and peat moss), available at most garden cen-tres, for the task. Straw and leaves can also be used for protecting roses, but should be weighted down with purchased rose collars or burlap. A thorough watering will also help prevent the mulch from blowing away.

Spring

You can use a variety of devices and techniques to protect tender plants from late frosts (see p. 64). Many of these aids also keep the ground and the air around the plant warmer than it might be without protection and therefore encourage early growth of your plants. For the northern Ontario vegetable gardener, these devices may very well mean the difference between harvesting juicy red tomatoes and hard green ones at the end of August, but the devices can also be used for early emerging perennials as well.

Make the most of winter

A co-worker of mine is a transplanted Ontario northerner and finds the winters of southern Ontario intolerable. During our wet, grey and dreary winter months, she waxes poetic about the brilliant sunshine, pearly white snowbanks and deep blue skies of her northern Ontario home town. It certainly sounds as if those of us in southern Ontario are in greater need

A number of commercially available devices are especially useful in the spring to protect transplants and tender seedlings from frost and wind:
Ⓐ *Water-filled cylinder*
Ⓑ *Plastic cloche*
Ⓒ *Plastic row covers*
Ⓓ *Floating row cover*
Plastic milk jugs also work well!

of making our gardens attractive in winter, but there is no doubt that gardeners in either location will find great pleasure in a garden that looks beautiful even without flowers or leaves. Check the January chapter of my *All Seasons Gardener* for how to plan for winter interest in your garden. There are wonderful tree and shrub choices for all Ontario zones.

Gardening at the Cottage

As I began to make notes for this chapter I found myself referring to it as "The Cottage Garden" chapter. Then I realized that this might be quite misleading to anyone browsing through the table of contents. "Cottage garden" in most gardening literature refers to a style of garden—specifically the English cottage garden look. I love this lush, irregular, natural-looking profusion of flowers, and it certainly has enjoyed periods of great popularity in Ontario. But when most people in this province hear "cottage" (or "camp" in northern Ontario), they think of a little place in the woods, by a lake, where summer days are spent away from town life. They think of the pristine inland lakes of Lake of the Woods, the Kawarthas, Muskoka or the Gatineaus. They think of quiet little places along the Trent-Severn waterway or the mighty St. Lawrence River. They think of the breath-taking vistas along the shores of all of our Great Lakes. This is cottage country to us, and this is where, if we are gardeners, we may find ourselves facing entirely different challenges than we meet in our city lots.

We are likely to be gardening in a growing zone that we are not used to, and with a soil structure that is markedly different than that in our city garden. We likely will have to deal with heavy shade, and we almost certainly will have to think about how we will manage any sort of garden when we may not be around on a regular basis. And of course, we will have a great many more insects and four-legged visitors in our flower beds. But before we make our first planting we should think about what it is we really want from our cottage landscape.

Take a good hard look around your cottage property. Perhaps you just want to enhance the natural environment, or, at the other extreme, completely morph your yard into something very personal. What do you like about the existing landscape? What would you like to change? Perhaps all that you want is to shape or finesse the transition between the woodland and the clearing around the cottage—to create a seamless, naturalistic look. Or maybe you are hankering for a splash of colour to contrast with the native greenery and the blues of the sky and water. Perhaps you find the cottage building itself looking a little exposed in its setting and want to work on foundation plantings or a few flower beds close by to soften the look of the structure. Once you have determined what your gardening design goal is, spend a little time thinking about how you might achieve this look and functionality. If you find yourself coming up with ideas you've used or have noticed in urban settings, ask yourself if these solutions are appropriate for your cottage. A cottage is, after all, an ideal place to try something a little different.

Of course, the next stage of planning your cottage garden is asking yourself how much time you really want to spend gardening at the cottage. You may have to admit that the answer is very little or none: sailing, swimming or simply relaxing with a good book may be far more appealing. If, however, gardening is your hobby and, like me, you find gardening a great way to relax, then you must be realistic about how much time you will be spending at the cottage and how much of that time will be available for gardening. Unless you are one of those lucky people who can move lock, stock and barrel to your cottage for the entire summer, you likely must be satisfied with a week or two here and there and as many weekends as you can cram in during the warm months. That means that gardening at a cottage is often a sporadic venture. If you really adore getting your hands into the earth during the summer months, that may mean spending your whole weekends gardening like mad, doing as much weeding and watering, pruning and deadheading as you can in two days. For others, it means creating gardens that thrive on neglect, that need only minimal attention to stay healthy and beautiful.

A third consideration when planning your garden should be an assessment of when you actually do spend the most time at the cottage. If, for example, you take your longest chunk of holidays at the end of the summer, you will want to plant late-blooming flowers. Why bother putting in a glorious bed of irises when you will be gazing at spent and flowerless stalks for your two weeks' holidays in August? Take a look at the Bloom Time chart on pp. 14–16 to help you plan the perfect cottage bloom cycle.

RULE OF THUMB
One of the most common questions I am asked is, "What plants can you recommend that will tolerate my hit and miss attention?" Surprisingly, it's really not such a tough question to answer—there are a good number of plants that thrive on neglect. Check out the extensive list of drought-tolerant plants in Chapter 9, Watering and Xeriscaping, on p. 182 for some attractive ideas.

Light

While planning the cottage garden, take into consideration the light levels in the areas you want to plant. Many cottages are set in relatively dense shadow or dappled sunlight at best. You may find that there are very few spots around the cottage that get the minimum six hours of sunlight needed for sun-loving plants. You should also consider the source of the shade. The shade is probably not caused by buildings, as it may be with urban gardens, but rather by trees which sap moisture from the soil. You will need to choose plants that like dry shade if planting in these conditions. Check out In Sun and Shade, for a list of dry shade plants and a host of other ideas for shade gardening.

Dealing with poor soil

As soon as we travel outside the "golden horseshoe" area of southern Ontario and away from the St. Lawrence Lowlands, we move into that vast, primordial area known as the Canadian Shield. Here the land is composed of great sheets of rock—primarily granite and limestone—with gravel, sand and sometimes, but not always, a thin dusting of soil clinging to it. Our woodlands are well adapted to these conditions, and nothing is more marvellous than seeing a canoe birch (my favourite) growing out of what appears to be solid rock, or noticing, after a forest fire, the first stages of succession as the mosses that will help break down the stone and create new soil work their way across blackened granite. But if we want to create our own garden in this setting, we may have to learn to adapt to this thin soil or find ways to enhance it.

You can always amend the soil in your cottage garden beds, but if you are putting in a new garden or expanding an existing one, you may find that you don't need to amend soil as much as replace or add soil to cover the rocky terrain. To do this you can create raised beds, but remember that raised beds need more watering as they lose moisture from evaporation on their tops and sides. If you don't want raised beds you will have to break up the existing topsoil, removing rocks or clay if necessary and replacing the soil with at least 35 cm (14 inches) of good-quality topsoil. If you are adding soil for a bed of moisture-loving plants, you might want to consider laying down a permanent lining material (like spun polyester landscape fabric) before adding the soil to prevent the new soil from washing away. To do this, dig a trough about 60 cm (2 feet) deep and line it with landscape fabric to cover the bottom and 30 cm (1 foot) up the side. Leave the rest of the side up to the ground open so that water can run off in very heavy rainfall.

You may also want to test the pH of your soil with a simple, inexpensive pH soil test kit (see p. 135). While most gardening experts agree that the fallen needles from a few pine trees on an urban lot are not going to have much effect on the acidity of soil, the soil under a coniferous forest is a different story. If the humus in your area is made up primarily of decaying pine needles, you might have quite acidic soil (spruce needles tend to be the most acidic, with pine and fir less so). Given that changing your pH is an arduous and never-ending process in any garden, you probably don't want to take on Mother Nature at the cottage. Choose plant materials that thrive in the pH range you have.

Native plant gardening

What better way to ensure the success of your cottage garden than by using plant, flower, tree and shrub species that are already growing naturally around your cottage? Not only will your landscaping perfectly blend in with the surrounding area, but your plantings will have the best possible chance of surviving if they are already thriving in these conditions. See Native Plants and the Ontario Naturalized Garden, for a more extensive discussion of native plant gardening. While it sometimes takes some research to figure out what plants might have originally been native to your *urban* lot, discovering the native state of your cottage land should be downright easy. Wander through the surrounding woods and fields and make a list of what you see growing there. Lorraine Johnson's *100 Easy-to-Grow Native Plants*—one of my favourite native plant guides—has some very helpful thumbnail photos that will help you identify plants. There is also a handy four-colour book available from some bookstores and the Federal Government Publications department (www.fedpubs.com) called *Forest Plants of Central Ontario* written by Brenda Chambers, Karen Legasy and Cathy V. Bentley. Also, the Natural Heritage Information Centre (a joint venture of the Ontario Ministry of Natural Resources, the Nature Conservancy of Canada, the Natural Heritage League and the Nature Conservancy) has a very thorough list of vascular plants native to Ontario listed on its Web site at www.mnr.gov.on.ca/MNR/nhic/nhic.html (under Lists of Ontario Species). Unfortunately, there are no pictures to accompany the list, so it is probably most useful as a way of checking to see whether plants you are interested in are native or not. Many native plants are now available at full-service garden centres in Ontario.

Xeriscaping

Using only drought-tolerant, hardy plants and designing your garden so that it thrives with very little water is an ideal approach for a cottage garden where regular and heavy watering may not be possible. See Chapter 9, Watering and Xeriscaping, for a discussion of low-water gardening.

Rock garden

If your cottage is set among rocky outcroppings, take advantage of it by using some of this rock as the base of a rock garden. Keep in mind that rock gardens are not low-maintenance gardens, and the weeding needed to maintain a rock garden may only be possible if you are at the cottage for most of the summer or can hire someone to do the weeding for you. But if you have the time and the inclination, what better use of an existing rocky outcropping or slope? Rocks can be useful if you are attempting to maintain soil on a slope, so you might even consider moving some of them around your property to create a new "rocky outcropping" and turn that into a rock garden.

The rock garden

If you are faced with a rocky outcropping on your property and don't relish the idea of hauling away all that stone, a rock garden is a wonderful way to transform this area. A rock garden is also a great idea for a slope. The slope aids the good drainage a rock garden demands, and the stones and plantings help prevent soil erosion on the slope. If you have no slope to transform but love the visual interplay between stone and tiny, delicate rock plants, you can construct your own rock mound or slope in which to plant your rock garden.

Choose a sunny, well-protected site. Most alpine and rock plants like full sun but will manage in filtered light in warmer regions. If the only available site for your rock garden is in the shade, you will be able to use only woodland plants.

Thoroughly plan the site before you begin. For every 30 cm (1 foot) in height, the rock garden will need to be 120 to 150 cm (4 to 5 feet) wide at its base. You will need rocks in a variety of sizes, including some quite large ones (remember that the rocks will be partially buried, so will not look as large once incorporated into the garden). Large rocks give the garden a more natural look as well. You will also need some mulch, either material that will decompose, like shredded bark or wood chips, or permanent mulches like stone chips, pebbles or gravel, which can give a lovely "scree" effect to a rock garden. This mulch will help control weeds (and therefore reduce the rock garden maintenance) and will also help hold the soil in place on the slopes.

Sandy soil really needs little preparation, other than thorough weeding and a light turning over. I also recommend adding finished compost (45 kg per 10 square m or 100 pounds per 100 square feet) unless you plan to use exclusively alpine (extremely drought-tolerant) plants, in which case compost can be reduced or eliminated entirely. Clay soil, however, will need to be dug out to a depth of about 45 cm (18 inches)—if you are moving up a slope, this may be a series of deep trenches—and gravel and stone laid in the bottom of the trench. Once the rocks are placed around the perimeter of the hole, the middle can be filled in with a loose, well-draining soil (you can make a mixture of loam, peat moss and fine gravel for this purpose).

In order to build a slope or mound, you may want to arrange your stones in a series of "L" or "V" shapes that form steps or terraces. Your biggest stones should be the corner stones of these angles, with rocks decreasing in size as they move farther away from the centre stone.

When setting and burying rocks in the slope or in the mound, place the weathered side of the rock facing out, and position the largest surface of the rock so that it sits on top (or is uppermost). For a natural look, equal portions of the rock should be buried and exposed. Burying a good portion of the rock also keeps the stone well anchored and provides for steady footing if you need to climb over it. It also ensures that there is plenty of cool soil under the rock for plant roots to seek out. When setting rocks in the ground, make sure you've laid them at a slightly upward angle so water flows back towards plants, instead of off the rocks. Also, try to lay the rocks horizontally by keeping the strata lines parallel to the ground. This will make the rock garden look more like a natural outcropping. Unlike brick laying, do not overlap the rocks to cover the space between two stones. Instead, keep the gaps between the stones lined up to aid drainage. Fill all gaps between the stones with loose, well-draining soil. Many gardeners also plant between these spaces, layer by layer, as they construct the garden. But you may want to add the soil over the course of several days, watering lightly after each fill, as soil may settle initially and need topping up before you begin planting.

Choosing rock plants

Rock plants are small and compact, but some are creeping and can grow quickly. Do not place these kinds near less vigorous growers or they may squeeze the smaller plants out. Also, traditional rock gardens use plants that need sun. The rocks absorb heat from the sun and radiate it to the soil and surrounding plants, so as long as there is plenty of sun, plants can thrive even if you are in part of Ontario that has cooler summers. If, however, the only place for your rock garden is in the partial shade, you may have to choose some plants that are not ordinarily considered rock plants.

If you're including dwarf upright shrubs and conifers in your rock garden, place them at the base of rocks. Spreading and cascading plants should be planted where they can fall down the rocks. Plants, like hens and chicks, that are small, compact and round or rosette-shaped can be tucked into vertical crevices.

Many alpine plants bloom in spring, so you may want to consider leaving a few spots where you can plant ground-hugging annuals for summer-long colour. Dwarf or minor bulbs like scilla, crocus and dwarf fritillaria will also add spring colour.

Plants for rock gardens

Alpine poppy (*Papaver alpinum*)
Alpine veronica (*Veronica allionii*)
Alyssum (*Lobularia maritima*)—annual
Anemone (*Anemone*)*
Aster, alpine types (*Aster alpinus*)
Beardtongue (*Penstemon*)*
Bellflower (*Campanula*), especially
   Carpathian bellflower or harebell
   (*C. carpatica*), fairy thimbles
   (*C. cochleariifolia*) and Serbian bellflower
   (*C. poscharskyana*)
Blue fescue (*Festuca glauca*)
Blue oat grass (*Helictotrichon sempervirens*)
Candytuft (*Iberis*)
Coral bell (*Heuchera sanguinea*)*
Coreopsis or tickseed (*Coreopsis auriculata* 'Nana')
Cranesbill geranium (*Geranium sanguineum*)
Creeping Jenny (*Lysimachia nummularia*)*
Creeping Veronica (*Veronica prostrata*)

Fernleaf bleeding heart (*Dicentra eximia* and *D. formosa* 'Luxurient')*
Gentian (*Gentiana*)*
Hens and chicks (*Sempervivum*)
Hosta (dwarf varieties) (*Hosta clausa* 'Normalis', *H.* 'Dorset Blue', *H.* 'Gold Drop', *H.* 'Grand Tiara', *H.* 'June')*
Lamb's ear (*Stachys byzantina*)
Pasqueflower (*Pulsatilla*)
Phlox (creeping types), especially Creeping phlox (*Phlox subulata*)
Pinks or dwarf carnations (*Dianthus*)
Potentilla or cinquefoil (*Potentilla*)
Primrose (*Primula*)*
Purple rock cress (*Aubrieta*)
Rock cress (*Arabis*)
Saxifrage (*Saxifraga*)
Stonecrop or sedum (*Sedum*)
Thrift (*Armeria*)
Thyme (*Thymus*)—annual and perennial varieties

*Can tolerate some shade

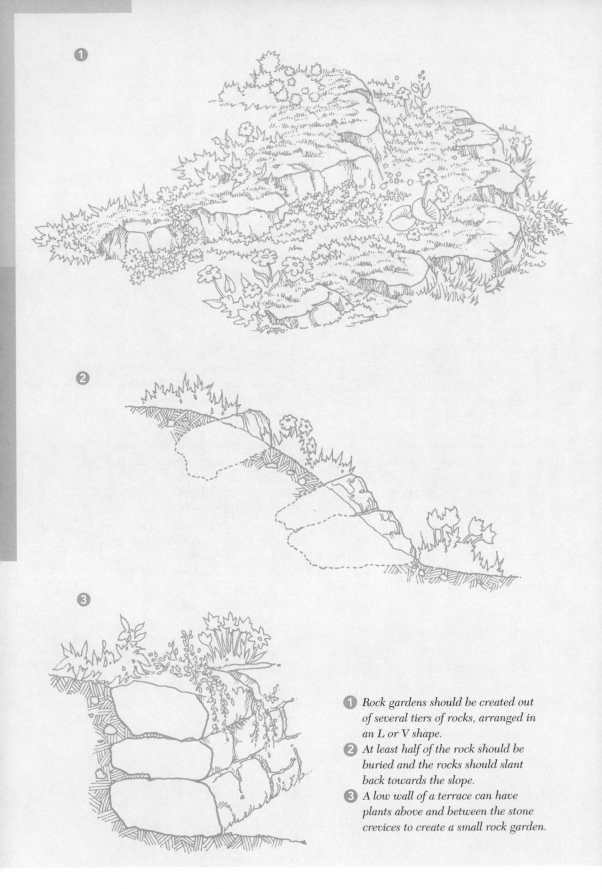

1 Rock gardens should be created out of several tiers of rocks, arranged in an L or V shape.

2 At least half of the rock should be buried and the rocks should slant back towards the slope.

3 A low wall of a terrace can have plants above and between the stone crevices to create a small rock garden.

Bog gardening

Establishing a bog garden is certainly something you can do in a city garden. You may have a naturally waterlogged area of your garden (this is especially true if your home lies on a former river bed, or where a creek has been diverted underground) that will be perfect for creating a bog garden. Some people are so fond of marsh marigolds, ferns, irises or the lush look of the bog garden that they will actually construct a special bed, lined with impermeable material like heavy black plastic, to plant their bog garden (see below). But the cottage is one place you are quite likely to find the perfect conditions for a bog garden. Huge areas of northern Ontario are indeed covered with bogs (and there are bogs extending into central and southern Ontario too)—waterlogged areas of acidic soil that sit on a substrata of peat. Other sorts of wetlands also abound, such as shrub- and tree-filled swamps and treeless marshes where reeds, cattails and wildlife flourish amid rich, fertile soil and areas of standing water.

Is your cottage located close to marshlands or swampy areas? Are there areas of wet land around a creek, river, lake or pond on your property? Is there a high concentration of clay or even muskeg around your cottage? If so, you may want to try creating an unusual and exciting bog garden.

The bog garden

A bog garden is one in which plants that like constant moisture or that have "wet feet" flourish. In a natural bog, the soil is acidic and waterlogged and sits atop a layer of peat. Poor drainage and the presence of the underlying peat means that the soil holds water and almost never dries out. If you have a low-lying area in your garden where water collects, this may be the ideal place to establish a bog garden. If you have heavy clay in this area, add peat moss and compost to break up the density and to make water accessible to the plants (see Chapter 7, Soil). If your soil is sandy, the drainage will be too good to create a bog. In that case, you can create a bog bed by digging down 30 to 45 cm (12 to 18 inches) and then lining the pit with plastic sheeting or a pond liner. Extend the plastic up the sides and over the ground edge. Make holes or small slits in the plastic sides, about 15 cm (6 inches) up and 10 to 12 cm (4 to 5 inches) apart. On top of the plastic, spread rocks, stones or wood chips or cover the bottom of the bog with pieces of sod laid grass side down. On top of this layer, add the soil, which should be equal parts topsoil and peat moss or cocoa fibre. Keep the soil in the bog garden damp at all times. Plant the bog densely—the visual effect will be much nicer, weeding will be reduced and the bog will not lose much moisture to evaporation. Top-dress the bog with well-rotted compost in the spring or fall. A winter mulch of shredded leaves or bark will help keep in moisture and add organic material to the bed.

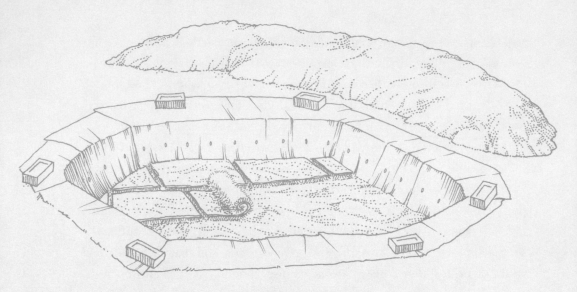

The planting area for a bog garden should be lined with plastic that has a series of holes or slits about 15 cm (6 inches) up the sides. The bottom can be lined with sod laid grass side down or with stones or wood chips.

Plants that like to have wet feet,
or bog plants
Arrowhead (*Sagittaria*)
Bergenia (*Bergenia cordifolia*)
Black chokeberry (*Aronia melanocarpa*)
  (it grows tall!)
Bog or water arum (*Calla*)
Calla lily (*Zantedeschi* spp.)
Cardinal flower (*Lobelia cardinalis*)
Cattail or bulrush (*Typha*)
Creeping Jenny (*Lysimachia nummularia*)
Eastern white cedar (*Thuja occidentalis*)
Elderberry (*Sambucus* spp.)
Globeflower (*Trollius*)
Hosta or plantain lily (*Hosta*)
Japanese iris (*Iris ensata*)

Lotus (*Nelumbo*)
Marsh marigold (*Caltha*)
Monkey flower (*Mimulus*) (an annual)
Primrose (*Primula* spp.)
Red maple (*Acer rubrum*)
Rodgersia (*Rodgersia*)
Siberian iris (*Iris sibirica*)
Sunshine (or New Guinea) impatiens
  (*Impatiens*) (an annual)
Sweet flag (*Acorus*)
Taro or elephant's ear (*Alocasia*)
Water canna (*Thalia*)
Water plantain (*Alisma*)
Watercress (*Nasturtium* spp.)
Willow (*Salix* spp.), especially the dwarf
  Arctic willow (*Salix arctica*)

Lawns and open areas

Even if you decide to keep all your ornamental gardening in your city garden, there is always the question at the cottage of what to do with the ground surrounding the house itself. If the cottage is set on rocks or close to the trees and surrounding woodlands, you may just let nature take its course. But many cottages are set in clearings of various sizes—places that seem to suggest a lush suburban lawn is in order. But this is a lawn that may not get the kind of regular upkeep your city lawn demands and receives. And to my way of thinking, mowing the lawn and "cottage life" do not go hand in hand. Why interrupt the lovely music of birds singing and breezes blowing through the trees with the roar of a motor (as if those dreaded jet-skis weren't enough). But even if you have the time and inclination to mow your lawn on a regular basis, you may not want to strain your well or your pump with lawn watering. You might therefore consider planting an attractive native groundcover, or if it is a large clearing, creating a native meadow on all or portions of it. Meadows are actually a transition stage in the development of a woodland that naturally occurs after the woodland has been cleared. It is therefore a wonderfully logical solution to your little clearing. Meadows, however, take a number of years to establish, so they are not low-maintenance at first. They also require periodic mowing and other maintenance (see p. 48) to ensure they don't revert to woodlands!

If you have small children or are partial to badminton or croquet, you may want to maintain an open space that can tolerate a good deal of foot traffic. Unfortunately, many of the really drought-tolerant, low-maintenance grasses, which sound ideal for a cottage setting, are not really great choices for play or for strolling. Many drought-tolerant grasses are bunch grasses rather than rhizomatous sod grasses (like those we grow on urban properties) and create a lumpy, bumpy surface that is not particularly pleasant to walk on. What's more, bunch grasses don't tolerate a lot of foot traffic.

If you have a very large open area, you can create two different lawns—the distant one that gives you the open visual perspective you want but requires little maintenance (see Watering and Xeriscaping, p. 180 for suggestions) and the more immediate lawn that will be pleasant to walk or lie on. When looking for seed or sod for this immediate lawn, look for seed mixtures that are labelled low-maintenance and hardy. These are now available across Ontario at garden centres, although they are relatively new to the market. They include some excellent low-growing and slow-growing grass seed varieties, and I highly recommend them for use at the cottage. Look for mixtures that include named varieties of creeping red fescue (*Festuca rubra* var. *rubra*), a pleasantly fine-textured grass that grows slowly and is drought- and shade-tolerant.

Fescues in general are wonderfully drought-tolerant and slow-growing. There are new cultivars that avoid their original "bunch-growing" nature. Look for mixtures that contain chewings fescue (*Festuca rubra* var. *commutata*) and hard fescue (*Festuca ovina* var. *duriuscula*). Drought-tolerant and slow-growing Canada bluegrass (*Poa compressa*) is also available in less clumpy cultivars. Other mixtures, however, that contain a high proportion of fast-growing grasses like Kentucky bluegrass (*Poa pratensis*) and perennial ryegrass (*Lolium perenne*) should be avoided as they need frequent mowing (and they tend to dry out quickly).

Establishing the cottage garden

Planning a low-maintenance, hardy or drought-resistant garden is a great idea for the cottage gardener, but how do you take care of your new plantings? Even hardy, drought-tolerant plants need frequent watering before they are established. The best bet is to get a neighbour to visit your garden during the week and water for you. If you can't arrange that (and even if you can), try one of these approaches.

Pop bottle spikes

The ingenious device, which is available in most gardening centres, is inserted into the mouth of two-litre plastic pop bottles. The bottles are filled with water and inverted so that the spike can be pushed into the soil right at the root zone of a thirsty plant. Water is gradually and consistently released through small openings in the spike. The water won't last long, and one of these devices won't be cost-effective or practical if you are putting in a large number of new plants, but a pop bottle spike just might help a few new plants to hang on until Friday night. They are also ideal for containers that may need more frequent watering than your cottage schedule will allow.

Mulch

Mulching is the most practical and attractive way to retain moisture in the soil. A layer of finely shredded bark covering the soil 5 to 8 cm (2 to 3 inches) in depth will protect new plantings from moisture evaporation caused by sun or wind while still allowing rainfall to penetrate the soil. See Mulch, Mulch, Mulch, for more details about mulching.

Ultimately, however, you may have to be resigned to losing a few plants, especially if you are trying to cultivate some semi-hardy varieties. Think of your garden like you would your investments—what is your risk level? How willing are you to lose a few plants for the chance of gaining a wider variety of bloom?

The big pests—animals

Living in a woodland setting means living with its wildlife too. And as any gardener knows, animals don't always see the same things in the lovely banks of flowers as we do. Of course, we share a more united approach to the vegetable patch—a great source of dinner—but this isn't any easier, as we scramble to get to the beans before our four-legged friends do! One cottage gardener I met told me of her mysteriously disappearing Asiatic lilies. Each weekend through the spring she would check on their progress, but invariably the buds that were promising to open when she departed on a summer Sunday night would be completely missing when she returned the next Friday evening. Even when she was down at the cottage full time, flower buds that looked ready to open one day would be snapped off by the following morning. She suspected that deer had acquired a taste for her tender lilies. Deer are also notorious for eating the bark off young trees in the winter and early spring, as are rabbits and other small creatures.

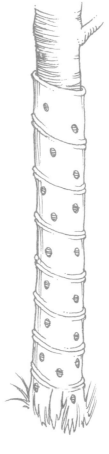

Is there any way to ward off these uninvited dinner guests? Yes! Young trees can be protected by covering their trunks with spiral plastic trunk protectors (available at garden centres and hardware stores). Some people have also found success with wrapping hardware cloth (actually a wire mesh) around the trees. Flowers and vegetables are another matter. A 60-cm (2-foot) high mesh fence may keep out rabbits but will not prevent deer, raccoons, dogs or cats from strolling through your garden. Discouraging deer requires a fence of at least 2 m (6 feet), but some deer can bound over even that with apparent ease. I recommend a fence that is 2.5 to 3 m (8 to 10 feet) high. Such barriers may be the answer for a vegetable garden, but it's not likely that fences like these

Protect the bark of young trees from deer and rabbits by wrapping the trunks in plastic trunk protectors.

are part of your cottage vision—nor are they practical when you are trying to protect flower beds. Bulbs can be protected with a small square of loose nylon mesh or hardware cloth (wire) placed over the bulbs and covered with earth (which should be removed in the spring if covering large bulbs). Squirrels aren't partial to bloodmeal (although raccoons like it), which can be dug in when planting bulbs. There are, however, good organic animal repellents in spray or solid form that are harmless to wildlife. These taste and scent repellents last for weeks (I always spray a little on the top of my spring-flowering bulbs at planting time, just before I cover them with soil). Thiram-based rodent repellents are useful and last the winter when painted on susceptible plants in late fall.

Some people swear by home-made preparations such as bags of human hair or soap scraps suspended near plants and trees to repel deer (Dial soap is highly recommended, but don't ask me what it's got that other soaps lack!), but if the animals around your cottage are hungry enough, they are not likely to be deterred by these things. For areas close to the cottage itself or to an electrical outlet, consider installing an outdoor light with a motion detector. The light will scare away most of your nocturnal visitors.

Another cottage gardener I met eventually settled on a different approach. She had planted a small vegetable patch behind her cottage, and the first year everything came up splendidly. However, just before she was about to harvest her first taste of Swiss chard, she discovered that every last leaf had been mown down, apparently by some animal. The leaf lettuce, the radishes, the beans and the carrots had been left untouched. She constructed a 60-cm (2-foot) high mesh fence around her garden and planted another crop of chard, only to wake up early one morning to the sight of a hare leaping over the fence with a belly full of greens. The following year she gave up planting chard, and the disgruntled hare ravaged her lettuce instead. From then on, she faithfully planted the chard—for the hare. That way, she figured, she could count on enjoying her lettuce and other vegetables.

You might consider taking the same approach with the ornamental cottage garden. While you can eliminate plants that seem to be favourites with the wildlife and introduce others that are reputed to be unappetizing to your four-legged neighbours, you might find the trial-and-error planting (they are sure to find other treats in your garden as you introduce new plants) just as time-consuming, costly and frustrating as a few ravaged flowers. Instead, plant your beds densely so that a few green, flowerless stalks are more likely to go unnoticed. And remember, some gardeners spend a great deal of time and effort creating gardens to *attract* wildlife. Why not keep a pair of binoculars handy for evening or early morning wildlife observation? You will know where to look!

"DEER RESISTANT" PLANTS

Anise hyssop (*Agastache foeniculum*)
Aster (*Aster*)
Astilbe (*Astilbe*)
Beardtongue (*Penstemon*)
Bee balm (*Monarda didyma*)
Bergamot (*Monarda fistulosa*)
Birdsfoot violet (*Viola pedata*)
Black-eyed Susan (*Rudbeckia hirta*), also sweet black-eyed Susan (*Rudbeckia subtomentosa*)
Blanketflower (*Gaillardia*)
Bleeding heart (*Dicentra*)
Bloodroot plants (*Sanguinaria canadensis*)
Bluebell bellflower or harebell (*Campanula rotundifolia*)
Branched coneflower (*Rudbeckia triloba*)
Butterflyweed (*Asclepias tuberosa*)
Canada milk vetch (*Astragalus canadensis*)
Cardinal flower (*Lobelia cardinalis*)
Catmint (*Nepeta*)
Columbine (*Aquilegia canadensis*)
Culver's root (*Veronicastrum virginicum*)
Daylily (*Hemerocallis*)
Dutchman's breeches (*Dicentra cucullaria*)
False indigo (*Baptisia australis*)
False Solomon's seal (*Smilacina racemosa*)
Fame flower (*Talinum rugospermum*)
Foxglove (*Digitalis*)
Globe thistle (*Echinops ritro*)
Goldenrod (*Solidago* hybrids)

Great blue lobelia (*Lobelia siphilitica*)
Green dragon (*Arisaema dracontium*)
Jack-in-the-pulpit (*Arisaema triphyllum*)
Japanese anemone (*Anemone × hybrida*)
Joe Pye weed (*Eupatorium maculatum*)
Lanceleaf coreopsis or tickseed (*Coreopsis lanceolata*)
Lupine (*Lupinus*)
Meadowsweet (*Filipendula*)
Monkshood (*Aconitum*)
New Jersey tea (*Ceanothus americanus*)
Nodding wild onion (*Allium cernuum*)
Pale purple coneflower (*Echinacea pallida*)
Purple coneflower (*Echinacea purpurea*)
Purple prairie clover (*Petalostemum purpureum*)
Rattlesnake master (*Eryngium yuccifolium*)
Red milkweed (*Asclepias incarnata*)
Sage (*Artemisia*)
Shasta daisy (*Leucanthemum × superbum*)
Snow-in-summer (*Cerastium tomentosum*)
Spurge (*Euphorbia*)
Stiff coreopsis or tickweed (*Coreopsis palmate*)
Turtlehead (*Chelone glabra* and *C. obliqua*)
Wild geranium (*Geranium maculatum*)
Wood poppy (*Stylophorum diphyllum*)
Wormwood (*Artemisia ludoviciana*)
Yarrow (*Achillea*)

PLANTS RABBITS MIGHT NOT LIKE

Cactus—yep, there are winter-hardy cacti for the Ontario garden, like prickly pear (*Opuntia polyacantha*)
Foxglove (*Digitalis*)
Gas plant (*Dictamnus albus*)
Lily of the valley (*Convallaria majalis*)
Monkshood (*Aconitum*)

Sage (*Artemisia*)
Spurge (*Euphorbia*)
St. John's wort (*Hypericum*)
Stonecrop or sedum (*Sedum*)
Thyme (*Thymus*)
Yarrow (*Achillea*)
Yucca (*Yucca*)

Ecological responsibility and the cottage garden

In planning your cottage garden I recommend that you avoid planting invasive, especially if non-native, plants. In a city or suburban garden there are plenty of constraints on a plant's travels. Your lawn and its regular mowing, the sidewalks, house foundations, roads and so on are natural barriers to a plant's spreading. What's more, plants that result from seeds that travel through the air to your neighbour's gardens and lawns are likely to meet the weed-picker's hands if they are not wanted. Most cottages, however, inhabit a different kind of environment altogether. The land surrounding a cottage, whether extensively landscaped or not, tends to blend in with the surrounding terrain, creating a large, relatively unbroken green expanse (that's what we go into the country for after all, isn't it?). Plants that like the conditions present can spread and multiply more aggressively than they might in the city.

I remember visiting a friend's cottage on the shores of Lake Huron a few years back. My friend's neighbour had used periwinkle (*Vinca minor*) as groundcover under a few of the silver birch on his property and around the foundation of his cottage. It was a lovely look—the dark, glossy green foliage against the white clapboard of the house and the shimmering silver bark of the tree. The problem was that the periwinkle didn't stop there. It had spread out under the pine trees at either side of his cottage, creeping along under the trees at the roadside for a considerable distance. What's more, it had travelled well into the bush and was alarmingly close to a section of Crown land that was a designated nature preserve. Yes, it was beautiful green carpet under the trees, but what native plants had it choked out? What essential elements of this forest's natural understory were now missing?

When you plant non-native plants around your country property, you have an ecological responsibility to ensure you are not introducing problem plants to the woods and fields around you. Be especially cautious about planting anything that is very quick-growing and invasive. Groundcovers like periwinkle and goutweed (*Aegopodium*)—one of the most aggressive—should be avoided. Invasive perennials like creeping bellflower (*Campanula rapunculoides*) and purple loosestrife (*Lythrum salicaria*) should definitely be passed over, and even aggressive "woody" plants like silver lace vine, Manitoba maple, Norway maple, willow and red twig dogwood should be avoided.

Other cottage considerations

❀ Plant hardy plants that can tolerate some neglect and a fairly wide range of temperatures. See the hardy plant list in The Northern Garden.

❀ Select plants that don't require much deadheading (I call these "self-cleaning": daylilies, hostas, bergenias, peonies and Chinese lilac.

❀ Select plants that are pest resistant—virtually all native plants are good choices for this!

❀ Use rain barrels to collect water from your roof and eaves troughs—this will take the pressure off your well or your pump.

❀ Compost at the cottage. Even though you may not be adding vast quantities of kitchen scraps to your cottage composter, yard waste can add up quickly and the cottage is a great place to compost. Usually you have more space to locate the composter than you do in your city backyard. If you are careful not to add meat or cooked foods, animals will generally ignore the composter. (When they do muck around in it, I see this as a good thing! Often they aerate the compost while having a meal.) And by all means collect a little "duff" and leaves from the forest floor and from around your cottage to add to your composter. It will provide much-needed carbon as a counterbalance to the green nitrogen.

❀ Plant densely. Closely planted beds require less frequent watering as they lose less moisture to evaporation from the soil. Densely planted beds also allow less room for weeds to become established.

❀ Keep the larger scale in mind. With all the space around a cottage, you may find yourself planning your plantings on too small a scale (likely borrowed from your urban lot). Consider planting fewer types of flowers but in greater numbers for wide swaths of colour.

❀ And don't forget that other constraint for country and cottage gardeners—the septic tank. While many people now have tanks that are more or less impermeable, it is best to avoid planting trees and shrubs with deep roots above or near to your septic tank. Choose shallow-rooted grasses and perennials for the areas covering and surrounding the tank.

PART 2

Fruits, Herbs and Vegetables

The Edible Garden

If you grew up in farming country or in a household that always relied on the backyard vegetable patch, then vegetable growing may already be one of the top priorities of your gardening plan. But I've noticed that a lot of people who come into the Weall & Cullen stores asking about vegetable growing are new to the activity, and I fully understand what is moving them to plant a little lettuce or a few tomatoes in their backyards. In the past few years we have begun to pay much more attention to the type and quality of produce we are consuming. Organic? Irradiated? Genetically modified? We now have many reasons other than freshness and superior taste to raise a few of our own vegetables for the table. What's more, we are moving away from that Victorian notion that vegetables are an inferior sort of plant, as far as their appearance is concerned, and should be kept well apart from their superiors, the ornamentals. Many gardeners are cleverly designing their sites to include spots for vegetables, sometimes slightly hidden from view and often beautifully complementing other areas of the garden. Indeed, you may have heard the expression "the potager garden," which refers to a long tradition of mixing ornamentals, herbs and vegetables. The potager garden is making a comeback after a long period of neglect, and it can be the ideal way to balance your desire for beauty, colour and design with a delicious harvest (see p. 92). So even if you've never seriously considered a vegetable plot, why not add a little lettuce or a few beans to your garden plans?

Planning the edible garden

Whether you have decided to plant a traditional vegetable patch or mix vegetables in with your other plantings, the best advice I can give is *start small*. Given that vegetables can be thirsty, heavy feeders, they will likely require a bit more attention than the hardy perennials in your garden that seem to take care of themselves from year to year. And anyone who has found a basket of zucchini left anonymously at their front door knows that sometimes even a modest planting will produce more servings than one family can possibly consume! If you try small plantings of a few vegetables the first year, you can increase your plantings the following year based on your consumption and growing success. Also remember the importance of good soil preparation and locating your veggies in the sun.

There are a number of ways to approach vegetable gardening. Read through the following to see what might suit your needs and your time and space.

Traditional row gardens

Planting your vegetable crops in narrow rows with wide foot paths in between gives the home plot the look and approach of a large farm in miniature. The rows provide good air circulation and generous exposure to sun, resulting in less disease and more even ripening of fruit. Unfortunately, this garden plan takes an awful lot of space—the paths have to be 50 cm to 1 m (20 to 42 inches) wide to allow room for the gardener to move down them. The plants themselves may take up no more space than 15 cm (6 inches) (or they may ultimately flank the path!). You can address this drawback by using a "wide-row" approach—that is, planting in rows that are 1 to 1.25 m (3 to 4 feet) wide. With this kind of bed, you can reach the centre of each row from both sides.

With either of these techniques, plant rows that run north and south so that no plants are blocked from the sun. Mulch along the sides of the rows and, in the wide rows, between the plants to reduce weeds and lessen the loss of moisture from the soil. If the paths are narrow, mulch them to prevent weeds. If they are wide enough, you can keep them mulch-free and use a tiller to reduce weeds. Whether you're planting in single or wide rows, this kind of vegetable plot is temporary: each year after harvest the whole patch is tilled. The following spring, rows can be established in slightly different spots so that plants are grown in soil not depleted from the previous year. Soil must be turned well, however, to break up compaction along last year's paths. The traditional row vegetable garden is labour intensive and only suitable for those gardeners who want to grow a large quantity of vegetables. On the other hand, if you do have the room and want to garden on this scale, tillers and irrigation systems can reduce the work load. And keep in mind that some vegetables, such as asparagus, raspberries, corn and potatoes, need space both for growing and for harvesting; for them, the single-row approach is ideal.

Permanent beds, raised boxes and container gardens for vegetables

Most urban gardeners and many rural gardeners will opt for garden plans that take less space and less labour.

Permanent beds

Permanent beds for vegetables have all the advantages of permanent beds for ornamental plantings—they can be planted densely to reduce weeding and evaporation; they can be separated by permanent paths that keep the gardener from stepping in the beds and compacting the soil; soil improvement can be ongoing from year to year with annual additions of compost or manure; and the beds can be designed to give each plant the optimum growing conditions and to create aesthetic appeal.

Like the traditional wide-row vegetable garden, the permanent bed should be no wider than 1 to 1.25 m (3 to 4 feet) so that you can reach the middle of each bed for harvesting, watering and weeding. You can create raised beds with wooden timbers (avoid pressure-treated wood or creosoted railway ties as these can affect fruit quality), bricks or stones, or you can keep the beds level with the surrounding ground. Choose raised beds if drainage is a problem on your site; avoid them if your soil is very sandy and dry. Keep in mind that raised beds require less stooping on the part of the gardener. Paths between or around the beds should be at least 70 cm (28 inches) wide and can be covered with paving stones, bricks, gravel or decorative mulch. If creating raised beds, remove the topsoil from the paths for use in the beds.

One popular variation on permanent vegetable beds is the "square-foot garden." This approach, developed by Mel Bartholomew in the United States, is designed to make the most efficient use of space when growing vegetables while reducing labour by careful seeding. The square-foot method advocates creating permanent raised beds 15 cm (6 inches) high and 1.25 m by 1.25 m (4 feet by 4 feet) wide. These beds are then divided into 16 small plots, each measuring exactly 30 cm (1 foot) square. Each one of these squares contains a different vegetable, laid out with taller vegetables behind (on the north or east side) and smaller ones in front (on the south or west side) so that sun exposure is equalized. How many seeds or seedlings are planted in each square is determined by the size of the vegetable when it is full grown. For example, a 30-cm (1-foot) square would accommodate one mature tomato plant or 16 radishes or four leafy greens such as lettuce or Swiss chard. Bartholomew also suggests putting just one or two seeds in each hole so that you can avoid the thinning process as the plants mature. I recommend that you add a few extra seeds and do the thinning as a little extra insurance against pests or poor seed germination. With the square-foot method, two such beds should produce enough for a family of four. And of course, as crops are harvested from each square, new ones can be sown. Like all permanent beds, the position of the vegetables should be rotated by family from year to year (see Rotation, p. 99).

The "square-foot" bed might contain the following in each of its squares:
First row: 1 tomato plant, 2 cucumbers
Second row: 4 Romaine lettuces, 9 dwarf French beans, 4 Swiss chards, 9 chives
Third row: 4 Boston leaf lettuces, 16 carrots, 4 salad bowl lettuces, 16 radishes
Fourth row: 4 marigolds, 9 mini-Savoy cabbages, 16 onions, 4 dwarf nasturtiums

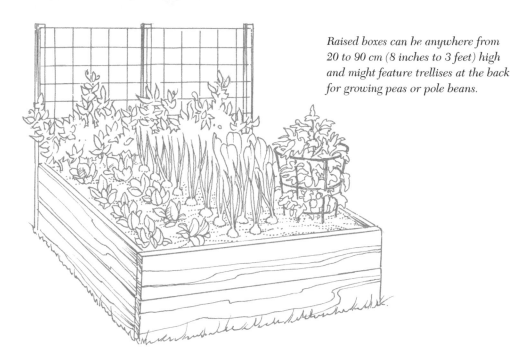

Raised boxes can be anywhere from 20 to 90 cm (8 inches to 3 feet) high and might feature trellises at the back for growing peas or pole beans.

Raised boxes

Another slight variation of the standard raised beds, which are generally about 15 cm (6 inches) high, is the raised-box bed. The box bed is a frame of wood that can be built anywhere in height from 20 cm to 60 or 90 cm (8 inches to 2 or as much as 3 feet) (for the tall folks). Like the wide-row or square-foot bed, the boxes are about 1.25 m (4 feet) wide so that it is easy for the gardener to reach the middle (if you have long arms, you can widen it slightly). Most box beds are about 2.5 m (8 feet) long (anything longer than 3.5 m/12 feet and the wood will be strained or become bowed). Raised boxes are really a form of container gardening on a large scale. They can be ideal for creating a tiny vegetable patch over poor soil. They drain well and warm up quickly—giving you a jump on the season. What's more, given their height, they virtually eliminate stooping and crouching.

One great advantage of raised-bed gardens is the opportunity you have to fill them with the very best soil possible (you don't have to work with the soil you inherit when planting in the ground). I like to seek out the best combination of topsoil, peat, finished compost and/or composted sheep, cattle or horse manure. It is this magical combination that will determine your gardening success, above all. The boxes can be built to have more than one level (like steps) and painted or otherwise decorated—I've seen a very attractive box painted in several shades of soft natural green that blends in beautifully with its ornamental garden backdrop. Raised-box beds also help you follow that important dictum for vegetable gardening: start small.

Containers

Even smaller containers can be used to provide fresh vegetables for your table. Clay pots, wine barrels, ceramic tubs, wooden planter boxes and so on can be both decorative and full of good things to eat. Other than herbs (which can be brought indoors for the winter), tomatoes and peppers are the most popular edibles for containers, but you can grow almost every-thing else in them too. Container vegetable gardening makes weeding almost disappear (there isn't much room for weeds to squeeze in!), and since many containers are small you can take advantage of all sorts of unused nooks and crannies of your site.

Place containers close to your house for easy access or hide them in an empty corner of your garden, as long as they'll get some sun. If you have a space along the side of your house (perhaps in the corridor between your house and your neighbours), that may be an ideal spot for a few containers—particularly if the wall is brick, stone or light-coloured, or south or west facing. In these positions, plants benefit from the ambient solar heat reflecting and radiating off the walls. You can use containers for rooftop or balcony vegetable gardens or for keeping your herbs close to the kitchen. Some gardeners like to place containers on castors so they can move the plants to follow the sun— the perfect way to get a full six hours of rays in a partially shady garden or balcony.

Peppers are an attractive and tasty choice for container vegetable gardening.

Ten-litre (2-gallon) minimum containers can be used for herbs, lettuce, radishes, green onions and other small vegetables. Most other vegetables should be planted in containers of at least the 20-litre (4-gallon) size. If using containers to grow beans or tomatoes, choose spreading varieties rather than climbing ones. Or insert small cages, a trellis or an obelisk in the containers to support tomato plants or any twining variety of peas, beans or other climb-ing vegetable.

Even crops that generally need plenty of space can be grown in containers of one variety or another. Potatoes can be grown in tall containers with removable sides, or other

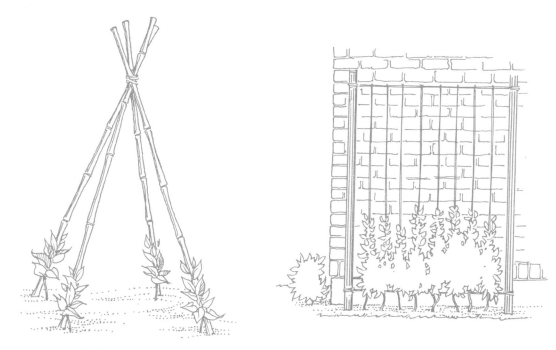

Peas and pole beans can be grown up a tepee made from slender stakes or up strings running between two posts.

structures (chicken wire and landscape fabric) that can be disassembled at harvest time. I have even heard of people using prefab compost bins with removable sides. This technique also works for strawberries and peanuts.

Remember that while containers have the advantage of warming up quickly in the spring, they need more frequent watering than beds. Daily watering is a must during hot, sunny weather. If using water-tight containers, perforate the bottoms with 1 cm (1/2 inch) holes for drainage. Keep in mind that containers must be filled with a top-quality potting soil or a blend of two-thirds soil-less mixture (peat, vermiculite and perlite) and one-third compost to produce the best crop. Soil-less mixes are less likely to produce weeds. Some commercially available mixes have slow-release fertilizer already in the mix.

PEANUTS IN A BASKET

Ontario gardeners are often surprised to learn that small, red-skinned "Spanish" peanuts are easy to grow here, up to zone 4 and even farther north when grown against a south-facing wall. Seeds are available on most garden seed racks. A few years ago, I picked up a package while visiting Picard's Peanuts in St. Thomas (they specialize in growing and selling Ontario-grown peanuts) and had great success with them.

If you want to treat yourself to home-grown peanuts, simply sow 10 to 12 peanut seeds in an old bushel basket ("old" because the bottom rots out of it by the end of the season). Light, sandy soil works best. Place the basket in a sunny spot (peanuts need a minimum of seven hours of sun a day). Harvest any time after the blooms are finished, and roast or broil the peanuts in a 150°C (300°F) oven before eating.

You will be impressed by the beauty of peanut flowers and quantity of peanuts when you harvest them in the late summer or early fall!

Mixing it up: The potager garden

Never overlook the beauty of edible plants. We all delight in apple blossoms and cherry trees, the beauty of a peach tree laden with golden fruit, but what about that spikey clump of chives with its soft mauve pompoms? Or the texture and colour of 'Northern Lights' Swiss chard? Or the twist of a pole bean dotted with bright scarlet flowers? The potager garden is an old French tradition of planting vegetables, herbs and flowers together in formal elegant geometric beds that are divided with foot paths and adorned with formal statuary, obelisks, trellises and other ornamentation. "Potager" actually comes from the French word for soup—*potage*—and these lovely mixes of edible and ornamental plants are a testament to the French passion for the culinary arts. The most famous potager garden today is the enormous exquisite garden at the grand château of Villandry in the Loire area of France. But the potager has had many less-vast incarnations throughout France and in pre-Victorian England as well.

Unfortunately, however, the Victorians disapproved of mixing "common" plants like vegetables with regal flowers, so discouraged the potager approach. Vegetable patches were moved out of sight. Today, however, gardeners have rediscovered the potager. Many take a far less formal approach to designs that incorporate vegetables, herbs and flowers than the traditional potager demands, and these gardens are often referred to simply as "kitchen" gardens. For a wonderful example of how beautiful a kitchen garden can be, visit Langdon Hall (Spa and Resort) outside of Cambridge, Ontario.

Traditional potager gardens use square or circular raised beds that are divided into smaller squares or wedges with intersecting paths. These beds can be combined into intricate patterns—I've recently seen a very attractive potager laid out in the shape of a Celtic cross. The beds are generally bordered by stone, brick or concrete borders, although you can also use untreated wood (cedar is the most resistant to rot). The smaller vegetables and herbs—leaf lettuce, greens, parsley, chives and so on—are kept at the front or edges of the beds, with the taller flowers or vegetables in the centres of the beds. Vegetables that will be harvested continually, like the ones mentioned above, must be kept within easy reach, but most beds in the potager garden are small enough that the gardener can reach the middle. The paths should be wide enough to move along comfortably once the plants are fully grown, and a metre (a yard) wide if you plan to use a wheelbarrow. They can be made with pea gravel or shredded bark over landscape fabric (to eliminate weed problems), or you can install permanent paths with brick or interlocking paving stones over sand (these can be mortared as well).

Hard furnishings can also be an important part of the potager—at the crossroads of the paths, for example, the area can be widened to feature a bird bath, fountain, pergola, urn or planting boxes. Arbours, trellises (for flowering vines or climbing vegetables) and furniture like benches are also wonderful additions. These furnishings, as well as shrubs and perennial vegetables and flowers, will remain much the same from year to year, but you can vary the design of your potager every year with the annual vegetables, herbs and flowers you plant.

While potagers were generally kept close to the kitchen (I suppose "close" is a relative term when we're talking about the grand manor houses of Europe!), the most important thing for any garden that features vegetables is that it is in a sunny location with good soil.

Here are a few ideas for beautiful vegetables and herbs that can be used in your potager design:

Alpine strawberries—delicate leaves, tiny flowers and bright fruit—what a wonderful combination!

Arugula—its small, low leaf works well in a rock garden and other low areas.

Basil—these dark glossy leaves look great anywhere. Purple basil is also a pretty and eye-catching herb.

Cabbage—creamy dense cabbage leaves look lovely among flowers. Savoy cabbage is especially attractive and one of my favourites.

Carrots—their tops also have a wonderfully feathery appearance that looks good as a border and complements many other flowers and vegetables.

Chives—the spikes and flowers are lovely in the front of beds.

Dill—the feathery herb looks great as a border or beside thick-leaved plants like cabbage or chard.

Egyptian onions—the tall tubular tops look good with broad-leafed vegetables.

Endive—this can be used for formal borders.

Kale—there are many attractive varieties to choose from and since it is frost hardy it can be left in the garden for fall interest. You can also choose purely ornamental varieties; flowering kale looks great in containers.

Leaf lettuces—the many varieties allow you to design with a wide choice of colours and textures.

Parsley—wonderful frilly leaves are attractive anywhere.

Peas and beans—the climbing varieties twisting through a trellis or up an obelisk make a lovely centrepiece to a bed or at the intersection of paths. Scarlet runner beans and hops, with their beautiful flowers, are especially pretty.

Radicchio—it makes beautiful borders.

Rhubarb—it takes up quite a lot of space, but the big broad leaves are dramatic. (When it gets out of hand, I just pull a few extra leaves to keep it in check.)

Spinach—the rosettes work well for informal borders (but don't allow spinach to bolt to flower!).

Thyme and golden lemon thyme—these tiny delicate leaves look terrific at the front of the beds and among other small flowers. Lemon thyme's lovely fragrance is a wonderful addition to your garden.

Tomatoes—try different colours for interest. Staking and climbing varieties, including cherry tomatoes, can look quite elegant growing up a trellis.

COMPANION PLANTING

Companion planting is the practice of placing certain plants, whether they are flowers, herbs or vegetables, close to one another to discourage harmful pests or encourage beneficial insects. Some "companions" also match such plants as peas and beans that add nitrogen to the soil with plants that tend to deplete the soil of nitrogen (heavy-feeding plants). I have listed here only a few suggestions. For a more thorough guide, check The *All Seasons Gardener* and my Web site, www.markcullen.com.

- Marigold (scented varieties) are said to repel all pests by covering the smell of other plants.
- Nasturtiums repel white flies and squash bugs, and attract aphids, drawing them away from other plants.
- Mints and catnip repel cabbage pests and aphids.
- Sweet basil is said to enhance the growth of almost any vegetable. It also apparently repels aphids, mosquitoes and mites.
- Aromatic plants and herbs like rosemary, sage, garlic and parsley repel some pests too.
- Parsley, mint, thyme, yarrow, lovage, lemon balm, hyssop, fennel, daisies, catnip and caraway attract beneficial insects.

Obelisks

Mulch Path

Arbour / Gazebo

Pergola

Brick Edging

Flag Patio

Pea Gravel Path

White Alyssum

Cucumber

Cabbage

Onion

Kale

Rhubarb

Radish

Carrots

Broccoli

Cauliflower

Swiss Chard

Sweet Peas

Interplanting

You don't have to commit to a kitchen or potager garden if you only want a bit of lettuce or a few tomatoes. Many gardeners I've talked to comment that they like to stick in a few vegetables among their ornamental plantings. Some choose locations where the vegetables are obscured from view; some choose attractive vegetables whose leaves and fruit complement the flowers and shrubbery (see p. 122 for suggestions for attractive edibles). Many people choose to plant vegetables near flowers and herbs that are reputed to repel harmful insects or attract beneficial insects (see Companion Planting, p. 93). The most important thing, however, if you are planting vegetables among ornamentals, is to keep in mind the needs of vegetables.

Most vegetables like full sun (six hours), although lettuce, spinach, chard and some other greens can thrive in filtered sunlight. They generally demand fertile, friable, well-drained soil, so if you are dealing with heavy clay, you will not want to interplant in beds, but rather choose containers or raised boxes. (Rutabagas, turnips and kohlrabi can, however, do quite nicely in clay.) Since most vegetables need plenty of water, you won't want to plant your veggies in a bed of drought-tolerant perennials. The watering the vegetables demand will be wasted on the less thirsty shrubs and plants. On the other hand, avoid planting vegetables in beds with poor drainage where plants that like wet feet can still thrive. The moisture will only lead to rot and disease. In short, when interplanting, try to match the cultural requirements of edibles and ornamentals as closely as you can.

If you would like to interplant, consider planning your garden so that perennials like rhubarb or asparagus, and perennial herbs like chives and parsley, are mixed with your other perennial plantings. Perennial vegetables also mix quite effectively with bush fruits like currants and gooseberries. Annual vegetables can be left to beds where you work the soil each spring as you plant your annual flowers.

RULE OF THUMB
Interplanting ornamentals with herbs and vegetables is a terrific idea, but remember, if you are growing food alongside your flowers you will want to be especially careful about the use of pesticides. Use synthetic pesticides as a last resort and choose organic treatments, companion planting and other non-chemical approaches to eliminating pests and disease.

The basics of vegetable growing

Once you've decided to try your hand at growing a little food for the table, it's time to consider the requirements of successful vegetable growing.

Soil, as always, is paramount. Most vegetables need a slightly acidic soil (approximately pH 6.5). Many vegetables are heavy feeders (see the chart on rotation, p. 99, for heavy, medium and light feeders). This means that soil has to be rich to start with—with plenty of organic matter and nutrients—and should be replenished either with a balanced 6-12-12 fertilizer or compost throughout the growing season. Other vegetables are less demanding but will thrive in good soil. The exceptions to this rich-soil rule are tomatoes, potatoes, carrots and rutabagas—nitrogen-rich soil will produce impressive leaf growth at the expense of the root, tuber or fruit of these plants.

Vegetables also like loose, friable soil in which the roots can grow easily and quickly (although some, like broccoli and rutabaga, will manage in clay soils). Root vegetables like carrots are especially dependent on loose soil—they will fork or become misshapen in compacted earth. But just because you are stuck with incorrigibly poor soil, you don't have to give up on vegetables. You can create a raised bed by mounding good topsoil 30 to 40 cm (12 to 16 inches) higher than grade to achieve good fertility and excellent drainage. Small raised beds, raised boxes and containers can all be filled with mixes (for example, equal parts peat, compost and topsoil) for vegetable growing.

Most vegetables and herbs need no less than six hours of sunlight a day; if the growing season is short, as it is in all of Ontario, vegetables and herbs just can't have too much sun. If possible plant your vegetables in a south-facing location. If that isn't available, choose a southeast or southwest exposure. Leafy vegetables like lettuce and spinach tolerate some shade.

You can increase the reflected light your plants receive by using light-coloured mulches and even foil on the surface of the soil. If planting in rows, lay the seeds or plants out in a north-south direction with the taller plants at the north end. If using small beds, the square-foot approach or boxes, design your planting so that the tallest vegetables are at the northern end with vegetable heights decreasing towards the southern end. Tall plants include any staked or twining vegetables like pole beans, peas on a trellis, staked tomatoes, corn or asparagus. Mid-sized plants include bush beans, potatoes and broccoli; lettuces, carrots and onions are usually the shortest vegetables.

Vegetables need daily watering when seedlings, with consistent watering as the surface of the soil dries thereafter.

Be wary of trees in any area you want to plant vegetables. Not only do they create shade but they also deplete the soil of nutrients. If possible, plant vegetables beyond the dripline of trees.

Keep in mind that wind has a very drying effect and that the water needs of your vegetables will be higher in a windy spot. See Watering and

Xeriscaping, p. 165 for ideas about protective windbreaks for your garden. If you want a food-producing windbreak to buffer your garden, try berry bushes like currants, gooseberries, saskatoon berries or highbush cranberries.

The best planting times for individual vegetables are often given in the number of weeks before or after the last spring frost. Likewise, late-harvest vegetables are often described by how many weeks before the first fall frost they can be sown. Obviously, unless you are prescient, you will have to know what the average last frost and first frost dates are for your area before you plant. Check the chart on p. 225. If it does not cover your area, contact your local weather bureau. It should be able to provide average dates for you.

If you choose cool crops for your first planting you shouldn't have to worry too much about temperatures. Remember, though, that while many early vegetables can tolerate a dip below zero, light frosts or even a dusting of snow on occasion (as long as the earth warms up again quickly), continuous unseasonably cool temperatures, even if the thermometer does not actually dip below zero, can kill tender seedlings. The combination of cold and wet spring weather can wreak havoc in the form of rot and disease with early-sown crops. If your spring weather is very slow in coming, protect your plants with thermal blankets, cloches and other devices (even an upside-down milk bottle can help a great deal) until the earth warms up.

Sowing seeds

Whether starting seeds indoors or planting directly outside, the rule of thumb is that seeds should be sown to a depth equivalent to two to three times their diameter. Very tiny seeds can be pressed lightly into the soil with a finger or can be spread on soil and then covered with a little soil. If planting in trays or outdoors, a furrow can be created with a stick or trowel or hoe tip to the appropriate depth for the seeds and then filled in after the seeds have been distributed.

Seeds that stick together can be mixed with a little talcum powder, and very tiny seeds can be mixed with a handful of sand (about three parts sand to one part seed). The sand mixture is then dribbled into the furrows, or a small quantity is poured into the holes. There is also a variety of convenient seed planters now available.

Seeds, whether started outdoors or in, must be kept in moist soil until they sprout. Water regularly and mist the surface of the soil covering seeds started indoors so that it doesn't crust over.

Hardening off

If seeds have been started indoors, they will need to be hardened off for about a week or two before they are transplanted. Hardening off prepares the tender seedlings for the rise and fall of temperature and moisture levels outside. Put your seedlings in a shaded spot outside for a couple of hours, then return them indoors. With each following day, leave them out for a little longer. Protect them from the wind and other harsh elements.

Pests and diseases

Keep plants well watered and well fed with nutrient-rich compost and plenty of sunlight—healthy plants are always more resistant to disease and pests. Inspect the plants regularly and get rid of pests as soon as you see them so they don't multiply. If you spot only a few interlopers, pick them off and kill them. If you are dealing with an infestation, use ladybugs and other natural pest predators. If you need to resort to insecticides, try insecticidal soaps and other organic solutions, like Green Earth AIM. If you need more help identifying pests or finding solutions, consult with your local garden centre or check out the Ontario Ministry of Agriculture's very helpful Web site, www.gov.on.ca/OMAFRA/english/crops. It has a section on insects, diseases and weeds that provides descriptions and photos of various fruit and vegetable diseases, with suggestions for prevention and treatment.

Harvest and clean up

Hot and warm crops will have to be harvested before fall frost damages them. Many cool crops can withstand frost, but they will stop growing once the temperature drops significantly. Tomatoes and squash will stop growing at 13°C (55°F), while lettuce stops at 4.5°C (40°F) and spinach not until 2°C (35°F). Beets, carrots and parsnips can be left in the ground over the winter if they're under a heavy mulch of hay or straw.

After harvest either remove all remaining plant material from beds and move it to the compost bin (leaving it in the ground can encourage the growth of disease and pests that can overwinter) or bury pest- and disease-free plants in the soil. The leaves and stem will rot down by planting time next spring, making good earthworm fodder. Burn or throw in the garbage any diseased plants you find.

Rotation

I have found that the majority of Ontario farmers, as stewards of our largest inhabited tracts of land, are very conscious of the impact their practices have on the environment. One of the long-standing farming principles that we can use to our advantage in the urban garden is "crop rotation." Plants, both vegetable and ornamental, in the same family tend to be vulnerable to the same insects and diseases. Certain families, like cabbage and potato, are especially at risk for soil-borne predators. So keeping plants from the same family in separate beds in one year, and moving and relocating those plants to entirely new beds the following year, may save both vegetables and heartache. What's more, rotating crops also helps keep the soil fertile by allowing light feeders to occupy soil depleted by heavy feeders while additions of compost or other organic material replenish the nutrients.

Plant families can be large, however, and often hold surprises. Hard to believe that the earthy, lumpy potato is related to the delicately graceful Chinese lantern, but there you are. When planning your vegetable garden, check the chart below so that you don't have family members side by side, or growing in the bed their cousins called home last year. Alternate from year to year between light feeders and heavy feeders where possible.

FAMILY	VEGETABLES & HERBS	ORNAMENTAL	ROTATION
Chenopodiaceae (Beet)	**Medium feeders:** Swiss chard, spinach **Light feeders:** beets		Rotate with Cruciferae, Leguminosae, Liliaceae, Solanaceae
Compositae (Sunflower)	**Medium feeders:** lettuce **Light feeders:** salsify, chicory, dandelion, yarrow, camomile, perennial tarragon, globe and Jerusalem artichokes, sunflowers, endive, cardoon	daisies, zinnias, dahlias, marigolds, asters, chrysanthemums	Rotate leafy Compositae plants with Cucurbitaceae, Leguminosae, Liliaceae, Solanaceae, Umbelliferae. Alternate sunflowers with tall or staked plants like peas or pole beans. Jerusalem artichokes are perennial—no rotation. Rotate marigolds with tomatoes.
Convolvulaceae (Morning glory)	**Light feeders:** sweet potatoes	morning glories	Rotate morning glories with pole beans, beans, Cucurbitaceae

FAMILY	VEGETABLES & HERBS	ORNAMENTAL	ROTATION
Cruciferae (Mustard)	**Heavy feeders:** cabbage, cauliflower, Chinese cabbage, mustard greens, cress, watercress, horseradish (perennial) **Medium feeders:** broccoli, Brussels sprouts, kale, kohlrabi, rutabaga, turnip **Light feeders:** radish	sweet allysum, arabis, aubrieta, aurinia, ornamental kale and cabbage, evening stock, Virginia stock, iberis (candytuft), lunaria, wallflower	
Cucurbitaceae (Gourd)	**Heavy feeders:** summer and winter squash, pumpkins, melons, cucumbers, gourds		When staked, rotate with other staked or climbing plants—pole beans, sunflowers, beans. If spreading, with potatoes or leafy Compositae.
Graminae (Corn)	**Heavy feeders:** corn		Rotate with legumes (is a very heavy consumer of soil nutrients)
Leguminosae (Pea)	**Medium feeders:** beans, peas, lentils	sweet peas, lupines	Can be left unrotated for years, but if turned under before fruiting, they add nitrogen to the soil so can improve the soil for plants that follow them
Liliaceae (Lily)	**Heavy feeders:** asparagus (perennial) **Medium feeders:** leeks **Light feeders:** onions, garlic, shallots, chives (perennial)	lilies (perennial)	Perennial onions and other perennials in family do not rotate; the family has few pests and can be interplanted with other families to discourage pests from neighbouring beds
Solanaceae (Nightshade)	**Medium feeders:** eggplant, peppers **Light feeders:** garden huckleberries, ground cherries, tomatillos	petunia, nicotiana, schizanthus, nierembergia, physalis, Chinese lantern	Vulnerable to fungus diseases and nematodes; members should be kept separate; rotate with plants of similar size and height from other families
Umbelliferae (Parsley)	**Heavy feeders:** celery, celeriac **Light feeders:** carrot, parsnips, parsley, dill, fennel, lovage (perennial), chervil, caraway, anise, coriander		Interplant and rotate with leafy or fruiting crops of other families—lettuce and tomatoes, for example. Deep-rooted plants that help break up soil.

Succession planting

Succession planting is simply the practice of re-sowing the garden as you harvest. By putting a little thought into what to plant when, you can keep your garden full of good things to eat right through the fall. Also keep in mind that succession planting is a good practice if you are going to inter-plant vegetables with ornamentals in your beds: once you harvest all that wonderful spinach you are going to have a bare spot. Do you want to replace it with some annual flowers or plant another vegetable that will grow well through the height of the summer? Whether a crop is "cool," "warm" or "hot" tells you at what point in the season it takes its place in your garden. Cool crops, like spinach, are ones that can be planted as soon as the soil can be worked. If they mature quickly they can either be re-sown or they can be replaced by a warm or hot crop. Warm crops are planted no sooner than one or two weeks after the last frost date. They can also be planted later, as a succeeding crop to an early-harvest vegetable. Hot crops can be planted only once the air and the soil are warm (i.e., above 20°C/70°F). They can replace any cool crop that matures relatively quickly.

* Leaf lettuce, mustard greens, spinach and radishes are quickly maturing and can be re-sown throughout the season. They can also be planted only in the early spring, making way for vegetables that must be planted only when the soil and air are warm (hot crops). They also make good late crops, as do peas, snow peas, beets and broccoli.

* Corn, carrots, beets and parsley are slow growing and will keep the ground occupied for most of the season: beets for eight weeks, carrots for about three months.

* Cabbage, cauliflower, broccoli, Brussels sprouts, endive, escarole and collard greens are warm vegetables that are relatively quick growing.

* Spinach can be planted early and late in the vegetable-growing season, but hates the hot weather of midsummer. Replace spinach with a warm or hot crop.

* For many vegetables there are early, middle and late varieties that can be sown and that mature at different points of the season.

Best bets for the Ontario garden

The following is by no means a complete list of vegetables that can be grown in Ontario. Instead, these are my suggestions for ease and success. For other vegetable ideas and information, check out

The New Greener Thumb, The All Seasons Gardener, seed catalogues or your local nursery.

When you're planning your vegetable garden, warm and hot crops may very well be high on your wish list, and no wonder. Biting into a bright red tomato straight off the vine can almost be a shock—the flavour is so intense, so sweet, so tart in comparison to the pale imitations available at the grocery store throughout the winter. (However, I think Ontario hot-house tomatoes deserve some credit—they're much better than the ones that are strip-mined in Texas and California, then shipped up here by the fumigated truckload!) But remember, all of these heat lovers are also finicky. The shorter your season, the more challenging it will be to produce a crop. What's more, even in southern Ontario, a summer of cool overcast days or an urban garden with just a shade too much shade will yield disappointing results. A few years ago I was talking with a friend about his experiences with his urban, zone 6, vegetable patch. Growing up on a southern Ontario farm, he was armed with vegetable-growing experience, and the first year he had spent a great deal of time preparing his small beds, improving the soil and bringing along his seedlings. When he got the plants into the ground, he nurtured them with judicious watering and regular feedings of compost tea. The sun cooperated and he got a bountiful harvest of snow peas and scarlet runner beans, cherry tomatoes and leaf lettuce. And his pepper plants seemed to be growing hale and hardy, but for one problem—there was no evidence of fruit. Eventually his three bushy plants produced one and only one moderately sized pepper. It was such a pathetic offering that he said he felt strangely reluctant to pick and eat this sole pepper progeny. The next year he considered planting the peppers in the only spot in the garden that was slightly hotter and sunnier, but abandoned the idea. It seemed wiser to devote his efforts to plants he knew would produce under his garden conditions.

By all means experiment with your vegetable patch, but if space and time are an issue, or you are facing one of Ontario's very short growing seasons in the north, choose quick-maturing vegetables from the cold-weather and warm-weather groups, plants like leaf lettuce, peas or beans. If you do put in hot crops, start seeds indoors, or buy seedlings or small plants for transplanting. Look for microclimates in your garden that may provide more sun and more heat than the rest of your garden. Lay down light-coloured mulches to reflect the sun, and avoid low-lying areas of the garden (frost pockets that will also be cooler all summer long). Amend your soil well and even consider using containers or raised beds to capture as much heat and sun as possible.

Cool crops

Arugula

From planting to harvest: 35 days

My former editor at Penguin Books, Jackie Kaiser, used to order arugula salad just to be able to say the word "arugula." It certainly does roll off the tongue nicely, but I love this wonderful salad green for its sharp, spicy flavour.

Arugula also has the advantage of managing quite nicely in dry, sandy soil, although it prefers rich, neutral soil. It can grow in full sun to partial shade. Sow seeds 2.5 cm (1 inch) apart in short or long rows approximately 6 cm (2 1/2 inches) apart, as soon as soil can be worked in the spring. Pick individual leaves when they are no longer than 15 cm (6 inches) (the flavour becomes stronger the longer the leaves) to extend harvest. You can sow new seeds every three to four weeks until six weeks before first frost.

Arugula will bolt in very hot weather. Water regularly.

Pests and diseases: Watch for slugs!

Beet

From planting to harvest: 50 to 60 days

Beets, with their deep green, red-veined leaves, can be a pretty addition to any garden and are easy to grow. The tops are edible as well as the beets—pick the greens early in the season for the best flavour. They are full of vitamins!

Plant as soon as the soil can be worked in early spring. Beets are frost tolerant and like a rich, sandy loam. Amend soil with compost or well-rotted manure.

Plant seeds to a depth of 1.5 cm (5/8 inch) in spring, 2.5 cm (1 inch) in summer, and space them 3 to 5 cm (1 1/4 to 2 inches) apart. Since each seed sprouts several beets, thin to 2.5 cm (1 inch) apart once the beets are 5 cm (2 inches) tall. Thin again to 7.5 cm (3 inches) when they reach 10 cm (4 inches). Larger winter-keeper types need to be thinned even more.

Plant at intervals until about ten weeks before hard frost is predicted. But do not sow beets in midsummer when the intense heat will damage the seedlings.

Early or late canning and bunching varieties are now available in red, white and yellow. There are also a great number of sizes to choose from.

Pests and diseases: Leaf miners, flea beetles and leaf spot diseases.

Broccoli

From planting to harvest: 60 to 85 days (from transplants)

Broccoli is one of North America's favourite vegetables. And a wide variety of broccoli types is available these days, including early and late varieties and a number of different colours. It is not particularly difficult to grow, but unlike many other vegetables, it doesn't do well in slightly acidic soil where it is susceptible to disease. It prefers neutral or slightly alkaline soil. Very few gardens in southern Ontario are naturally acidic, so broccoli will do fine here. In northern Ontario, where acidic soil is prevalent because of the predominance of evergreen trees, the addition of sharp sand and horticultural limestone will raise the pH to an acceptable level.

Plant broccoli transplants about two weeks before the last expected spring frost. Sow two or three seeds 6 mm (1/4 inch) deep at 60-cm (2-foot) intervals. Thin out all but the hardiest shoots when 5 cm (2 inches) tall. Depending on the length of your growing season, you can plant successive crops through July for fall harvest.

Broccoli is a heavy feeder that likes a nitrogen-rich soil, so you should fertilize every two weeks or side-dress the bed with mature compost at longer intervals. Keep the plants well watered, as broccoli has shallow roots and can dry out easily. It also tends to bolt to seed in the heat of the summer. Don't plant too much; harvesting often will prevent bolting.

Once you have harvested the main head, smaller shoots will appear and can be harvested as well. Pick broccoli by cutting the stem just above where leaves join it. Mature broccoli can survive a light frost.

Pests and diseases: Cutworms, root maggots, aphids, cabbage worms, clubroot and blackleg diseases.

Carrot

From planting to harvest: 60 to 80 days (baby carrots: 45 to 50 days)

Carrots like light, friable soil that is loose (work the soil to a depth of 20 to 25 cm/8 to 10 inches) and stone-free. Heavy, compacted or rocky soil will produce stunted, misshapen or split carrots.

Sow seeds up to four weeks before last frost (as soon as the soil can be worked) 1 cm (1/2 inch) deep and about 5 cm (2 inches) apart or scatter seed across a 15- to 20-cm (6- to 8-inch) width. I recommend that you intensely sow seeds without using rows, re-sowing every three weeks until about 60 days before hard frost is expected, for a succession of crops.

Weed carrot beds well—seedlings can be choked out by faster-growing weeds. Water regularly—at least once a week and more than that in the first few weeks and during hot weather. Top-dress with mature compost or fertilizer (6-12-12) at mid-season.

You can begin to harvest carrots when you can see the orange tops from the base of the leaves. If you want to pick only at full size, wait until the visible tops are about 2 cm (3/4 inch) wide, but small young carrots are especially delicious. For the winter, store carrots in bushel baskets filled with clear, dry play sand. While frost may damage the tops, the carrots themselves can withstand it, so you can also "store" carrots in the ground right up to the point that it freezes solid.

Pests and diseases: Carrots are fairly disease and pest resistant, but by mid-season, carrot rust fly larvae and carrot beetle might make an appearance. Also, rodents and rabbits consider carrot tops a delicacy.

Chicory, radicchio, witloof and endive chicory
From planting to harvest: 85 to 110 days

These leafy greens are growing in popularity and are often added to salads for interest and flavour. Their colours and textures also make them attractive additions to the garden.

Radicchio, the increasingly popular red leaf that grows in a small tight head, is actually one form of chicory. It is very expensive at the grocery store, so if you like this flavourful leaf, you might want to grow some. Chicory also comes in several other forms. Witloof or Belgian chicory grows upright like romaine lettuce. Endive chicories feature smooth Bibb-type or scalloped loose leaves.

Chicory is very cold resistant (more so than lettuce) and withstands light frosts well. Like lettuce, chicory is relatively easy to raise. In Ontario's zone 6 it may actually overwinter, if it is mulched well.

Chicory likes moist, rich soil and full sun. Seed most chicory varieties directly in the soil, as soon as it can be worked, 5 to 10 mm (1/4 to 1/2 inch) deep and 2.5 cm (1 inch) apart. Thin radicchio and other head varieties so that plants are 20 to 30 cm (8 to 12 inches) apart.

Harvest while young and do not allow to flower or the plant will be bitter.

No serious pests or diseases.

Kale

From planting to harvest: 50 to 80 days

In my experience, you either love kale or you hate it. If you do love this flavourful, attractive leafy green, it's a great one to try in the home garden. It not only tolerates frost both at the seedling stage and in its mature state if planted for a late harvest, but unlike so many other vegetables it does quite well in poor soil. Kale will also tolerate shade and will actually prefer shade if your garden is particularly hot.

Sow seeds as soon as the soil can be worked, about 1 cm (1/2 inch) deep, 2.5 to 5 cm (1 to 2 inches) apart. Thinning is not usually necessary and leaves can be harvested when they reach 15 to 20 cm (6 to 8 inches) in length. As with leaf lettuce, you can pick individual leaves as you need them, but keep in mind that the smaller the leaves the less bitter the taste (you can eat the first miniature leaves). The flavour is also enhanced after a heavy frost, so by all means plant a second crop or use kale as a late vegetable to succeed an early one in your garden.

Pests and diseases: Cutworms, root maggots, aphids, cabbage worms, clubroot and blackleg diseases.

Lettuce

From planting to harvest: Loose leaf—40 to 60 days; Butterheads—60 to 75 days; Romaine—75 days; Iceberg (and other "crisphead" varieties)—90 days

There are many varieties of lettuces to choose from these days, some of them extremely decorative. You may also want to look for slow-bolting varieties.

Lettuce likes neutral to slightly acidic soil rich in organic material. Sow seeds as soon as the earth can be worked in the spring. For continual harvest, sow only as much as your family will consume in a week, but sow new seeds every week, until mid-May. Since lettuce that matures in hot weather bolts quickly, either go without re-sowing until mid-July or plant only slow-bolting varieties in June and early July.

Leaf lettuce can be planted closely; head lettuce should be thinned to 20 to 25 cm (8 to 10 inches) apart. As the lettuces mature, pick the outer leaves for consumption. Romaine lettuce should be harvested by cutting at the base when it is about 30 cm (12 inches); butterhead should be cut when it is 25 cm (10 inches) in diameter.

Pests: Slugs, aphids, earwigs, leafhoppers and cabbage worms.

Mesclun mix

From planting to harvest: 40 to 45 days

Mesclun is a mix of lettuce and small salad greens such as arugula and cress, and it's a great way to get a variety of greens in a small space. Sow as soon as soil can be worked and every three weeks after. Make short rows, approximately 10 cm (4 inches) wide. Harvest when leaves are 10 cm (4 inches) tall, cutting 2.5 cm (1 inch) above the ground. You should get four cuttings from each sowing.

Mustard greens

From planting to harvest: 35 to 40 days

Here is another green that makes a delightful addition to salads, as well as a delicious cooked green. Some varieties are striking additions to any garden, with colours ranging from bright green to dark purple, and textures that are crinkly or frilly.

Mustard greens like full sun to partial shade and average to rich soil with a neutral pH. Plant as soon as the soil can be worked and again in the late summer or early fall. Sow seeds 2.5 to 3.5 cm (1 to 1 1/4 inches) apart, about 1.5 cm (5/8 inch) deep. Keep rows 35 cm (14 inches) apart and thin seedlings to 15 cm (6 inches) apart. Harvest the greens 35 to 40 days after sowing so that plants don't go to seed. Pick outer leaves first and use leaves 10 to 15 cm (4 to 6 inches) long for salad; longer leaves can be cooked.

Pests and diseases: Flea beetles, aphids.

Onions and scallions

From planting to harvest: 90 to 120 days (from sets); 65 days (from transplants)

While vegetables like onions, leeks and scallions may not be ones that spring to mind when you think about how much fresher or more flavourful homegrown vegetables can be, you should consider planting a few in your edible garden. Not only are many of the varieties quite attractive on their own or interplanted with ornamentals, but this family of plants is also easy to grow and very space efficient. Hardy perennial onions include bunching or Welsh onions and Egyptian onions.

Onions can be grown from seeds or "sets" or small bulbs. Most Ontario gardeners will want to use sets or start seeds indoors in February in order to guarantee a good harvest. Shallots are difficult to grow from seed; I recommend that you use sets instead. Sow seeds or sets as soon as the soil can be worked. Seeds should be spaced 13 mm (1/2 inch) apart;

sets should be spaced 13 to 20 cm (5 to 8 inches) apart with their tops crowning just at or above soil surface. Soil should be rich and well drained.

Large onions should be thinned when stocks are 20 cm (8 inches) tall by removing every second onion. Thin three times before harvest for globe and Spanish onions. Regular watering and weeding are needed for good growth; adding compost or fertilizer in mid-season is also a good idea.

Harvest by pulling green onions out of the soil as you need them; dig up large onions when the tops turn yellow. Dry large onions in the sun for two days before storing in a cool, dry place to prevent rotting.

Pests and diseases: Watch for thrips and root maggots.

Pea—shell, snap and snow peas
From planting to harvest: 55 to 80 days

Peas like rich, slightly acidic soil. Sow seeds as soon as the soil can be worked—peas like long cool days and can withstand frost, so plant early in the spring or late in the season for a fall harvest. (Pea plants stop producing fruit when the temperatures rise above 24°C/75°F.) You can either choose peas with different maturity dates and plant all at the same time, or sow another planting three or four weeks after the initial spring sowing to prolong your summer harvest.

Set seeds about 2.5 cm (1 inch) deep, 5 cm (2 inches) apart. Peas like moist soil, so water deeply in dry weather. Most pea varieties (with the exception of dwarf varieties) need to be against a trellis or fence, chicken wire or other support.

Peas are medium feeders, but will produce more foliage than fruit if the soil is very nitrogen rich. Side-dress the beds with compost or feed with low-nitrogen fertilizer when the plants are 15 to 25 cm (6 to 10 inches) tall.

Pick regularly so that the peas don't get tough—shelling peas and snap peas are harvested when the pods are rounded and plump; snow peas are picked when the pods are still flat.

Pests: Flea beetles when young.

Spinach
From planting to harvest: 40 to 60 days

Like mustard greens and Swiss chard, spinach thrives in cool temperatures; unlike chard it does not do well in hot weather, bolting to seed quickly.

Spinach likes full sun to partial shade and average to rich well-drained soil with a neutral pH. Plant seeds as soon as soil can be worked and every three weeks after that until the daytime temperatures become a consistent 21°C (70°F). Planted after that point, spinach will mature during the height of summer, when it will bolt to seed very quickly in the heat. You can resume planting in July through to six weeks before first frost (it will overwinter and reappear in the spring). Sow seeds 1.5 cm (3/4 inch) deep in furrows 35 cm (14 inches) apart. Pick individual leaves to prolong the harvest.

Pests and diseases: Cutworms, leaf miners, aphids, flea beetles, mosaic virus (blight).

Swiss chard

From planting to harvest: 45 to 55 days

Swiss chard is a cool crop that tolerates both frost and heat. It has an attractive leaf and is lovely in a potager garden or interplanted with ornamentals in your flower beds.

Sow seeds as soon as the soil can be worked (or three to four weeks before the last frost), 1 cm (1/2 inch) deep. Thin seedlings to 7.5 cm (3 inches) apart. As the chard grows, thin until remaining plants are 25 cm (10 inches) apart (you can eat the plants you pick out). Then remove outer leaves for eating when they are no more than 25 cm (10 inches) long.

Chard likes fertile, neutral soil. Feed with a high-nitrogen fertilizer (try 20-20-20) at least three times during the growing season (more often if the soil is poor) and keep the chard well watered to prevent bolting.

Pests and diseases: Chard is relatively pest and disease resistant. Watch for aphids, caterpillars and four-legged pests.

Warm crops

Beans, snap

From planting to harvest: Pole varieties—60 to 70 days; bush varieties— 45 to 60 days

Snap beans, also called string beans, green beans or wax beans, are easy to grow and a great vegetable for those short on space. "Pole" varieties or climbing beans can be grown up a trellis, string or pole. Not only are many of these varieties very attractive (my favourite is the scarlet runner bean), but they can even be planted in containers, as long as there is a vertical support for them to cling to as they grow. Bush beans do not need to be supported but require a bit more room to accommodate their spread. Snap beans need no special soil preparation, providing your garden is friable, but they will not germinate until the soil reaches 16°C (60°F) or warmer.

Sow seeds outdoors just before the last frost until about mid-June. Place seeds about 2.5 cm (1 inch) deep, 2.5 to 3.5 cm (1 to 1 1/4 inches) apart for bush beans, five to six seeds around the pole or string for pole beans. Water regularly, especially during and immediately after flowering and once pods have appeared. Beans are medium feeders, so give them a side-dressing of mature compost or a low-nitrogen fertilizer when they reach about 15 cm (6 inches) tall.

Pick beans when pencil-thick (left to grow any thicker than this and they will become tough). During the harvesting period (about three weeks) this will probably mean checking your plants every two or three days. Pick large tough beans that you've missed so that new beans will be produced. Add the older beans to the composter—they are full of nitrogen!

Pests and diseases: Bean seeds have a tendency to rot. Choose fungicide-treated seed for early plantings or plant seeds more densely to accommodate some seed loss. The plants themselves may develop rust, although rust-resistant varieties are available. Watch for aphids, Japanese beetles and Mexican bean beetles.

Cabbage, napa and bok choy

From planting to harvest: From transplants—early varieties: 60 to 70 days; mid-season varieties: 70 to 85 days; late varieties: 100 days

There is a wide variety of cabbages to choose from, including ones with beautiful ruffled leaves (Canada Savoy) or deep red heads (like Meteor). Many hybrid varieties are also now available, as well as some that are pest resistant, and others that are hardy in a variety of weather conditions.

Cabbages, however, take a long time to mature, so unless you plant from transplants and have a relatively long season, you may not be able to grow some of the mid-season or late varieties. If you want to start them from seed, sow indoors six to eight weeks before the last expected spring frost. Harden these seedlings off in a cold frame. Set out seedlings and transplants when the danger of frost has passed, spacing 45 cm (18 inches) between plants.

Cabbages like rich, well-drained soil, and they are heavy feeders so amend soil well with compost or well-rotted manure before planting and side-dress with compost or fertilize with 6-12-12 every month after planting. (Also check the rotation chart to avoid planting cabbage where similar vegetables have been previously.) Cabbages have shallow roots, so keeping them well watered and mulched is important. Careful weeding will also help young plants survive. Mulching around the plantings will help with both weeds and moisture needs. Cabbage can split in hot weather or after sudden periods of growth. You may be able to prevent this by inserting a shovel into the earth to one side of the stem and cutting off some of the roots. I've talked with other growers who simply give the head a good pull until they hear some of the roots snap.

Michihli and napa varieties of cabbage are head-formers and take two months or more to mature after transplants have been planted. Bok choy grows like chard and can be harvested in about 40 days.

Pests and diseases: Cutworms and root maggots are the most common pests.

Cucumber

From planting to harvest: 50 to 70 days

You can choose from a wide variety of cucumber types these days. New varieties include lemon, white and long gourmet cucs. "Burpless" cucumbers are mildest and thinnest skinned. Vining cucumbers can be grown vertically on uprights (like pole beans), but the fruit may need to be supported by cloth slings or netting. Compact varieties (like 'Patio Pic') work very well in containers.

Sow plant seedlings (that have been started indoors) once all danger of frost has passed. Cucumbers need good air circulation and well-drained soil. Before planting, prepare a hole 15 cm (6 inches) deep and 60 cm (2 feet) in diameter and fill with well-rotted manure. Mix a handful of 6-12-12 fertilizer with the soil you removed from the hole. Return this soil to the hole, covering the manure. Plant three to five seeds, 2.5 to 5 cm (1 to 2 inches) deep, in this hill of soil. Space hills 2 m (6 feet) apart. Mulch and keep cucumbers well watered (never allow the plants to wilt from dehydration).

Pollination: See Peppers, p. 112.

Harvest pickling cucumbers when they've reached about 7.5 cm (3 inches) in length, slicing varieties when 15 cm (6 inches), and the long English seedless type at 35 cm (14 inches) or longer. All should be picked before they turn yellow. Always remove ripe or overripe cucumbers to encourage the plant to produce more fruit.

Pests and diseases: Powdery mildew, bacterial wilt, anthracnose, squash vine borer.

Zucchini

From planting to harvest: 50 to 60 days

Zucchini is the most popular of the summer squashes, and it is relatively easy to grow. Keep in mind that one plant produces about 16 fruit and that zucchini does not store very well. Depending on the size of your family and the number of zucchini recipes you have, one or two plants may be all you need!

Zucchini like warm, rich, well-drained soil and a sunny spot protected from wind. Sow seeds 1 to 2.5 cm (1/2 to 1 inch) deep about a week after the last frost date. If planting more than one zucchini bush, plant seeds 15 cm (6 inches) apart and thin plants so that they are 30 cm (12 inches) apart. Feed with a low-nitrogen veggie fertilizer and water deeply once a week, especially during dry spells.

Pollination: See Peppers, p. 112.

Zucchini can grow to enormous sizes but the flavour and texture are much nicer when the plants are quite small—10 to 15 cm (4 to 6 inches) long. Picking the vegetables early also encourages the plant to produce more fruit. Harvest all fruit before damaged by frost.

Pests and diseases: Blossom-end rot, squash vine borer.

Hot crops

Peppers

From planting to harvest: 60 to 80 days (from transplants)

For the Ontario gardener, there just can't be too much sun for pepper plants. They like about eight hours of full sun a day and lots of heat.

Peppers like warm, loose, well-drained soil. Seeds should be started indoors about ten weeks before the last frost, but most Ontario gardeners will probably want to purchase small plants from their garden centres to give them a good head start. These transplants should be set out when the weather and soil are warm and all danger of frost is long gone (usually early June for most of the province). Sweet pepper plants should be spaced 20 to 30 cm (8 to 12 inches) apart, while hot peppers need 35 to 45 cm (14 to 18 inches) between them. Pinch off bottom leaves of the plants and set the plants a little lower in the soil than they were sitting in the pot to encourage new root growth. Consistent, generous watering is important for good growth—give the plants a good soaking twice a week or as soil becomes dry past the top 2 cm (3/4 inch). Fertilize with 6-12-12 once a month.

THIS PAGE *Hard furnishings can be an attractive addition to any garden. A willow bench graces a large site; a smaller site features a wrought-iron chair.*

FOLLOWING PAGES CLOCKWISE FROM LEFT *Interplanting bulbs with perennials guarantees a burst of colour early in the season.* ❀ *In my garden, I create vibrant, long-lasting colour by mixing perennials and annuals.* ❀ *Leaves of various shapes, sizes and colours, like those of the hosta, fern and Canada anemone, along with well-chosen accents, add interest to the semi-shade under a tree.*

TOP AND FAR RIGHT *Even small gardens can use "rooms" to create interest and depth. Here the space is divided by fences, tall flowers and gravel paths.*

RIGHT *Ornamental onion (Allium aflatunense).*

CLOCKWISE FROM TOP LEFT *A shady garden is the perfect environment for native woodland plants such as foamflowers and ferns* ❊ *This zone 4 garden features hardy daylilies, irises, lupines and ornamental onions.*

CLOCKWISE FROM TOP LEFT

The paper or canoe birch is one of my favourite trees for the Ontario garden. ❀ *At the cottage, the use of native plants, like these trilliums and foam-flowers, creates a harmonious transition from woodland to clearing.* ❀ *Wet areas are ideal spots to plant bog gardens, like this one featuring primulas.*

CLOCKWISE FROM TOP LEFT *Meadow gardens can feature large groupings of native flowers such as purple coneflower, Joe Pye weed and the ornamental grass miscanthus 'Morning Light.'* ❁ *A large site is the perfect setting for wide swaths of one flower, like the sunflower.* ❁ *Even a garage or a shed can be an attractive part of a garden.*

CLOCKWISE FROM TOP LEFT

The natural rocky outcroppings of the Canadian Shield are perfect for rock gardens, like this one at an Ontario cottage. ✽ *Front entranceways benefit greatly from container gardening.*

CLOCKWISE FROM LEFT *Rock gardens can feature plants of various heights, such as low-lying sedum and bergenia, taller dianthus, chives and irises, and even shrubs like euonymus.*
❀ *Groundcovers can be anything from flagstone paths to ground-hugging plants, like creeping jenny.* ❀ *Don't be afraid to plant vegetables and ornamentals together. Here kale nestles beautifully between French marigolds to the left and cleome to the right.*
FOLLOWING PAGE *A beautiful native Ontario woodland garden with lady slippers, wild phlox, foamflower, wild geranium, columbine and, at the centre, a Jack-in-the-pulpit.*

Pollination: If you are gardening on a balcony, rooftop or in an area where you don't see evidence of honey bees, I recommend that you pollinate your peppers yourself to ensure fruit production. Simply use a paintbrush to wipe some pollen off the stamens (the long stalks or "filaments" inside the flower petals that are topped with a powder-covered nodule) and then apply it to the pistils of other flowers (the tube inside the flower petals that's topped with a sticky cap). You can also simply shake the stamens until you see pollen fall onto other parts of the flower (it only takes a grain of pollen to fertilize each fruit). If your pepper plants are in a windy location, this kind of assistance may not be necessary at all. But if the weather is humid (making the pollen sticky), the paintbrush method works best.

Peppers are good candidates for container growing, which may provide them with the extra heat they need. Just make sure they don't dry out!

Harvest peppers frequently to encourage the plants to produce more fruit.

Pests and diseases: Colorado potato beetles, flea beetles, cutworms.

Tomatoes

From planting to harvest: 60 to 80 days (from transplants)

A couple of years ago, southern Ontario had an unseasonably cool, wet summer. People were frustrated with the lousy weather at the cottage, and the need for sweaters in July, but their despair over the state of their tomatoes come August was the keenest disappointment I witnessed. Ontario loves its tomatoes. And tomatoes like the conditions that much of Ontario affords: with good reason Heinz chose to locate its Canadian headquarters in Leamington.

There is now a huge variety of tomatoes to choose from. Colours range from white to yellow to orange to red. You can find early and mid-season varieties and ones resistant to disease, and even "square" tomatoes that won't roll off the table! Choose from a wonderful selection of cherry tomatoes (these work very well in containers), medium and large tomatoes and varieties ideal for sauce and paste making. The two basic types of tomatoes are bush tomatoes (often referred to as "determinate" varieties) and staking varieties (called "indeterminate"). The former are generally grown in cages and produce their fruit in a

TOMATOES FOR CHRISTMAS!
One of my radio listeners called in to say that he was "harvesting" tomatoes from their original plants the first week of the new year. He had pulled the plants out of the ground in September—roots and all. Then he hung the plants upside down in his basement cold cellar. As the fruit ripened on the plants, he picked and ate it!

concentrated period of time. Staked varieties, however, need to be supported up a pole or trellis and bear fruit progressively over the growing season. These types need to be pruned.

Tomatoes can be started from seed indoors six to eight weeks before the last spring frost. Many gardeners opt for plants from a nursery, but if you have your heart set on a specialty variety, you may have to start with seed instead. If you are purchasing seedlings, look for dark glossy leaves and a short, sturdy stem. Put seedlings or transplants into the ground once the temperatures are warm (a minimum 20°C/70°F) throughout the day and night—generally a week after the last frost date. My good friend Lois Hole in Edmonton recommends taking a chance on an earlier harvest by planting just after the last spring frost date. If you decide to follow suit, be prepared to cover the seedlings with an inverted milk bottle or cloche for protection. Plant the seedlings deep, at least up to their first leaves. I recommend you also pinch off the bottom leaves and plant so that the soil covers this area. New roots will develop along the stem, producing a stronger plant. For staked varieties, space the plants 45 to 60 cm (18 to 24 inches) apart and stake within the first month after planting to avoid root damage. Leave 8 to 13 cm (3 to 5 inches) between the plant and the stake and make sure the stake is deep in the soil for stability. As the plant grows, tie it to the stake loosely. For bush varieties, leave 90 to 120 cm (3 to 4 feet) between plants if you are going to let them sprawl or 90 cm (3 feet) between cages.

Tomatoes like plenty of sun—a full eight hours a day, in fact. They also like heat and shelter from the wind. They are heavy feeders so the soil should be rich with organic material at planting time (I can't say enough about compost!). Fertilize with 10-52-10 once a week for the first two weeks, then feed with half-strength 20-20-20 once every ten days to two weeks. Water regularly (at least twice a week), more frequently if the weather is dry and hot.

Prune staked varieties by cutting out suckers growing between the main stem and the branch, as often as twice a week when plants are growing most vigorously. You can also prune back the top of the stem if it outgrows its stake or at the end of the season when you want the plant to spend its energy on the remaining fruit.

Pests and diseases: Blossom-end rot (caused by calcium deficiency or extremely dry weather). Watch for tomato hornworm, which can be removed by hand, and early blight, which you can prevent with an application of all-natural Bordeaux mixture or fixed copper, in July.

Perennial bush fruit and vegetables

Asparagus
(to zone 2)

Asparagus is a perennial vegetable, and as such is a great addition to your perennial flower beds or potager garden. What's more, it can really only be grown in cool, northern climates (up to zone 2)—perfect for Ontario gardeners! It does, however, take some space, so you will need to plan your garden accordingly. It can be grown from seed (which requires patience) or from root sections (crowns). Growing from seed can take years before you see a harvest, so many gardeners choose to plant crowns to cut a year or two off the process. Asparagus planted from crowns can be harvested after two years' growth (in its third year).

Asparagus likes fertile, well-drained soil that is slightly acidic (6.5 pH). Since it is a perennial and will be occupying the same space for years to come, it is important that you amend the soil well before planting. Dig out the bed and mix in organic material (a mixture of peat moss and compost works well) to create a trench or hole 15 to 30 cm (6 to 12 inches) deep. The deeper the crowns are planted, the fewer and thicker the spears will be. The crowns should be planted in the trench 60 cm (2 feet) apart and barely covered with rich soil. Over the course of the season, as the shoots grow, gradually fill in the hole with loam. Mulch, and water regularly.

Because asparagus is a heavy feeder it is important to keep competitors—weeds—out of its beds. Fertilize or work in mature compost as spring growth begins. For white European-style asparagus, mound soil over the spears as they grow in the spring to blanch them. Protected from sunlight, they remain white.

In the third season, you can harvest the thick spears. Pick when they are 15 to 20 cm (6 to 8 inches) long, breaking them off below ground. After a few weeks, thinner spears appear. Very thin spears (0.5 cm or 1/4 inch or smaller) should be left to develop foliage, which will feed the roots for the next season. The harvest lasts about four weeks. When the fern-like foliage turns yellow in the fall, it can be removed. Apply additional compost or composted manure to a depth of 7.5 cm (3 inches) in autumn and a layer of chopped leaves or organic mulch.

Pests and diseases: Asparagus beetle may be a problem, but there are varieties, like Viking and Mary Washington, that are resistant to asparagus's other attackers: rust and fusarium wilt.

Blueberries
(hybrids to zone 6; native varieties to zone 3)

If you live in northern Ontario, you may not want to bother with cultivated blueberries. After all, nothing is as heavenly as wild Ontario blueberries. But for those of us who don't have access to this bounty, backyard blueberry bushes provide a real treat in summer!

Blueberries like acidic soil (pH between 4 and 5) that is richly organic but well drained. They are best planted in fall.

Blueberries cross-pollinate, so plant two or more varieties and alternate the types in the row or bed. Space the plants 90 cm to 1.5 m (3 to 5 feet) apart. Some varieties need more—check with your garden centre or the information provided with the plants.

Dig holes wide enough to accommodate plant roots. Add water to the hole and let it drain before placing the blueberry plant in it. Once in the hole, the plant should be just low enough that the soil added to fill in the hole reaches to the existing soil line on the plant. After adding soil, mound it around the plant, matching the diameter of the roots to make a small well. Fill this well with water. About a month after planting, fertilize with a 20-20-20 solution.

Mulch with an organic mulch (an acidic mulch, if possible—pine needles, for example) in the spring and keep soil damp but not wet. You can remove flowers in the first year to allow the plant to conserve energy. In the next two years, prune only dead or damaged branches. From the fourth year on, remove up to four of the oldest shoots to encourage new growth.

Birds and rabbits love blueberries, so you may need to cover the bushes with netting to protect your precious harvest!

No serious pests or diseases.

Currants

(to zone 4)

Currant bushes are attractive ornamentals as well as practical. Growing up to 90 cm (3 feet) high and 90 cm (3 feet) wide, they can serve as hedges as well as a food source. Once established, they are hardy and low maintenance.

Currant bushes like cool, moist soil. If you have sandy loam, mulch the root zone well to retain moisture.

Plant in either spring or fall. Space bushes 1.2 m (4 feet) apart and prune to 15 cm (6 inches) above ground level. Do not prune for another four years. After that time, prune in fall to leave only six healthy canes on each bush.

Pests and diseases: Currants, as well as gooseberries, can be host to white pine blister rust (a fungal disease). Some horticulturists suggest planting no closer than 250 m (800 feet) from white pine (or 400 m/about 400 yards from nursery-grown white pine).

Garlic

(to zone 2)

Garlic is a perennial and the cloves should be planted, base down, 5 to 7.5 cm (2 to 3 inches) deep, in late summer or fall for harvesting the next year. Apply a good layer of winter mulch in the late fall. If snow covering tends to be poor over the winter, you can plant in spring, up to five weeks before the last frost date. Garlic likes light, well-drained soil.

Water and weed regularly, and feed with a nitrogen-rich fertilizer in the spring. Harvest when leaves wither (generally in August). Harvesting is easiest if soil is dry.

Pests and diseases: Not only does garlic suffer few diseases, it is reputed to repel pests. Interplant garlic with other vegetables or ornamentals like roses.

Gooseberries

(to zone 3)

A variety of gooseberries are available for the home garden. Some, like the green Pixel, are sour and wonderful for jam. Others are sweet enough for eating fresh.

Gooseberries develop on thorny canes that grow 90 cm (3 feet) high and tend to spread and ramble. They like cool, moist, rich soil and partial shade. They need watering only when the growing season is very dry.

Plant bushes about 1.5 m (5 feet) apart and prune to ground level. Mulch with compost or well-composted manure.

After the first summer, prune all but four or six of the healthiest canes, cutting 15 cm (6 inches) above the root stock. Do this each fall, ensuring that a few of the older canes remain (fruit is produced on new canes or new shoots on older canes). On older stalks, cut back canes to 15 cm (6 inches), leaving at least one bud.

Pests and diseases: Gooseberries are vulnerable to birds, aphids, sawfly and mildew. Like currants, they can harbour white pine blister rust (see Currants, p. 117).

Raspberries
(to zone 4)

Raspberries prefer established beds to reduce the threat of cutworm. They like rich, fertile soil that is well drained. They also need acidic soil (pH 5.5).

Plant in spring or fall, with 45 cm (18 inches) between plants (and 2 m/6 feet between rows). Rooted canes should be planted so the soil meets the soil line on the canes. Add water to the hole as you fill with soil. Mulch the soil and water in dry weather.

In the first growing season, remove flowers to allow the plants to conserve energy. In the second year, pick fruit carefully so as not to damage the delicate berries.

Prune fall-bearing varieties in October or November; prune July-bearing varieties right after the last berries have been picked in mid-summer. Remove the canes that bore fruit and prune out suckers that grow between established plants.

Pests and diseases: Cutworms, aphids, fruit worms, cane borers, cane blight, cane spot (anthracnose).

Rhubarb
(to zone 4)

I always look forward to my wife Mary's garden-fresh rhubarb crisp. It is one of the "rites of spring." Indeed, rhubarb is a staple in many Ontario gardens—not only, I suspect, because we are a province of rhubarb devotees, but because rhubarb is so darn easy to grow. If you have the room (a mature rhubarb plant likes to spread itself over a full metre at least), then this ultra-hardy perennial "fruit" is a lovely addition to both your table and your garden (it does, in my opinion, possess some "ornamental" qualities in the right place).

Rhubarb likes rich, well-drained soil and a relatively sunny location. Rhubarb roots (available from a neighbour or a garden centre) should be planted in the early spring or late fall in a 60-cm (2-foot) deep hole that has been half-filled with compost or well-rotted manure. Fill hole with well-amended soil until the crown is covered by 5 to 5.5 cm (about 2 inches) of soil. Rhubarb is a heavy feeder so periodic feedings of 20-20-20 fertilizer or compost will help the plant along in its first year, and an annual feeding of compost will keep it in trim in coming years. Don't harvest stalks in the first year, and only the thickest stalks for just the first two weeks in the second year. By the third year, you can harvest stalks for most of the late spring and early summer before the stalks thin. If the plant bolts to seed, remove the seed stalk before it flowers. This preserves the plant's energy for root and stalk development.

No serious pests or diseases.

Strawberries
(to zone 6)

Strawberries like rich, fertile soil that is slightly alkaline (pH 7.5), in an established bed (to reduce white grub problems).

Double-dig strawberry beds in the fall, adding plenty of compost or composted manure. Plant 50 cm (20 inches) apart for spring-bearing varieties and 20 cm (8 inches) apart for ever-bearing types. Rows should be 75 cm (30 inches) apart. (The additional space between spring-bearing strawberries provides room for runners to grow. These should be removed in the first year and placed in another bed to mature.)

Holes for plants should be wide enough to allow for root growth. Place plants in holes so that the crowns are level with the surrounding soil. Water new plantings well and mulch (straw makes a clean dry mulch that keeps fruit off the ground).

In the first year, remove all initial flowers from all varieties. Ever-bearing strawberries will produce a second set of blossoms and then a light, midsummer crop.

Fruit production will be strongest every second year, so you may want to plant a second crop a year after the first, to have a robust harvest each year. Cut back strawberry tops in the fall and cover with an organic winter mulch.

Pests and diseases: Strawberries can be susceptible to disease so look for disease-resistant stock and cultivars and practise crop rotation. Remove diseased plants immediately and burn them.

Watch also for aphids, Japanese beetles, leafhoppers, leafrollers, slugs, thrips, mites, weevils, spittlebugs and earwigs. Keeping leaves and fruit off the soil with straw or plastic mulch will help deter pests. Protect fruit from birds with netting or aluminum-plates suspended over plants.

Herbs

While you may be new to the idea of a potager garden, or interplanting vegetables and flowers, you will no doubt know of many gardens, including your own perhaps, where you can find herbs tucked in with ornamental plants. Herbs are also commonly grown in containers, and tender herbs are often brought in to spend the winter on sunny window ledges. Herbs like chives and mint are perennial in most zones in Ontario, to zone 2.

Generally, herbs need five hours of direct light per day; if you are growing them indoors, place them in south- and west-facing windows, as close to glass as possible. Most herbs like rich, fertile soil that is neutral in pH. They don't, however, do their best in soils with high nitrogen levels—this reduces the flavour in the leaves and stems. You don't need any supplemental fertilizers during the growing season. Most of our popular herbs originated in the Mediterranean region and therefore require little moisture.

You can start most herbs from seed, but to get a jump on our short season, many gardeners prefer to buy small plants at their local garden centre.

Basil

Basil is available in a wide number of varieties. It is extremely difficult to grow from seed—most Ontario gardeners buy young plants in the spring. Basil does not like to be overwatered, which can lead to root rot.

Plant in a sheltered spot that receives full sun, two weeks after the last spring frost. If putting in more than one plant, space 30 cm (1 foot) apart. Given that basil is fussy about the amount of water it receives, it is a good candidate for containers, where you can monitor the moisture it gets.

Chives

Chives are a perennial hardy to zone 3 and a very decorative addition to the garden. They are easy to grow and can be started from seed, from young plants purchased at a garden centre or from roots taken from a mature plant. Plant chives as soon as the soil can be worked (they are wonderfully frost resistant). They like full sun or light shade and need only average soil.

Cilantro

The plants are also called Chinese parsley and the seeds, coriander.

Cilantro can be seeded directly or grown from young plants. It likes light, well-drained soil that is not nitrogen rich. It needs a location that is sheltered but has full sun and must be set out only after all danger of frost is past.

You can pick the leaves as soon as they appear (the lower leaves are more flavourful). You may also pick and eat the flowers, but even if you are eating only the leaves, you should pinch off the flowers to allow more leaf growth. Seeds should be harvested at the end of the growing season when they are hard and brown.

Dill

Dill is easy to grow but needs quite a lot of space. It likes full sun and will tolerate poor, well-drained soil. Seedlings are difficult to transplant, so it is best grown from seed sown directly in the garden. Sow early, approximately at the date of the last spring frost. You can use all parts of the dill plant and can begin picking it when it is very young, continuing throughout the growing season. Harvest the flower heads before they open fully.

Mint

There are many varieties of mint available and all are easy to grow. The only drawback to mint is that it is highly invasive. Growing it in a pot or container may save your flower beds from being overrun.

Mint prefers some shade but can tolerate full sun. It likes moist, rich soil, but it isn't overly fussy! Mint is best started with young plants from a garden centre or from plant division. Keep mint 60 to 90 cm (2 to 3 feet) apart from other plants. Mint requires regular watering and individual leaves can be picked at any time or the whole plant can be cut (10 cm/4 inches from the soil level) twice during the season.

In most Ontario zones, mint is a perennial but in the colder zones it should be protected with a good snow cover. After three or four years, mint plants become woody and should be replaced.

Parsley

Parsley is a tender biennial but can usually be grown only as an annual in Ontario. Curly and plain leaf parsley varieties are available. (I have seen curly parsley used as a border plant in an ornamental planting—and it looked good, too!)

Parsley likes moist, average to rich soil. It is easiest to grow from young plants as the seed germinates slowly and only when the soil is quite warm. Plant parsley approximately a week before the last spring frost date, spacing plants 20 to 25 cm (8 to 10 inches) apart.

Parsley does well in cool temperatures but will withstand heat quite admirably. It doesn't need a great deal of water, except if planted in containers, which should be watered every day.

While most people like to harvest all their parsley at the end of the season and either dry it or freeze it for future use, I have heard of gardeners who leave it in the ground and continue to snip the frozen leaves throughout the winter!

Rosemary

Rosemary is a perennial in zones 8 and warmer, but for most Ontario gardeners it is an annual. I have, however, been bringing our rosemary "tree," which now stands about 60 cm (2 feet) high in a clay pot, indoors for the winter for several years. It provides a wonderful scent of summer all year round, especially when my wife, Mary, makes toasted rosemary bread.

Like parsley it is often difficult to raise from seed—most gardeners purchase young plants or propagate from cuttings (there are upright as well as trailing varieties). Plant around the last spring frost date. It is well suited to containers.

Rosemary likes poor, well-drained soil and a sunny location. It will tolerate some shade and needs regular watering only when it is getting established.

Thyme

A huge assortment of thyme varieties are available, some perennial in Ontario zones, some annual. Not only are there all sorts of delightful flavours and colours but thyme is often grown as a groundcover as well.

Thyme can be grown from seeds but is easiest from young plants. Set out as soon as the soil can be worked (it can tolerate light frost). Thyme likes light, well-drained soil and will tolerate poor soil. It likes full sun and doesn't like to dry out. Overwatering and too much fertilizer, however, will produce less flavourful leaves. Pick leaves at any time; remove flowers to make leaves more flavourful (these can be eaten as well).

PART 3

Gardening
Basics

Soil

Ninety per cent of the success you enjoy in your garden is the direct result of proper—thorough!—soil preparation. And while there are certain types of soil that will make gardening easier or more challenging, understanding the type of soil you have and its strengths, weaknesses and needs will largely determine what you can get out of it. Making sure your soil is healthy and fertile will not only lead you to vibrant blooms and verdant foliage, but will also reduce your need for pesticides and fertilizers. If you are keen to garden organically, soil improvement is the essential first step and maintenance is an important follow-up.

Soil composition

Good garden soil is composed of air (25 per cent), water (25 per cent), minerals (45 per cent) and organic matter (5 per cent). The bulk of the soil, the mineral portion, is made up of very small fragments of rock. Chemically, these tiny rock particles provide some of the mineral nutrients that plants need. The rock particles also largely determine the texture of the soil. They vary greatly in size, the very smallest being those that make clay, the next in size being silt particles, with sand the largest of these particles. The size of the mineral particles and the amount of each in the soil determine how well that particular soil holds and drains water and have a significant impact on the air circulation of the soil. Sand is coarse, and because the spaces between sand particles are big, the particles do not stick together or compact. Sand therefore cannot hold water or nutrients well—they tend to flow through and out of sand quickly. Sand, however, does warm up faster in the spring, and, in moderate quantities, is a useful ingredient in any good-quality garden soil. Clay particles hold nutrients well, but they tend to stick together and create compaction and even "hardpan," which is extremely dense, hard soil.

Mixtures of clay, silt and sand are called "loams." My dad always swore by "sandy loam" as the best possible start to a garden. It is easy to dig and easy for plants to root in (good for you, good for your plants!). The ratio of the mineral portion of the soil that most gardeners feel is ideal is anywhere between equal portions of all three components to 40 per cent sand, 40 per cent silt and 20 per cent clay. A soil composition in this range means pore space between soil particles will account for between 30 and 50 per cent of the volume of the soil, allowing air and water to circulate freely.

We don't often think of soil as being composed of "air" but, indeed, if we have good soil, a quarter of its volume will be air (the three primary components of which are, of course, nitrogen, oxygen and carbon dioxide). The microorganisms that live in the soil, keeping the cycle of decomposition moving and manufacturing a good deal of the nutrients our plants rely on, need oxygen to survive. Nitrogen in gas form is also essential in soil so that nitrogen-fixing bacteria can consume it and turn it into a water-soluble form that plants can absorb. What's more, roots need to "breathe," so they depend on good air exchange between soil and atmosphere.

The necessity for the water component in soil is obvious to any gardener. Water not only carries nutrients from the soil to the roots in a form that the roots can absorb, but it also maintains the cell structure of the plant. But the mere presence of water in the soil may not be enough for your plant. While sandy soils don't retain water well and therefore plants may go thirsty without vigilant watering, clay soils also pose a problem for thirsty plants. Clay soils hold water well; in fact, they can hold it too well. Water and clay bond together strongly (not unlike a magnetic attraction), so the plant roots may not be able to remove the water molecules from the clay bond. Much of the water in a clay soil may therefore not be available to your parched plant. And with this tight bond between water and clay, pore spaces are filled with water, squeezing out the necessary air as well.

The smallest component of soil, yet the one that can have the greatest effect on how the other three interact and how well your plants do in your soil, is organic material or humus (found in finished compost). Humus is the decayed remains of organic or once-living material—in other words, decomposed plant and animal material. Humus provides food for microorganisms, bacteria, fungi, insects and earthworms that convert the nutrients it contains into soluble forms that plant roots can absorb. It also can contribute macronutrients (nutrients that plants need in large quantities) such as nitrogen, phosphorus and potassium, as well as micronutrients or trace elements (nutrients plants need in small quantities) directly to the soil as well.

Organic material like compost and leaf mould also affects the composition of the soil. It makes clay more workable or friable (it will crumble more easily). And by increasing pore space, it also improves air and water circulation (sometimes referred to as improving a soil's "tilth"). In sandy soil, it allows the soil to retain more moisture and nutrients.

So what kind of soil do you have? If you have been digging in your garden, you no doubt know if you are dealing with very sandy soil or very heavy clay. But if you have been fortunate to escape the extremes, you may want to try one of the following simple tests to see where your soil composition lies between these two extremes (the chart on p. 130 illustrates the range of soil types depending on their composition).

RULE OF THUMB: BALANCE
"All work and no play...." Life demands that we find balance: work, play; eat, sleep; drink— but moderately. So it is with good soil. Some sand, some clay and lots of finished garden compost. Balance: not too much of any one thing. This, to my way of thinking, is a good example of how the gardening experience teaches some wonderful life-long lessons.

Testing composition

Jar test

Take 250 mL (1 cup) of garden soil and place it in a 1-litre (4-cup) jar (tall skinny jars work best). Fill the rest of the jar with tap water and shake until the soil and water are mixed. Let the jar rest undisturbed for at least 24 hours. You will begin to see the soil settle. When the water at the top is almost clear, you should see that the soil has separated into layers. Sand will settle at the bottom. The next layer will be silt, and clay will settle on top of that. The organic matter will float on top of or in the water. Check the ratio of sand, silt and clay against the diagram below to determine what kind of soil you have.

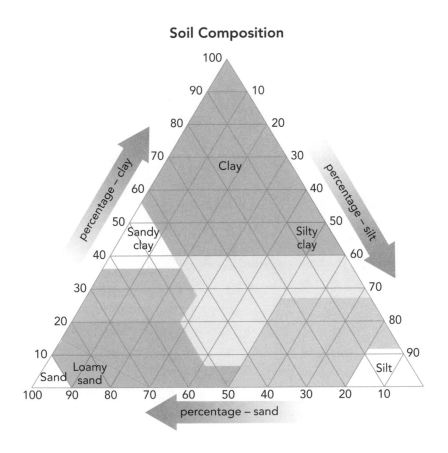

Soil Composition

Hand test

You can also determine your soil type by appearance and feel. Clay soil is generally yellowish-tan in colour, loam is usually light to dark brown and sandy soil tends to be greyish-tan in colour. To identify your soil type by feel, try this test two or three days after it has rained. Pick up a small quantity of soil (about the size of a golf ball). Squeeze it between thumb and index finger, or close your hand around it, and then let go. If it feels gritty and falls apart as soon as you release it, it contains a high proportion of sand. If it feels smooth and silky, but holds its shape for a short time before it crumbles into chunks, it is loam. If it feels like moist talcum powder (some people say it feels "greasy"), it is high in silt. If it is slippery or sticky, and holds its shape even after you have released it, it is mostly clay.

Soil fertility

While the physical composition of the soil will affect aeration, water percolation and the ease with which you can work the stuff, the fertility of the soil is an essential factor in determining how healthy your plants will be. Plants consume CO_2 from the atmosphere and water from the soil, but they also feed on naturally occurring chemical elements available to them through the soil. Their primary need is for nitrogen (N), phosphorus (P) and potassium (K) (these are the three main ingredients in all commercial fertilizer mixes). They also need magnesium, calcium and sulphur (often referred to as secondary nutrients).

As well as these macronutrients, plants need many other elements in much smaller quantities (micronutrients), such as iron, manganese, zinc, chlorine, boron, copper and nickel. These nutrients are literally consumed by the plants, so some of the elements (usually just the macronutrients) need to be replaced in the soil on a continual basis. Decomposing organic material does just this by slowly releasing the elements over a long period of time. Synthetic fertilizers add the elements directly to the soil for consumption by the plants. If you are adding plenty of organic material, like compost or composted cattle manure, to your soil each year, you generally do not need to worry about further feeding your garden. But some plants, like vegetables, are fast growing and therefore need and absorb a great deal of these nutrients from the soil. You may need to fertilize your vegetable beds or feed them regularly with compost tea (compost steeped in water overnight, usually in a burlap sack, to create a liquid that contains the nutrients that are now dissolved in the water).

How nutrients affect plant growth

NUTRIENT	HOW TO TELL IF IT IS ADEQUATE IN YOUR SOIL*	HOW TO TELL IF IT IS DEFICIENT IN YOUR SOIL
Primary		
Nitrogen (N)	Aids stem and leaf growth; plants with adequate nitrogen have lush green foliage.	Leaves yellow and drop, starting with oldest leaves. Stunted growth: weak stems, undeveloped leaves and reduced root growth.
Phosphorus (P)	Encourages strong, healthy roots and vigorous plant growth. Also encourages plants to bloom and to bear fruit more quickly. Increases seed production. Aids in a plant's resistance to disease and ability to withstand winter cold.	Stunted, retarded growth of all plant parts. Some plants develop red, purple or very dark green leaves (older leaves first). Little flowering or fruit production.
Potassium (K)	Plays a key role in plant cell division and growth. Helps plants use available nitrogen and balance the effects of excess nitrogen and calcium. Thought to increase drought tolerance and resistance to disease and winter cold. In the growth of fruit, nuts and vegetables, helps in the production of starches, sugars and oils, improving colour, flavour and texture.	Retarded growth; weak stems. Leaf edges and tips turn brown (older leaves first). Small fruit or shrivelled seeds.
Secondary		
Calcium		Poor growth and death of buds and young leaves.
Magnesium		Veins on leaves remain green but rest of leaf yellows (on oldest leaves first). Black spots can develop near veins.
Sulphur		Leaves yellow (youngest first). Plant becomes stiff.
Trace		
Zinc		Area between veins of young leaves turns yellow; veins stay green (oldest leaves first). New leaves are stunted.
Iron		Area between veins of young leaves, as well as small veins, turns yellow.
Manganese		Area between veins of young leaves turns yellow (veins stay green). Black or brown spots develop on leaves.

NUTRIENT	HOW TO TELL IF IT IS ADEQUATE IN YOUR SOIL	HOW TO TELL IF IT IS DEFICIENT IN YOUR SOIL
Copper		Stunted growth and dead spots on leaves (beginning with newest leaves). Wilted leaf tips.
Boron		Buds die, causing fans of stiff shoots along the stems. Plant becomes brittle.
Molybdenum		Paleness and yellowing of leaves. Leaf edges curl up.
Chlorine		Wilting and loss of colour.

*A lab test is needed to determine if your soil has adequate secondary and trace nutrients.

Understanding pH

When it comes to soil and soil improvement, it is a good idea to spend some time determining the chemical nature of your soil as well as its physical composition. This means understanding "pH"—not always an easy thing to do. Years ago, a local politician made a gaffe by swearing his commitment to getting the pH level of rain in the area back to zero. Ouch. The letters "pH" stand for "parts hydrogen" and the scale measures the concentration of hydrogen ions in a substance. This concentration determines the relative acidity or alkalinity of a substance. The most extremely acidic end of the pH scale is 1. Concentrated hydrochloric acid, for example, would be around 1, and white vinegar around 4. Seven is the number the politician meant to say—the midpoint of the scale, indicating neutrality. And 14 is the extreme alkaline end of the pH scale (household ammonia ranks about 10 on the pH scale). PH can be a confusing concept, but it is one worth getting a handle on as the pH of your soil can seriously affect not only what plants thrive and which suffer in your garden, but how nutritious your soil is for your plants.

In soil, extreme pH (below 5 or above 8 is generally inhospitable for plants) affects the availability of soil nutrients, although pH itself is no indication of the nutrient content of soil. In highly acidic soil or soil with a low pH, for example, phosphorus and potassium

RULE OF THUMB: FOOT SOLDIERS OF THE GARDEN

I love earthworms! Their presence is not only good for your soil, it is an indication of its fertility and level of organic matter. Earthworms aerate the soil, pull organic material from the surface of the soil down through it (they can burrow at least 2 m/6 foot down and sometimes much farther), then consume the organic material and turn it into castings (580 g/20 oz. per year per worm), providing high levels of nitrogen, phosphates and potassium for your plants. They also maintain the pH balance in your soil. A 30-cm- (1-foot-) square patch of soil housing ten or more worms is in good shape (keep in mind that earthworms will be fewer in evidence in very cool or very dry soil). An absence of earthworms may indicate insufficient organic material in the soil, a mineral imbalance or soil that is either too acidic or too alkaline. You will want to investigate further.

cannot be readily taken up by plants even though they may be present in the soil. In very acidic soil some heavy metals, like lead and cadmium, break down easily and may be absorbed by plants in harmful quantities. What's more, many helpful microorganisms (including nitrogen-fixing bacteria) cannot live in highly acidic soil. At the other end of the scale, in alkaline soil, iron cannot be taken up by plants, even though the soil itself might be quite rich with the mineral (this is a problem for those plants, such as rhododendrons, that need unusually high quantities of iron). All these are reasons why pH is often mentioned when the topic of soil improvement is raised.

Most plants do best in soil that ranges between neutral and slightly acidic—in other words, 6 to 7 on the pH scale (to be even more specific, most plants like the 6.3 to 6.8 range). Plants that like acidic soil, such as ferns, azalea, camellia, rhododendron and blueberries, thrive in pH between 4.5 and 5.5. If you are told that a plant prefers a mildly alkaline soil, as do asparagus, spinach and cacti, we are talking about soil in the 7.5 pH range. Those number ranges might sound rather slight, but the pH scale is logarithmic, meaning each number indicates a value ten times the previous number, so that a soil with a pH of 9 is 10 times more alkaline than a soil with a pH of 8, and *100* times more alkaline than a soil of 7!

Most soil in southern Ontario, where the bedrock is primarily limestone, is in the neutral to slightly alkaline range. In most of northern Ontario and other areas where the bedrock is granite, the soil is neutral to slightly acidic. And if you live in an area where acid rain has been a problem, your soil may be somewhat or even very acidic.

Because the underlying rock has such a great effect on soil pH, amending soil by adding minerals and so on (see the chart on p. 139) is a bit of an uphill battle. Adding lime to raise the pH, for example, or digging in sulphur to lower the pH will generally change the soil chemistry for only one growing season before the soil reverts to its natural pH. You will either have to commit to amending on a continual basis or work with plants that thrive in your type of soil. Organic material will, however, have a longer-lasting effect on pH. Humus keeps soil in the neutral range and helps plants to thrive in soil outside their pH comfort zone.

Some gardeners decide to create a separate bed for plants that like soil conditions not found elsewhere in their garden. If they have neutral or slightly alkaline soils, for example, they may create an "acid" bed where they will plant their rhododendrons or azaleas. Amending one moderately sized bed is a far easier task than trying to convert your entire garden, and you may find that if you are working on only one spot, you won't mind the continual upkeep. To create an acid bed, you might dump your coffee grounds straight onto the soil instead of in the composter, or grind and add your citrus fruit rinds to the topsoil. You may work in the pine needles that fall from trees. In other words, you may engage in a continual variety of small acts to reinforce the acidity.

RULE OF THUMB
Hydrangeas can take a wide pH range but blue varieties will bloom blue only in acidic soil. "Pink" hydrangeas require somewhat alkaline soils.

ACID- AND ALKALINE-LOVING PLANTS

ACID-LOVERS (OPTIMUM PH: 5 TO 6)

Bleeding heart (*Dicentra formosa*)
Blueberries (*Vaccinium corymbosum*)
English daisy (*Bellis perennis*)
Goldenrod (*Solidago*)
Heathers (*Erica* spp.) (hardy to zone 6) (pH can be as low as 4)
Holly (*Ilex*)
Japanese andromeda (*Pieris japonica*) (hardy to zone 7: in Ontario, the Niagara region only)

Lily (*Lilium*)
Lily of the valley (*Convallaria*)
Magnolia (*Magnolia*)
Maidenhair fern (*Adiantum*)
Rhododendrons and azaleas (*Rhododendron* spp.)
Serviceberry (*Amelanchier canadensis*)
Veronica (*Veronica*)
Wild ginger (*Asarum canadense*)

VEGETABLES (PH 5.5 TO 7)

Artichoke (hardy to zone 6)
Carrots
Corn
Eggplant (to 6.5 pH only)

Potatoes (to 6.5 pH only)
Sweet potatoes (to 6 pH only)
Turnips and rutabagas

ALKALINE-LOVERS

Asparagus (6 to 8)
Baby's breath (*Gypsophila paniculata*) (7 to 7.5)
Canna (*Canna*) (6 to 8)
Cotoneaster (*Cotoneaster*) (6 to 8)
Crocus (*Crocus*) (6 to 8)
Delphiniums (*Delphinium elatum*)
Forget-me-not (*Myosotis*) (6 to 8)
Forsythia (*Forsythia*) (6 to 8)

Hepatica (*Hepatica*) (6 to 8)
Honeysuckle (*Lonicera*) (6 to 8)
Lilacs (*Syringa* spp.) (6 to 7.5)
Pasque flower (*Pulsatilla vulgaris*)
Peonies (*Paoenia lactiflora*) (6 to 7.5)
Phlox (*Phlox*) (6 to 8)
Poppy (*Papaver*) (6 to 8)
Sweet William (*Dianthus barbatus*) (6 to 7.5)

How to test for pH

Home soil-testing kits, available at most garden centres, generally include a pH test. Remember, when performing any sort of home pH test, you must use distilled water. You can also purchase portable pH meters, although they can be quite expensive. Inexpensive pH-testing kits are available from most garden centres. Simple litmus paper (you remember this stuff from high school chemistry class) can also give you quite reliable home results and is a good deal cheaper than meters. To use litmus paper, add distilled water to a small quantity of soil until you have a thick liquid consistency. Let this mud stand for an hour (adding water if it dries out). Then dip the strip of litmus paper in the mud and leave it for a minute. Rinse the strip with distilled water and match the colour of the paper to the chart that comes with the paper to see the pH. You can also send soil samples for professional testing (see p. 144) that will include a pH test.

You can also make a rough estimate of the pH of your soil by assessing the wild plant life that grows on your property or in your neighbourhood. Sorrel or horsetail weeds, dandelion, plantain, knotweed, mosses, nettles, oxeye daisy, ferns, blueberries, rhododendrons and trees such as hemlock, red spruce, oak and white pine all thrive in acidic soil. Pennycress or stinkweed (*Thlaspi arvense*) prefers alkaline soil.

Remember that soil can vary from spot to spot in your garden so test a number of areas, especially if you have a large garden. You may find slightly more alkaline conditions next to your house, where calcium can leach from the concrete foundation.

Replacing and amending soil

Soil improvement may be a long process, especially if you are starting with very poor soil (two to four years), but all soil benefits from a yearly or bi-yearly application of fresh organic matter; otherwise your soil will become less fertile over time. I recommend that you add no less than 2 to 4 cm (3/4 to 1 1/2 inches) of new organic material—finished compost, or if that is not available, well-rotted manure—to your beds each year (40 kg/ 90 pounds of compost over a 10 square m/100 square foot area). You can apply this material in the spring or fall. Some gardening books insist that this sort of soil amendment must be dug well into the soil, but of course this poses a problem when you've got established perennial beds, especially if they are closely planted. I simply lay the compost on top of the beds in the early spring before too much has come up. Earthworms and other soil organisms will pull the organic matter down into the soil, doing the work for you (and causing the beds to settle or sink so that even with yearly applications your beds won't be raised in height by these additions).

There is no better proof that this works than looking at the soil in a wooded area. No one works the leaf mould that gathers on the forest floor into the topsoil, but it does make its way in, leaving the soil rich with humus. If, however, you are establishing new beds, by all means work compost, manure and other soil amendments in well. Always add organic material or other amendments when planting new plants, but remember that you can't adjust just one "spot" for a plant—for example, if your soil is alkaline and the plant likes acidic soil, once the roots have moved past the amended soil area, the plant will have a shock (and the amendment would have to be renewed constantly at any rate). It is the same with soil composition. If a plant needs well-drained soil and you have clay, an area amendment is not going to do it.

If your soil is very poor or unsuitable for the plants you have your heart set on, you may want to consider digging out some beds, removing the existing soil and ordering a high-quality topsoil or a triple mix to replace it. Be careful, however, if you buy topsoil: order your soil from a reputable company or purchase by the bag from a garden centre or nursery. Very often "topsoil for sale" ads in the classified section of the newspaper are put in by people who are clearing land for building and development and who therefore are not in the soil business. What they consider "good" topsoil may be no better than the stuff you are already struggling with in your garden! Triple mix may be more expensive if you are replacing a large area, but it has the advantage of already containing soil amendments and conditioners. It is an equal mix of topsoil, peat moss and compost.

If your soil is so hard and clay-like that you need a pickaxe to dig it, you will need to remove it to a depth of at least 45 cm (18 inches) for annuals and perennials and 60 cm (2 feet) for evergreens, shrubs and roses. Make sure that new soil is 10 cm (4 inches) above grade because the new bed will settle by about 20 percent in the first year. Also, organic microbial activity in the soil will cause it to settle further *each year* (another reason why you should add 2 to 4 cm (3/4 to 1 1/2 inches) of finished compost to your garden yearly).

RULE OF THUMB: QUADRUPLE MIX
Recently our retail garden centre experimented with various "triple mixes" and came up with a superior product: a quadruple mix of equal parts natural peat, loam, compost and composted bark fines. My garden's foundation consists of this stuff. I have never had such excellent results. We call our quadruple mix "Super Grow Soil."

Organic vs. synthetic

Organic fertilizers and amendments improve soil structure as well as add fertility to the soil. The decomposing organic material aerates and conditions the soil, making it friable, as the microorganisms work their way through. And of course organic material attracts the insects and micro-organisms in the first place. Indeed, organic gardeners believe in feeding the soil, before the plants, for all these reasons. Synthetic fertilizers, while doing an adequate job of feeding the plants, do none of the above—they simply sink into the soil and are taken up by the plant.

Ask any successful Ontario farmer and he or she will tell you that synthetic fertilizers must be measured carefully and applied with great caution to avoid overdoses that can kill or burn plant roots and foliage. The exclusive use of synthetic fertilizers is a bad idea. This practice will leave the soil compacted and dense, with little air circulation (leading to plants and microorganisms being starved of air); in sandy soil, synthetic fertilizers do nothing to add water retention and may, in fact, not get to the plant at all. Air pockets between soil particles are so large that water and fertilizers can sink right through, bypassing the plant and its roots altogether. This leaching of synthetic fertilizers can pollute groundwater.

There is some concern that extensive use of synthetic fertilizers may alter the populations of essential soil microorganisms. Synthetic fertilizers do have their advantages and uses, however. They can be less expensive than manure and less messy than compost. And if chosen correctly, they give a plant a quick fix of exactly what the plant needs in the way of nutrients. They are particularly helpful with new plantings or transplants where the roots need immediate feeding to help them quickly overcome transplant shock.

> **RULE OF THUMB: MYCORRHIZAL FUNGI— MOTHER NATURE'S HELPERS**
> As long as plants have existed, so have the beneficial fungi that facilitate all root growth and development. By affixing themselves to the roots, mycorrhizal fungi boost the plant's ability to move water and nutrients from the soil to wherever the plant requires them. The association between roots and fungi is called "mycorrhiza," and in recent years a Canadian company, Premier Tech Bio-technologies, has found a way to increase this activity in your garden. They grow the microbial fungi in the laboratory and package them in a form that's easy to add to planting mixes and garden soil. They call this product Myke.
>
> I have been adding Myke, along with a quality fertilizer, to the soil at planting time with excellent results. When you use Myke, add it to your planting mix according to package directions and be sure that it makes contact with the plant roots.

Professional soil testing

As mentioned earlier, professional soil testing is available through various soil-testing services across the province as well as many full-service garden centres (like Weall & Cullen). A listing of accredited soil-testing laboratories in Ontario is available on the Ontario Ministry of Agriculture, Food and Rural Affairs Web site at www.gov.on.ca/omafra. Look under Agriculture/Soil Management for the list. You can also call the Ministry of Agriculture

Organic

Bloodmeal

- A good source of nitrogen; NPK: 10-0-0.
- Releases nutrients more slowly than synthetic fertilizers (therefore apply spring and fall).
- Add to soil when planting bulbs to deter squirrels.
- Apply 4.5 to 13.5 kg per 93 square m (10 to 30 pounds per 1,000 square feet) depending on soil fertility.

Bonemeal

- A good source of phosphorus and calcium; NPK: 1-11-0.
- Releases nutrients more slowly than synthetic fertilizers (therefore apply spring and fall).
- Apply 4.5 to 13.5 kg per 93 square m (10 to 30 pounds per 1,000 square feet) depending on soil fertility.
- Has little effect on pH.

Citrus rinds

- Ground rinds worked into soil will lower pH slightly (make soil more acidic).

Coal ash

- Little nutritional value.
- Can be used as a soil conditioner for heavy clay.

Coffee grounds

- A source of nitrogen.
- A good addition to compost, but can be dug into the soil as well.
- Will lower pH (make soil more acidic).
- Tea leaves and teabags have similar properties.

Compost (I can't get enough!)

- A great source of organic matter.
- Contains trace elements such as zinc, copper, manganese.
- Naturally slow release (apply spring and fall).
- Attracts earthworms and other beneficial insects and microorganisms.
- Improves drainage and air circulation in clay soils.
- Improves water retention, texture and volume of sandy soils.
- Use backyard composters to produce your own or check to see if compost is available from a municipal large-scale leaf composting service. Good-quality "cattle manure compost" is a fine substitute.
- Soil with lots of compost is darker in colour, absorbing heat faster in the spring and therefore giving plants a quicker start.
- Helps keep soil pH neutral; helps plants succeed in pH levels outside their comfort zones.

Egg shells

- Provide calcium and some trace minerals.
- Can be added to composter or soil.
- May deter slugs when placed around plants.
- Useful when planting tomatoes to deter blossom-end rot (add the shells from two eggs per plant).

Feather meal

- Ground feathers from poultry.
- A slow-release source of nitrogen; NPK:11-0-0.
- Apply 4.5 to 13.5 kg per 93 square m (10 to 30 pounds per 1,000 square feet) depending on soil fertility.

Fertilizers, organic granular commercial

- Generally derived from fish meal, rock phosphate, greensand, gypsum and kelp meal.
- See package information for NPK.
- Slow release.
- Apply to soil as required.
- May contain trace elements.
- Do not improve soil structure.

Fertilizers, organic liquid commercial

- Can be applied to foliage—plants absorb nutrients through leaf pores readily.
- More quickly released than granular: use once a month or every two weeks.
- See package information for NPK.
- Usually contain trace elements.
- Do not improve soil structure.

Fish emulsion

- Made from fish by-products dissolved in water.
- A good source of nitrogen; NPK: 4-4-1.
- Contains trace elements.
- Can be applied in liquid form to foliage.
- Doesn't smell as bad as you might think if used outdoors.

Ground bark or sawdust

- NPK: 0.2-0-0.2.
- Not recommended for clay soils, but adds texture and volume to sand.
- Decomposes slowly.
- Should be added with a nitrogen-rich fertilizer (it will rob nitrogen).
- Sawdust should be well rotted before use.
- Apply sawdust 45 to 113 kg per 93 square m (100 to 250 pounds per 1,000 square feet) depending on soil composition.

Hoof and horn meal

- Slow-release source of nitrogen; NPK: 12-2-0.
- Apply 4.5 to 13.5 kg per 93 square m (10 to 30 pounds per 1,000 square feet) depending on soil fertility.

Humus

The terms humus and compost are often used interchangeably, but humus is actually the very final stages of decomposition of organic matter, while compost is material that is largely decomposed, but which may contain as yet identifiable bits of matter—eggshell, leaves or twigs and so on. Compost is therefore rich in humus, as is leaf mould. It is nutrient rich and its texture is soft and sticky and contributes greatly to the friability of the soil. See benefits listed under compost.

Kelp (seaweed)

- A good source of potassium, iron, trace minerals; in meal form: NPK: 1.5-0.5-2.5.
- Available in dried meal form or as a liquid.
- Liquid can be applied to leaves.
- Meal helps friability (texture) of soil.
- Extracts contain growth hormones so must be used sparingly.
- Extracts can be used as rooting solutions and growth stimulants.

Leaf mould

- A good source of humus and therefore nutrients.
- Improves soil structure.
- Will decompose rapidly so is not a long-lasting source of nutrients.

Manure or compost tea

- Contains small quantities of macro- (primarily nitrogen) and micronutrients.
- Can be used frequently as a nutrient booster.
- I water with a dilute form of compost tea all of my container plants *all* season long.

Manure (rotted)

- A naturally slow-release source of nutrients (apply spring and fall).
- Sheep manure (dry)—NPK: 4-1.4-3.5. Apply 11 to 45 kg per 93 square m (25 to 100 pounds per 1,000 square feet).

- Cow manure (dry)—NPK: 2-2.3-2.4. Apply 45 to 90 kg per 93 square m (100 to 200 pounds per 1,000 square feet).

- Horse manure—NPK: 1.7-0.7-1.8. Apply 45 to 90 kg per 93 square m (100 to 200 pounds per 1,000 square feet).

- *Must* be composted, not fresh, or will burn plants (raw manure can be added to your compost pile to break down with the other material).

- Loosens clay soils and improves drainage.

- Improves the texture of sandy soils.

Mushroom compost

- Same benefits as compost, but it will make soil more alkaline (this can be offset by adding sulphur).

Oyster shells

- Contain 33.5 per cent calcium and trace minerals.

- Can be used instead of limestone.

- A great addition to the composter.

- Apply 11 to 45 kg per 93 square m (25 to 100 pounds per 1,000 square feet).

Peat moss

- Adds acidity (pH range 3.0 to 4.5).

- Improves water retention in sandy soil (can hold up to 20 times its weight in water).

- Improves water and air circulation in sandy and clay soils.

- Always wet peat moss before adding and dig well into soil.

Soybean meal

- A good source of nitrogen; NPK: 7-0.5-2.3.

- A good food for soil microorganisms.

- Apply 4.5 to 23 kg per 93 square m (10 to 50 pounds per 1,000 square feet).

Wood ash

- A good source of potassium (potash) and calcium; NPK: 0-1.2-2 leached/0-1.5-8 unleached.

- Will raise pH (make soil alkaline); twice as strong as lime.

- Apply 2.25 to 9 kg per 93 square m (5 to 20 pounds per 1,000 square feet) leached and 1.4 to 4.5 kg per 93 square m (3 to 10 pounds per 1,000 square feet) unleached; apply only once every several years.

- Make sure ash is from plain untreated wood or paper.

- Wood ash mixed with water creates lye, which is caustic. Therefore mix ashes with other soil amendments (but not with fresh manure, which leads to the breakdown of nitrogen) before adding to beds and make sure it doesn't touch leaves or stems of plants.

- Sprinkled on the earth around plants repels slugs, cutworms, snails, root aphids, vine borers and other pests (they don't like crawling over it). Make a depression around a plant and fill with a little ash.

- You can "leach" the wood ash by running water through it to remove the lye.

- Watch for nails, screws, staples, etc.!

Worm castings (I love this stuff!)

- A good source of nutrients and microorganisms.

- Contain 50 per cent organic matter and 11 trace minerals.

- Improve water retention.

- You can get worm castings by using worms to compost your kitchen waste. They may also be available from the fishing worm industry.

Synthetic

Clay

- Add to sandy soils along with organic material to improve water retention.
- Can use unscented, plain kitty litter.

Epsom salts

- Add magnesium (10%) and sulphur (13%).
- Apply 0.5 to 2.25 kg per 93 square m (1 to 5 pounds per 1,000 square feet).

Fertilizers, synthetic

- Easy to use; relatively inexpensive.
- Can give plants the right balance of nutrients.
- Some synthetic fertilizers (vs. organic fertilizers) may lack trace elements.
- Do not improve soil structure.
- Some organic gardeners feel that synthetic fertilizers are too concentrated, leaving the soil with a chemical imbalance that reduces microbial and earthworm presence.

Horticultural gypsum (or land plaster)

- A source of calcium (22%) and sulphur (17%). Gypsum is calcium sulphate.
- Helps correct excess magnesium or sodium content of soil.
- Loosens clay soil.
- Does not affect soil pH.
- Apply 2.25 to 18 kg per 93 square m (5 to 40 pounds per 1,000 square feet), depending on soil composition.
- Don't apply if pH is below 5.8.

Limestone (dolomitic)

- Finely ground limestone.
- Raises soil pH.
- A source of calcium (51% calcium carbonate) and magnesium (magnesium carbonate 40%).
- Apply 11 to 45 kg per 93 square m (25 to 100 pounds per 1,000 square feet), depending on soil composition.

Perlite

- Superheated volcanic material.
- Can be used instead of sharp sand to improve aeration and drainage.
- It will also absorb water, aiding water retention.
- Often used in potting soil.
- Lasts longer than vermiculite.
- Lightweight and dusty (don't breathe it in).
- No nutrients.
- pH 7 to 7.5.

Profile

- Ceramic granules made from Fuller's earth—a natural mineral.
- Breaks up clay soils and prevents compaction, allowing air and water to circulate.
- Helps maintain moisture in sandy soils.
- Is a permanent amendment—it does not break down over time.
- This stuff works!

Rock phosphate

- A source of phosphorus, especially in acidic soils; NPK: 0-3-0 (32% total phosphate, 33% elemental calcium).
- Contains 11 trace minerals.
- Apply 4.5 to 27 kg per 93 square m (10 to 60 pounds per 1,000 square feet).
- Best way to use rock phosphate, however, is to add to the composter where the phosphate can be converted in the decomposition process to forms that are readily available for absorption by plant roots.

Sharp or coarse sand

- Add to clay soils to improve air circulation and drainage.
- Use with other organic amendments for fertility.
- Avoid sandbox sand, which is too fine and smooth and will compact.

Sulphur

- Reduces pH (makes soil more acidic).
- To lower pH one unit, apply 4.5 kg per 93 square m (10 pounds per 1,000 square feet), depending on soil composition.
- Overuse can damage plants and disrupt the chemical balance of the soil.
- Sulphur may be ineffective on strongly alkaline soils.

Superabsorbent polymers

- Can be added to sandy soil to improve water retention.
- Expensive.

Super phosphate (0-20-0)

- A good source of phosphorus.
- Apply 1 kg per 93 square m (2 pounds per 1,000 square feet), in the fall, once every five years.
- Great for bulbs and assists root development.

Vermiculite

- Shiny, porous flakes of superheated mica (a natural element).
- Can be used in sandy soil to improve air circulation and water and nutrient retention.
- Larger granular size than perlite.
- Less expensive than perlite, but does not last as long.
- Is not dusty like perlite.
- Contains small amounts of potassium and magnesium.
- pH 7 to 7.5.

RULE OF THUMB

Make your own organic fertilizer (mixture will range from 4-5-4 to 5-8-5). Combine one choice from each column.

Nitrogen	Phosphorus	Potassium
2 parts bloodmeal	3 parts bonemeal	1 part kelp meal
or	*or*	*or*
3 parts fish meal	6 parts rock phosphate or colloidial phosphate	6 parts greensand

at 1-888-466-2372. These labs will screen the soil for pH, macronutrients and organic matter, and can test for specific micronutrients or other chemicals and elements at your request (generally, the labs have an agronomist who will speak with you about your specific concerns and can help you determine what other things should be tested for). The basic tests are usually relatively inexpensive, but all other specific screens can be quite costly. A professional test should come with a summary that tells you how you should treat the soil to remedy any deficiencies.

But do you need a professional test? There are several reasons you might want one. If your home test indicates deficiencies or problems that you might need to address with the addition of lime, rock phosphate, greensand, gypsum, sulphur or Epsom salts, you may very well want to reconfirm these results with a professional test before adding any of these sorts of ingredients. Too much of any of them may cause other problems, and you will need to know quite specifically how much is demanded.

You may also want to have a professional test done if you have a history of plants doing poorly in an area even though they have been given appropriate care. You may also consider a professional test a wise investment if you are putting in a vegetable garden, as vegetables demand adequate levels of nutrients to flourish.

If you have any concerns about contamination on your property (whether from a nearby industry or previous use of the land), consider getting a professional test done. You will have to know what chemicals or elements you are looking for, however, and the lab may be able to help you there. Keep in mind that if the land your home was recently built on was previously the home of any industry, the developer may have had to have the soil tested and approved, and these documents should be available for you.

Preparing samples for a professional test

If you decide to get a professional test done, make sure that you get accurate results by preparing your samples properly. Use only stainless steel or plastic trowels or other tools (instruments of other metals may leave traces of metals or minerals that will alter your soil sample). Dig a small hole to a depth of 15 cm (6 inches) for beds or 10 cm (4 inches) for soil under lawns and then take a slice all the way down the side of this hole. Make sure that the sample is free of mulch or other debris from the surface.

As with home testing, you may want to have a number of areas of your yard tested, but this will be more expensive. If you wish to do a follow-up each year to see if your amendments are improving the soil, make sure to take samples at the same time each year (soil content can vary throughout the season). And keep in mind that fall is usually a less busy time for testing labs, so you may get your results faster then.

Planting
Tips

"**L**et's play in the dirt again!" When I was a kid, this was my idea of fun, and I confess that things haven't changed very much. In fact, when I talk to gardeners, new and experienced, I get the sense that apart from creating beautiful growing landscapes, what *most* gardeners really love about gardening is getting down on their hands and knees and getting their hands dirty. (One gardener I know refuses to wear gardening gloves for this very reason. "What would be the point?" she says.)

Planting, I think, is often the highlight of gardening tasks for many. But apart from the sheer joy of working good rich soil, our goal when planting is to get precious seeds, bulbs, young plants and transplants into the ground, while minimizing the shock or trauma. We also want to make sure that their new home is as comfortable and inviting as possible and the conditions for their future growth are well in place. To achieve this, spend some time before you plant—in fact, before you even choose your plants—on deciding where they will go. Keep in mind the mature size of the plants, both horizontally and vertically, and their needs—for sunlight, for moisture and for soil nutrients and pH. Avoid putting plants in spots they will quickly outgrow and keep in mind that large roots (like those of trees) can create havoc if shrubs and trees are planted too close to walls and paved areas. The right plant in the right place will not only ensure the plants' success but will also save you labour and heartache.

Early morning or late afternoon is my favourite time for planting young, soft annual bedding plants and perennials. Working at this time keeps the plants out of the strong midday sun and ensures that the water you give them while planting and immediately after will not evaporate so quickly. Planting on overcast days also works well, and while some gardeners advise against working in the rain, I've never experienced problems planting in wet conditions. In fact, those in the U.K. would never be able to garden if they could work only in dry weather!

Bedding plants and young nursery stock

As it is important to get young annual flowers and bedding plants into the ground quickly, it is a wise idea to have their holes already dug in the beds before you bring the plants home. If you do have to keep plants in their trays or flats for a day or more, make sure they stay well hydrated and out of the scorching sun. But also remember that they need light—storing trays or pots of plants in the garage for a few days until you are

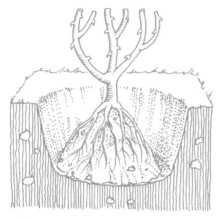
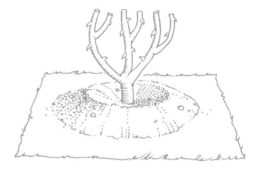

When planting roses, woody shrubs or trees (see p. 159), make sure the hole is larger than the root ball or nursery pot. Make a small hill of soil at the bottom of the hole and place the plant on top of this, spreading the roots down over the mound. After filling the hole, use soil to create a small well around the plant where water can collect and drain over the root zone.

ready to plant them could mean that you are planting light starved and weakened plants in your garden.

Once they are in the ground, new plantings need to be kept in moist but not waterlogged soil. Regular, gentle watering is necessary. I like to use a "water wand" or "water beaker" to water newly planted annuals and perennials. The soft flow of water is just what they need for the first few weeks as they put their roots down. Check the specific types of plants listed below for more details about watering.

"Nursery stock" (trees, shrubs, evergreens, roses and even large perennials) are not nearly as fussy about when they are planted. Plant any of them at any time of the day and in virtually any weather, bearing mind that

❋ no plant likes to sit in the sun to dry out before planting

❋ all plants benefit from a well-prepared planting hole (read on for more!)

❋ if you cannot plant for a few days or more after taking delivery of nursery stock, it is best stored on the shady side of your home and hand-watered as the top 2 cm (3/4 inch) become dry. Different plants will have different watering needs, and windy weather will necessitate more frequent watering

Annual bedding plants are planted in the spring for summer and early fall bloom. Most gardeners also do all their perennial planting in the spring. I can understand this—the garden centres are bursting with new plant stock, the days are tantalizingly long and gardeners have itchy fingers after months in winter gloves. But I contend that many perennials, like most trees and shrubs, are better off when planted in the fall. Peonies and iris, in particular, do very well when planted in the fall. The cool, moist days of autumn prevent soil and plant dehydration. Fall planting also allows the roots to develop before winter brings on plant dormancy, meaning that the plant will get a strong, early start on growth in the spring.

Most garden centres (I can speak for the Weall & Cullen centres) provide excellent discounts in the fall as they reduce inventory before winter sets in. If you choose to plant in the fall, apply a winter mulch of fallen leaves or finely ground-up bark to the beds to prevent heaving during freeze-thaw cycles. Fall planting is also a great option if you are interested in growing your own seedlings. These can be started in a protective area over the summer (plant seeds in midsummer) and then transferred to their permanent homes in the fall. If buying young plants from a nursery for fall planting, make sure they are in good shape—not leggy, root bound, diseased or dehydrated—before you purchase them.

Avoid planting annuals and perennials on a hot day if possible. Morning and late afternoons will provide some protection from strong sun that may stress or dry out the young plant before it is in the soil. Overcast days are good planting days. Plant perennials once the soil has reached a temperature of at least 5°C (40°F) and annuals in soil that is 15 to 20°C (60 to 70°F) (pansies and violas can be planted in cooler soil). These young plants have been growing in a warm greenhouse, and cold soil at the time of planting can give the roots a shock and set these plants back.

To plant seedlings and young plants, whether annuals or perennials, dig beds or individual holes to a depth of 15 to 20 cm (6 to 8 inches). If the whole bed has been turned over and the soil loosened, the holes for individual plants need only be slightly wider than the root ball. If you are "pocket planting" in an existing bed or other area where the soil is unprepared, make the width of the planting hole considerably wider than the root mass of the plants. Amend the soil well with compost, well-rotted manure, and/or moistened peat moss. A new product called Myke (a form of beneficial mycorrhizal fungi) is another excellent addition (see Rule of Thumb, p. 138). Mix the soil well. I recommend that you water the plant holes before adding the plants to ensure that roots get immediate access to moisture when they enter the soil. Applying a mild transplanting fertilizer, like a 5-15-5 solution, to the plants while they are still in their pots or trays is a very good way to give your new plants a head start.

RULE OF THUMB: EARLY BIRDS
If you want to get a jump on the growing season, try these hardy annuals. They can be planted just as soon as the ground can be worked and can tolerate a light frost: godetia, pansies, poppies, primrose, ranunculus (buttercup), violas and Virginia stock.

Apply liquid transplanter to the root zones of new plants after planting as well. Space most annuals 20 to 25 cm (8 to 10 inches) apart to allow for growth. Border plants such as alyssum, ageratum and lobelia can be planted closer together for a denser look. Large-growing annuals such as geraniums, cleome and tall marigolds should be planted with greater space between them.

Follow the directions provided by the nursery on how to space specific perennials. Plant tags now provide much of the cultural information you'll need. The important thing is to take into account the mature height and spread of the plant.

When removing potted plants from their container, turn the container over and push gently on the bottom. If necessary, you can run a clean knife between the pot and the soil to loosen the plants. Resist the temptation to pull the plant from the pot by the stem as this can damage the plant. For most container-grown plants, the roots can simply be left as they are, although I like to loosen them by gently pulling them apart if the plant seemed root-bound in the pot. With any bare-rooted stock, spread the roots gently and carefully before planting (removing any damaged roots) and place in the ground with the roots spread. Container-grown nursery stock should be planted to the same depth it was growing in the pot. Paper or peat fibre pots can be left on most plants when planting, but be sure the rim is below the soil level or it will draw water away from the plant.

After planting annuals, keep the soil moist for the first two weeks so that the plants become well established. Perennials need to be generously watered for their first full growing season. (This is not to say, however, that any newly planted plant likes to exist in bog-like conditions. Let the soil be your guide by pushing your finger into it from time to time. When it is dry a centimetre or two/up to an inch down, water generously enough to ensure that moisture has percolated down to the root zone. See Watering and Xeriscaping, p. 165, for more watering advice.)

If you are planting a perennial that grows vigorously or aggressively, consider isolating it in the garden by planting it in a restricted area (a bed surrounded by stone or wood borders, lawn or patio and path stones). Or plant it in a container. Some gardeners I know like to plant aggressive growers in plastic or clay containers that they then lower into a garden bed. The container helps contain root spread, for a time at least!

Staking perennials

Nothing is sadder than going into the garden to find a delphinium with its gorgeous colourful blooms hanging limply off a snapped stem. For very tall flowers such as delphiniums, lupines, foxglove, gladioli, hollyhock, bearded iris and lilies, a little support is very often necessary if they are to make it through their blooming season undamaged. Even if a plant is not top-heavy when in bloom, it may require some form of support if its stems tend to bend over or if it is in a windy, exposed site. There is now a wide variety of commercial plant supports available—from single-stem supports, to stakes with attached wire loops that can support a number of stems to stakes that link together (link stakes) to form a cage or are attached to a small grid that can support several plants at one time.

You can also make your own supports with small wooden or metal stakes; small branches or cane; and twine, raffia or twist ties. As a matter of fact, my Uncle Tom has created a very "traditional" Canadian garden by using broken hockey sticks to stake his tomatoes. He found an endless source of these free hardwood stakes at his local arena. Whatever type of support you choose, however, there are a few things to keep in mind.

- A plant should be allowed some movement—gentle swaying in a breeze helps strengthen stems. Leave some room between the stake and the stem when tying plants (i.e., don't tie them too tightly).

- Keep stakes far enough away from the base of the plant to avoid damaging the roots.

Stakes for supporting single stems can be purchased (there are several types) or made from wooden or metal supports and twine.

- Stake or support a plant while it is still small—attaching the stakes or putting a support around a mature plant is cumbersome and awkward. Putting the stakes in early in the season also means you are less likely to damage the spreading roots. What's more, if the plant blooms early or you are delayed in getting the stakes in, you may not get to it in time.

- Stakes should reach to just below the flower spikes, so keep the mature height of the plant in mind when putting in the supports.

- Stakes are easiest to put in when the soil is slightly moist.

One of the best ways to deal with a group of tall perennials is to create a grid from twine and narrow stakes. In the early spring before the plants have begun to really take off, place the stakes (garden centres often carry green-dyed bamboo stakes that are virtually unnoticeable among the stalks of the flowers) around the perimeter of the tall plants. Use four stakes to create a square, or more if covering a very large area. Thread green garden twine along the outside of the stakes (wrap it around the stake a few times to prevent slipping) and then criss-cross the twine between the stakes to create a loose grid. Do this at several heights and if necessary add another level of twine if the plants grow very tall over the course of the summer. The plants will grow up through the grid, and as long as you have made the horizontal spaces between the twine large enough, the plants will have room to move in the breeze (which gives their stalks strength) but will not fall over when they get buffeted by strong winds or get too top heavy.

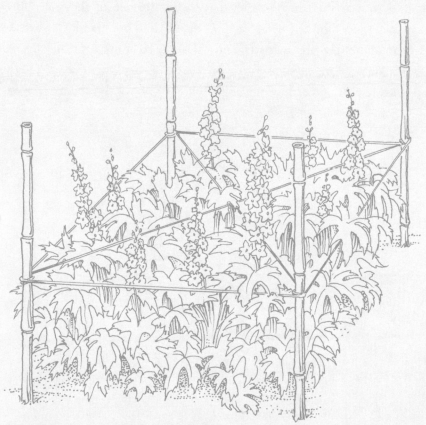

A grid made from twine and slender stakes is a great way to support a group of tall plants.

Bulbs

I love the flowers that bulbs produce—particularly spring-flowering bulbs like daffodil, crocus, tulip and hyacinth. Spring-blooming bulbs are planted in the fall, are winter hardy and stay in the ground from year to year. Bulbs planted in spring for summer bloom, like gladiolus, tuberous begonia, dahlias and canna lily, also produce beautiful flowers. They usually need to be lifted from the ground in the fall and stored indoors over the winter.

Bulbs (for example, hyacinth, tulip and daffodil), rhizomes (for example, iris, lily of the valley and canna lily), corms (for example, crocus, gladiolus) and tubers (for example, begonia, anemone) are generally planted in the same fashion. Most bulbs like neutral to mildly acidic soil that is loose and well drained. The deeper the bulbs are planted the more important this drainage is (many bulbs are susceptible to fungus and mildew diseases). If your soil is heavy, dig in generous quantities of sharp sand to improve drainage. Soil should be moist but not wet before planting.

Rhizomes and plants with short tubers, like begonia, need to be planted so that their tops are level with the surface of the soil. Other tuberous roots (for example, daylily, dahlia and ranunculus) must be planted so that the fibrous roots with the stem buds are near the surface. The rhizomes of iris should be no more than 2.5 cm (1 inch) deep, and the top third to half of the rhizome can actually be above the soil.

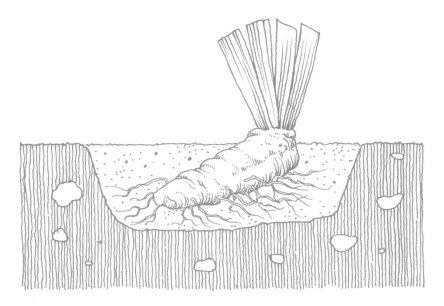

Rhizomes must be planted so that their tops are level with the soil.

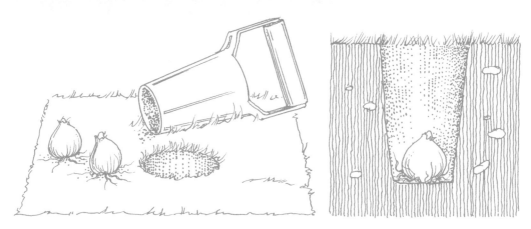

When planting bulbs make sure that the bottom,
with its hairy roots, is in direct contact with the soil.

The rule of thumb for bulbs is that they should be planted three times as deep as their diameter (measuring soil depth from top of bulb). Usually this means small bulbs like crocus and scilla are covered with 1.25 to 2.5 cm (1/2 to 1 inch) of soil and large bulbs with 15 to 20 cm (6 to 8 inches) of soil. When the bulbs are set in the soil, it is important that the root end of the bulb is in direct contact with soil (don't leave air pockets under or around the bulbs when the holes are filled with soil). Sometimes trying to tell the top from the bottom of a bulb is difficult. On the whole, the top is more pointed or has pale-coloured growing buds and the bottom may have tiny roots growing from it.

Bulbs can be planted deeper than this if squirrels and other small animals are a problem, but keep in mind that particularly small bulbs may have to concentrate on root and foliage growth at the expense of blossoms if planted too deep. Certain big bulbs, like those of tall-variety daffodils and hybrid tulips, can be planted up to 30 cm (12 inches) deep as long as the soil has good drainage. The depth not only will support the tall plants, but will also protect the plants from dividing too quickly and therefore producing smaller flowers. If your soil is clay, you may have to plant more shallowly than is optimal to avoid rot. In Ontario's coldest zones of 4 or above, bulbs should be planted a bit more deeply than the "three times" rule would suggest, as intense freezing and sudden cold snaps may damage the bulbs. In these climates it is particularly helpful to mulch over bulbs (see Mulch, Mulch, Mulch, p. 185).

Plant bulbs in groups in a wide hole or use a bulb-planting tool, dibber or narrow trowel to cut holes for individual bulbs. If you are planting bulbs individually, space them with twice the diameter of the bulbs between each one to avoid overcrowding.

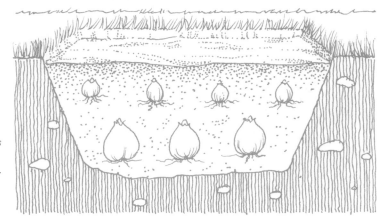

Planting different varieties of bulbs together, with smaller bulbs above larger ones, can provide a lovely succession of blooms.

Remember, flowers from bulbs most often look best if planted in groups or wide swaths. You can even plant bulbs in layers with larger bulbs on the bottom and smaller bulbs up top. Not only does this make a great use of a small space, but if you choose bulbs that bloom at different times, the successive blooms will cover the spent foliage of earlier flowers.

Many hardy bulbs can be planted so that they naturalize—or multiply and spread naturally throughout an area. To create a natural look in a grassy area or beneath trees, scatter bulbs by hand across the area. Then, using a sharp spade or shovel to open up the soil, plant the bulbs where they fell. Crocus, muscari and scilla are all good choices for naturalization and should be planted in the lawn by peeling back the turf and placing bulbs underneath it (they will come up through the turf next spring). Hyacinth, iris and daffodil also spread, but they do so more slowly, especially in dry or cold climates. If you do plant bulbs in a grassy area, remember that after the bloom has wilted, the leaves should not be cut or removed for several weeks, as they are necessary for food storage and future flower reproduction. Corms are less reliant on foliage, so plants like crocus and scilla can be cut earlier and are therefore great choices for lawns.

I recommend that you scratch in a handful of super phosphate in the bottom of the hole before planting bulbs to encourage root development in the fall.

Bulbs and their predators

Anyone who has experienced an invigorating fall afternoon planting bulbs will also, no doubt, have experienced the annoyance of watching squirrels cheerfully carrying away those bulbs a few days later. Take heart—there are a number of ways of protecting bulbs from squirrels and other rodents during the fall and winter. Bloodmeal dug in around the bulbs often discourages squirrels (although raccoons find it tasty). You can also place chicken wire or loose plastic mesh, covered with mulch, over the soil that covers the bulbs to dissuade rodents. Remove the chicken wire in the spring if it is covering large bulbs. Narcissi bulbs are toxic and animals avoid them, so you can plant them among or encircling other bulbs to discourage predators. Some gardeners plant bulbs in paper bags (which will rot by spring). These hide some of the bulb odour from the squirrels. Other gardeners recommend adding broken oyster or clam shells or crushed eggshells on top of the bulbs when planting. Rodents dislike digging through the shells. There are also a number of safe, organic rodent repellents now on the market. Some come in both granular and liquid form. I use them in the spring and summer as well, but I find them particularly helpful in the fall when I spray a little on the top of my spring bulbs at planting time, just before I cover them with soil.

RULE OF THUMB
Don't cut or braid the foliage once the flowers of bulb-grown plants are gone. Plants need the foliage to continue their food storage activities for next year's growth and reproduction. This process stops only once the foliage is thoroughly wilted. Then you are free to cut the foliage off.

Seeds

When planting seeds, always make sure that the soil is well prepared and mark beds and rows before beginning. Plant seeds to the depth and spacing recommended on the seed packages, although if you're planting in mid-season you may want to put them in slightly deeper to prevent them from drying out in the summer sun. Water soil lightly with a fine spray so as not to disturb freshly planted seeds, but keep the soil moist to prevent the seeds from dehydrating. Make sure the soil does not "crust over" after a rainfall or during a dry spell—this will prevent the seedlings from developing properly and may make it difficult for the soil to absorb water in the future. I recommend that you cover the seeds with a soil substitute like vermiculite, worm castings or sand after planting to prevent this.

Getting small seeds into the soil is sometimes tricky. Grass seeds and other widely spread seeds can be broadcast by hand or by hand-held seed spreaders available at most garden centres. But evenly distributing tiny carrot seeds along a furrow can be more of a challenge. If you're pouring the seeds from your hand, they may stick together or fall in uneven streams. If so, when the plants begin to sprout, you may have bare patches along the row or you may find yourself doing a lot of thinning (and therefore wasting a lot of seed). Garden centres offer a variety of inexpensive hand-held devices that make even seed distribution much easier. I mix one part seed with two or three parts sand, which helps to even the distribution when pouring seed along a furrow by hand. Some small seeds, like radish, are best tapped directly from the packet.

You can also create a straight row of seed by making your own seed tape. Roll out toilet paper on a kitchen counter. Place seeds evenly along the middle third of the paper. Fold the toilet paper over the seed from both sides, then fold or roll the paper for easy carrying. Unfold or unroll the "seed tape" on the ground, then sprinkle loose soil over the tape to the appropriate depth and water.

Trees and shrubs

Timing

When it comes to planting trees and shrubs, there is quite a debate among gardeners about when to do it. Some advocate the spring, while others suggest the autumn. I fall into the latter camp—I like to get new trees and shrubs into the ground in September (or late August if you live in northern and northwestern Ontario) while the earth is still warm and the plants have a chance to set new roots before going dormant for the winter. Cooler fall days reduce evaporation from plant leaves and the ground, keeping the plant well hydrated as it settles in. Once the cold weather arrives, plants will go dormant; deciduous trees and shrubs lose their leaves and evergreens naturally harden their new growth to withstand winter. Planted in the fall, trees and shrubs will begin their new growth as soon as the ground thaws and the air temperatures warm, rewarding the gardener with more spring growth than those planted in the spring, and leaving the trees well established by the time growing season is in full swing.

Most shrubs and trees are very hardy, and you can delay planting them as late as two or three weeks before the ground freezes. Rhododendrons, magnolias, birch and daphne do best when dug from the field in the spring and transplanted in the fall. For spring planting, I prefer to choose only trees or shrubs grown in fibre containers that can be placed directly in the ground to minimize shock to the roots.

Method

Before purchasing your tree or digging its hole, spend some time choosing the best location for it. Keep in mind its mature size and the extent of its future root system. Avoid planting it too close to other trees—you don't want to have to be removing large trees simply because they are cramped or the area is too crowded. Also factor in the amount of shade the mature tree will cast and how that may affect other trees, shrubs and plantings. Don't plant your new tree too close to walls and buildings. Not only may you have crowding and shade problems later but the mature tree's root system will extend to at least the width of the widest portion of the tree branches (this is referred to as the dripline). The roots of an aggressive tree variety or cultivar can wreak havoc with sewer pipes, masonry and foundations. Large branches of the newly planted tree should be directed away from paths and areas you want to keep open.

When preparing the new home for your tree, don't be stingy with the size of the hole. It should be at least two to three times as wide as the root ball or the nursery pot, and slightly deeper than the root ball or pot. Once the hole is dug, check its drainage (see Watering and Xeriscaping, p. 168). If the drainage is poor, you may have to amend the soil in an area that extends past the usual planting hole. Keep in mind, however, that the root system will cover a large area when the tree is mature, and once the roots have grown past the amended portion of the soil, they may experience shock or simply push up to the surface. If you are not prepared to amend the soil to the breadth of the dripline, check with your local nursery about what sort of tree would thrive in your soil conditions.

Even if the drainage is adequate, it is a good idea to add lots of organic matter to the hole—I recommend compost, well-rotted manure or moistened peat moss (two parts topsoil to one part peat and/or compost). Also amend the soil you have removed before you use it to fill around the tree. Before adding the soil amendments, pierce the inside walls of the hole with a garden fork if your soil is clay-based so that the tree's roots will be able to grow through this porous soil more easily. Add water to the hole before putting the tree into the ground.

If your tree has bare roots, you may want to soak the roots for 24 hours before planting. When it is ready to go into the earth, make a mound of soil in the middle of the hole and place the tree or shrub on top, spreading roots down over the mound. This will prevent air pockets around the roots. Roots should be loosened and spread apart to encourage straight, even root growth. Very long roots can be trimmed to fit the hole. Prune any that appear broken or discoloured.

Trees in fibre or peat pots can be planted with the roots still in the pot. You should slit the sides of the pot right to the bottom and remove the rim so that it doesn't draw water from the soil up to the surface. It's a good idea to soak the pot in water before planting the tree.

If the tree has been grown in another type of container, it must be removed before planting, keeping the root ball intact. Try to leave the dirt surrounding the roots undisturbed to reduce trauma to your tree. If the container is root bound, loosen the circling roots and spread them outward, or cut through these roots so that they and others can spread.

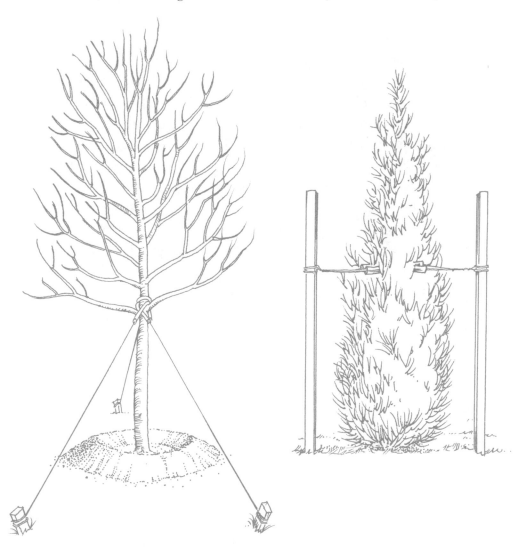

When staking trees, use two or three stakes at regular intervals, and protect the tree's bark by covering the ends of guy wires with rubber tubing.

If planting a tree in an exposed site, place the tree so that it leans about 5 degrees towards the direction of the prevailing wind. It will straighten as it grows and not appear to be bending backwards in a strong wind when it is young and supple.

After placing the tree in its hole, fill with amended soil (or "triple mix"), watering the roots thoroughly when the hole is half-filled with soil. Once the hole is filled, step on the soil to remove any air pockets, and then heap earth in a small wall encircling the base of the tree at the edge of the roots' reach. Fill this basin with water immediately and again in a few days. For the rest of the season, water as the soil becomes dry 2 to 4 cm (1 to 1 1/2 inches) down. Add mulch around the base of the tree to reduce evaporation and prevent competition from weeds. Water your new tree deeply before the ground freezes for the winter to protect the roots from freeze-thaw cycles.

There is some debate among gardeners and arborists about whether staking young trees is a good idea. Some research suggests that staking actually weakens the tree. You should, however, consider staking if your tree is in a windy, exposed spot, is very top heavy or taller than 60 cm (2 feet). If you do need to stake your tree, a single stake is rarely sufficient. If you have ever seen newly planted trees listing towards their stake, you will know why. Use three stakes at regular intervals, 60 to 90 cm (2 to 3 feet) away from the tree. They should be inserted at least 25 cm (10 inches) into the ground. Before attaching heavy guy wire to the stakes, cover the tree ends of the wire with lengths of rubber tubing (an old hose works well).

Wrap the trunks of young fruit and flowering trees with a rodent-proof plastic tree wrap (not just any old plastic) or tar-impregnated crepe paper to protect the trunks from winter damage and animals.

Bed prep

Digging

Digging is digging, right? Well, yes and no. Like cookbooks, gardening books and gardening instructions often use a number of terms to refer to different techniques. *Forking* is a method of loosening soil by pushing a garden fork or other similar implement into the soil and twisting it to loosen the dirt (there are a number of "fork substitutes" on the

RULE OF THUMB
Avoid walking in your flower bed, whether newly dug or established. The pressure of your footsteps compacts the soil, reducing aeration and impeding drainage. Consider placing stepping stones or flat rocks in strategic places throughout the beds to allow to you move around on the stones rather than the soil when weeding and deadheading. Garden centres also sell low stool-like devices that you can kneel on so that only a small area (the legs of the stool) presses against the soil.

I have always felt that gardeners can learn a great deal from Canadian farmers. The "no-till" approach is a good case in point.

What happens when you turn the soil over by "double-digging" or rototilling? Many of the beneficial insects, such as earthworms, are disturbed and millions (literally!) of the microbes that make soil work are destroyed. Today many Canadian farmers are realizing that if they leave the soil undisturbed, except where seeds or plants go into it, the soil is greatly improved and the plants mature as quickly and are of equal quality as those in the rototilled fields.

To combat weeds, the surface of the soil is covered with organic mulch and the previous year's crop residue. Farmers know the other benefits of leaving the previous year's crop residue on the surface of the soil. It helps shield and cushion the force of falling rain and creates many mini-dams that hold the rain, slowing runoff and giving it more time to soak into the soil.

Unless you need to replace or heavily amend soil in large areas, you can use the "no-till" approach in your garden. Dig up only as much of the garden bed (i.e., the planting hole) as you need to get new plants in. In established perennial beds, spread compost or well-rotted manure on top of the soil. Then spread a 5- to 7-cm (2- to 2 3/4-inch) layer of shredded bark mulch over your entire garden. It will conserve moisture throughout the growing season and contribute to healthy soil structure. (See Mulch, Mulch, Mulch, for more information about the benefits of mulching!)

market that make the lifting and twisting motion slightly easier). This helps aerate the soil and improve drainage. It's a good way to improve soil that has been compacted by heavy rains or foot traffic. It also helps loosen the roots of shallow weeds so they can be removed. *Digging* generally refers to removing soil to the depth of your spade and turning it over on the spot or removing it altogether.

Single- and *double-digging* are ways to prepare beds, small and large, for planting. The techniques are similar, although double-digging involves going down much deeper and/or loosening the subsoil. Single-dig your beds if you are preparing a site that has not been used for gardening before or for several years. Double-dig your bed if the drainage is poor or your soil is very poor and needs a great deal of amending and improving before planting. This method of "soil enrichment" is especially beneficial to root crops such as carrots and beets.

Single-digging a bed

Mark the area to be dug and divide it into sections about 30 cm (1 foot) wide (their length will depend on the size of the bed you are digging and how much room you have to store the soil from the first trench). Dig down about 25 cm (10 inches) in the first trench and place this soil in a wheelbarrow or on a tarp. Move this soil near the last trench if possible. Starting in an adjacent section, dig down again (25 cm/10 inches), moving the soil into the empty trench next to it. This is your opportunity to enrich the soil with quantities of compost or composted cattle manure. Continue to dig the sections this way until you reach the last trench. Fill this last trench with the soil removed from the first one you dug. And remember to always remove weeds, stones and other debris from the earth as you dig it.

Double-digging a bed

Double-digging uses the same method of moving soil from one trench into the previously dug trench, but compost is added and the digging is deeper. With this method you may either choose to dig down a full 60 cm (2 feet) or dig out 30 cm (1 foot) of soil and simply loosen the next 30 cm (1 foot) at the bottom of the trench with a fork. Either way, you should spread a layer of compost or well-rotted manure along the bottom of the trench before soil from the next trench fills the space. You may want to mix the compost with the soil as you add it or cover the entire bed with another layer of organic material when you've finished the bed.

When single- or double-digging a bed, create a series of trenches and move soil from one trench into the previously emptied trench.

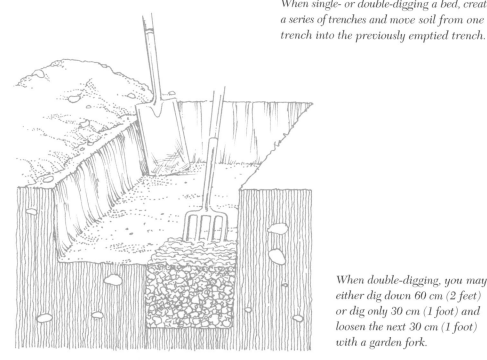

When double-digging, you may either dig down 60 cm (2 feet) or dig only 30 cm (1 foot) and loosen the next 30 cm (1 foot) with a garden fork.

Watering and Xeriscaping

Travelling through the English countryside where the great swaths of uncultivated meadows and the strips of untended roadside are a lush, verdant green, you realize how much toil an abundance of rain can take out of a gardener's life! Really now, as a Canadian, all you have to do is look to Victoria or Vancouver on our west coast to see the up-side of a damp, drizzly spring and summer. Most of us in Ontario have to "put up" with balmy summer sunshine and a significant number of dry clear days each growing season. Not a burden really, but it does keep most of us occupied with watering our gardens more often than our west coast friends (check out Appendix II for average annual precipitation levels in your city).

As a matter of fact, I find that I am asked the same questions about watering over and over again on my radio phone-in show. How much? When? How often? And there is a fourth common question, not always asked directly, but often implied in the other questions: "How can I do less watering?" Watering is time consuming and resource consuming, and while water is essential to the health and beauty of your garden, overwatering does little good and may cause significant problems for your soil and your plants. In fact, I often say that programmed lawn and garden sprinklers are a plant's biggest enemy! Knowing the water needs of your garden is an indispensable component of gardening success.

While plants need water to maintain cell structure and therefore continue growth and photosynthesis, water also affects the availability of soil nutrients and fertilizers for the plants. Plant roots can absorb soil nutrients only when those nutrients are dissolved in water. Even a very fertile soil will do a plant little good if it is completely dried out—the nutrients are there but the plant has no way of taking them up. Similarly, there is no point to fertilizing your lawn or plants unless the soil remains moist enough for the plants to absorb the added nutrients. Inadequate watering can therefore cause a host of problems for your garden.

Knowing how often to water and how much to water is based on knowing your plants and their moisture requirements and knowing your soil and how well it retains moisture. When choosing plants, always make note of their water requirements. If possible, group plants with similar water needs together (more on this on p. 175). This will not only help you to remember which plants need more or less water, but will prevent you from having to water individual plants within a bed. And remember that newly installed plants need more frequent watering than established plants. Quite simply, the established plants have deeper roots and better access to ground moisture. You should water the new plants as the soil becomes dry to the touch, and give them extra water for up to a year.

Careful observation of your garden can assist you in watering, but you cannot rely on the appearance of plants to tell you when they need watering. If some plants look limp or wilted in the heat of day, it does not necessarily mean they need watering. Wilting may be the plants' natural reaction to high temperatures. But if a plant is wilting at night, chances are that it has gone thirsty and serious damage has been done. When the plant is lacking sufficient water, the fragile hairs on the roots of the plant can dry out and die, seriously inhibiting the plant's ability to absorb water in the future. Therefore even short-term underwatering can cause long-term damage (especially with newly planted plants), and watering a wilted plant may not be enough to save it.

Your decision to water, then, must be made before your plants get this dry. Keep in mind that the hotter the weather, the more water your garden requires—not only does the soil dry out faster, but your plants will be losing more moisture through transpiration (the process by which plant leaves give off moisture along with oxygen to the surrounding air). Winds also have a drying effect on the soil and on the plants (although some plants, if shaken by winds, will react by stopping transpiration for a time).

One good way to judge the water needs of your garden is to inspect your soil. Pushing your finger into the soil will tell you a lot. If soil is dry below 2.5 cm (1 inch), your garden needs watering. If the soil crumbles and will not hold shape when you squeeze a handful, you need to water.

The best rule of thumb for watering both gardens and lawns is to water deeply—2.5 cm (1 inch) will provide moisture for a 30-cm (1-foot) depth—usually no more than once a week. (You want to have at least 20 to 22.5 cm/8 to 9 inches of moist soil.) Infrequent but generous watering forces the roots of plants to grow deeper in search of moisture, without starving them for water. Deep roots mean that your plants can better survive short periods of drought and that those roots are protected should the soil surface heat up in very sunny and hot conditions. Not only are deep roots less susceptible to scorching and damage, but they also anchor plants well, so during the freeze-thaw cycles of fall, winter and early spring, your plants are less likely to be heaved out of the ground!

If too much water is applied too frequently, not only is shallow root growth encouraged, but air circulation in the soil can be reduced by filling up air pockets with water. Reduced air circulation can lead to plant damage, damping off, crown rot and a host of soil fungi and diseases. Watering too much can also cause nutrient and fertilizer run-off, driving essential elements from the soil around the plant roots and leaching them into the ground water.

Unfortunately, no one can tell you exactly how long to run that sprinkler to water your garden sufficiently. Each sprinkler or irrigation system is different; each soil type retains a different amount of water. To check how much water your system is distributing in a given period of time, try the following simple test.

RULE OF THUMB
Most gardeners worry about getting enough water to their plants. But overwatering can cause all kinds of plant problems too. Even wilting leaves can be an indication of overwatering. Given the challenges of providing the right quantities of water to your garden and lawn, I always stress the importance of providing well-draining soil when planting and amending. Unless you are planning a bog garden, good soil will give you a good deal more leeway with watering!

Measuring water distribution

Take a small, shallow can (a tuna or cat food can is ideal) and mark on the can a 2.5-cm (1-inch) depth line. Place it on the lawn or soil. Start your sprinkler or watering system and time how long it takes for the can to fill up to the 2.5-cm (1-inch) mark. Now you know how many minutes of watering time you need per 2.5 cm (1 inch) of water you want to apply. (If you are using an oscillating sprinkler, place more than one tin across the lawn or garden area and average the results to find the minutes per 2.5 cm/1 inch of water.)

Once you know the capacity of your watering system, you must determine how much of that water you are applying actually stays in the soil. If you have sandy soil, it will drain quickly and have more difficulty retaining moisture. You will need to increase the time you leave the water running to achieve the same effects that a shorter watering spell would have on organically enriched loam. This is just one of the many reasons why I recommend that you incorporate generous quantities of compost into your garden soil. Try the following test to see how your soil fares.

Drainage tests

Dig a hole 15 cm (6 inches) wide and 30 cm (1 foot) deep. Fill with water and let drain. Fill again, this time, timing how long it takes to empty. If the water takes more than half an hour to drain from the hole, you have a drainage problem, perhaps due to compaction or high clay content. If water drains from the hole in minutes or right before your eyes, there is no drainage problem. (Remember, when you plant something new, particularly something large like a tree or a shrub, it is the perfect time to perform a drainage test in the hole you've dug for the plant.)

Another way to test if your soil drains too quickly is to water an area very deeply (at least 5 cm/2 inches). After two days, dig down in the same spot 15 cm (6 inches). If the soil is already dry to the bottom, it is probably draining too quickly and you will want to amend the soil to help moisture retention (compost or composted cattle manure is the best choice for this purpose).

Drainage problems

If drainage in your garden or your lawn is sluggish, you should be careful not to overwater, but you will probably need to improve the soil if you don't want problems in the long run. If you have heavy clay, amend the soil with compost, well-rotted manure or even a bit of sharp sand to improve drainage and air circulation (see Soil, p. 127). If the problem is hardpan clay in the top 60 cm (2 feet) of soil, you can break it up by double-digging (see Planting Tips, p. 163). Digging in lots of fallen leaves in the autumn can help a lot. I also recommend planting sweet clover to help with drainage, as the roots can penetrate hardpan, and may be able to break up hard soil that goes down more than 60 cm (2 feet). If amending the soil or digging it out is too onerous, consider creating a raised bed on top of the poorly draining area.

You can also use a soggy area of your garden to create a "bog garden" (see p. 73), full of plants that thrive with "wet feet."

If your problems with drainage are severe (especially if melting snow or heavy rains create periods when whole areas are awash), consider constructing "catchment basins" to collect surplus water. This is best done with the help of a reputable landscaping company, which will identify areas on your property where the water flows to naturally and will construct large basins, approximately 120 cm (4 feet) deep and filled with crushed rock, where runoff water can collect and drain to the soil below rather than onto your beds. It can also bring in fill if necessary to raise areas of the garden to correct flow to basins. Flagstone can be used to disguise the crushed rock and incorporate the hidden basins into a pleasing landscape design.

If your soil is sandy, the best solution is to amend it heavily, across a large area, with compost or well-rotted manure (see Soil, p. 127).

Where to water?

Water is best applied at a slow, consistent rate, in the morning or evening, so that the soil gets a chance to absorb the water before any runs off, puddles or evaporates. Water should also be applied as close to the ground as possible to avoid excess evaporation as the droplets travel through the air, and it should be directed over the root systems of your plants. Some plants have a very deep root (a tap root) that extends far down into the soil to anchor the plant and find water, but most other roots are found within 60 cm (2 feet) of the surface (this includes roots that are most active in water and nutrient absorption and in respiration). Most gardeners used to believe that the longest root grew no farther out than the equivalent extension of the longest branch of a tree or shrub, but everyone who has had the headache of tree roots growing in their sewer systems or through their underground pipes will tell you that roots can travel much farther than that. Nevertheless, the idea of a "dripline," a circle drawn around

Most roots grow within a tree's "dripline"—the area around the base of the tree that is equivalent in diameter to the circle created by the tree's longest branches. To be on the safe side, extend watering just past this dripline.

your plant that corresponds to the diameter created by measuring the longest branch, *is* useful—most roots grow within a metre/a yard either side of this circle. When watering trees and shrubs, always water to the full extent of the dripline. During very dry conditions you might also want to "bucket-water" your young trees. At the bottom of two 1-litre (4-cup) plastic pails, puncture a 6-mm (5/16-inch) hole on two sides of each pail and place them against the base of the tree. Fill the buckets with water and allow them to drain slowly. In dry conditions, fill the pails once or twice a month.

When to water?

A friend of mine recently reseeded her front lawn and then was called out of town for a few days just after the first shoots appeared. The afternoon she returned she immediately turned on the sprinkler to water her seedlings—desperate to get moisture to the soil before the new growth died. As the water began to run, no fewer than three neighbours and passersby dashed over to tell her that she shouldn't be watering on a hot, sunny afternoon. If there's one thing that gardeners seem to agree on, it is when not to water!

There is a popular misconception that watering on a hot afternoon will burn or scorch plants and grass as the water standing on leaves "boils" under the sun. The theory sounds convincing until you think of what happens when you get out of a pool or lake on a hot afternoon and lie down in the sun to dry off. No, water doesn't get hot enough to do damage, but watering in the middle of the day will not do nearly as much good as watering at other times. The sun and the heat of the day will cause much of the moisture you are applying to evaporate before it is absorbed by the soil. Conversely, if you are using a soaker hose or drip system in which water is applied directly to the soil, and that soil is somewhat shaded from the sun by the foliage of plants, then there isn't a reason not to water in the light of day! But when is the *best* time to water? My vote is always for early morning. After a long, cool night, before the sun begins to heat up the air and the ground, there will be the least amount of evaporation. And if the weather has been hot, plants will be less stressed after a long period without sun and high temperatures. My second choice is to water in the evening, after the sun has begun to set but before it is really dark and cool. However, watering at night is not ideal. In the coolness of the night, dew collects on the surface of grass and soil. This dew is a combination of moisture that condenses out of the air and moisture that is drawn up from the surface of the soil by capillary action. Therefore, watering at night means that some of the moisture added will return to the surface as dew and less moisture will ultimately be absorbed. What's more, this surface moisture can increase the potential for slugs and fungi, and therefore disease and damage. Roses, especially, do not like evening watering, except during long, hot spells. And remember, it often rains at night, so watering then may be redundant!

Also keep in mind that watering on a windy day will be less effective, as air movement increases evaporation. And watering during cold weather is not advisable, as root absorption of water is retarded and there is the chance of surface water freezing and damaging plant stems, foliage and shallow roots. Most shrubs and evergreens, however, do need a thorough watering just before the ground freezes—for most parts of Ontario this is in late October or November. Be particularly generous when watering around the foundation of your home—houses should be constructed with excellent drainage around their foundations so that water will flow away quickly.

Watering systems

These days you can select from a wide range of methods to deliver water to your lawn and garden. Your choice will be determined by your gardening budget and the amount of effort you are willing to put into watering your plants.

In-ground systems are without question the most labour-saving of watering systems. Some have the added advantage of potentially conserving water, as they can be set on timers (especially helpful for those who tend to forget they've turned the sprinkler or soaker hose on!). I say "potentially" because, unfortunately, many people leave their timers set on the same schedule from month to month even though their garden's need for water changes dramatically through the season.

A variety of different types of sprinkler heads are available for these systems, but they should be set to spray water as close to the ground as possible to help reduce evaporation while still covering the necessary area. Bubbler heads keep water closer to the ground but cover less area and can cause puddling or run-off if left on too long. After installing an in-ground system, make sure that you adjust the timer to respect water restrictions in your area during dry spells; override automated systems when there has been rainfall and extra watering is not necessary. On average, set your system to come on for two to three hours once a week. Make this watering period during the very early morning or at night to reduce evaporation. An in-ground system is not inexpensive (automated systems are more costly and more difficult to install than manually operated systems) and should be installed by a reliable professional installer who has first worked with you to determine your gardening needs.

A *drip irrigation* system is an ideal watering solution for a vegetable garden, tree plantings or orchards—anywhere non-spreading plants are grown in rows. The system slowly distributes water from a series of low-lying pipes that run alongside the plants. Little if any water is lost to evaporation, and the soil in the root zones can be kept consistently moist. A drip system requires less excavation to install than in-ground systems and is not difficult to install yourself.

Soaker hoses, made from porous synthetic rubber, are long and flexible and can be curved and threaded through your flower beds, around shrubs and along rows of vegetables. They are left in place for the season and can even stay out all winter if need be. As water flows through them, they "weep" or produce beads of moisture along their length that drip directly into the soil. To maximize their effectiveness (and reduce evaporation), you can spread loose mulch over the hoses. Soaker hoses are sold in a variety of lengths, but avoid ones that are longer than 16 m (50 feet), as these will not provide uniform water distribution. (Use several shorter ones instead.)

And since the water is released directly to the soil, keep in mind that the hose is watering only a small area on either side of it—you may need quite a series of hoses to cover your whole garden, or you may choose to use them only for moisture-loving plants or hard-to-reach areas. If you opt for soaker hoses, keep an eye on them—they can sprout "leaks" or bigger holes and send out unwanted sprays of water. Replace the hose if you notice this happening.

Sprinkler hoses are another handy alternative. These long rubber or plastic hoses have a series of small holes running along their length, and they generally are slightly flattened to lie neatly along the ground. Like soaker hoses, they can be threaded through gardens and even along lawns. If the holes are laid facing down, the sprinkler hose acts much like a soaker hose and can be mulched over. If the hose is placed with the holes facing up, the water is distributed to a greater area, but some water will be lost to evaporation.

Keep in mind when using drip irrigation, soaker or sprinkler hoses or any other method that provides water directly to the soil, that water percolates quickly through sandy soil and much more slowly through clay soils. Therefore, the area directly below the hose or pipe in sandy soil will get wet to a good depth quite quickly, but the moisture will not travel very far from side to side. Alternatively, a clay soil will hold the water that trickles onto it for a greater length of time, allowing the moisture to spread horizontally much farther than in the sandy soil, but to a shallower depth. You will need to have more area covered with hose or pipe on sandy soil, but will have to run the system for less time.

There is also a wide variety of *conventional sprinklers* to choose from, and these models vary in effectiveness. Sprinklers, besides requiring you to drag them back and forth to where they are needed, are not the most efficient deliverers of water. It is often difficult to adjust them to cover only the area required (and not your porch or the neighbour's driveway), and the higher the water flies in the air, the more is lost to evaporation during the day, meaning that most of the water they spray may *not* make it to your lawn or plants.

The traditional *oscillating sprinklers* that move back and forth are fun for children to run through, but they can lose up to an astonishing 50 per cent of their water through evaporation when used in the middle of the day. And while these sprinklers cover large areas, they may spray more water at either end of their arc as they pause to change direction. Some models have new features to address uneven water distribution, so check with your garden centre if you have concerns, and water in the early morning to reduce evaporation.

The *revolving* type of sprinkler in which the rotating arms are moved by the water pressure you provide from the hose work well to cover a large area, but delivery is difficult to control with these. To get the arms revolving, a certain amount of water pressure is needed, so there is a minimum distance they have to cover in order to work properly. Too much water pressure or too little can result in uneven distribution. The *fixed* type of sprinkler (generally a ring with small holes) can be effective, but only if it is well made and does not leak or puddle around the base.

Impulse sprinklers (the type that delivers water through a gun-like head that swivels back and forth) provide the most uniform distribution of water and are generally available in a variety of precipitation rates.

When choosing any model of sprinkler, remember that more often than not, you get what you pay for. Brass is still the best material for sprinklers, although it is the most expensive. Plastic sprinklers can be affordable and serviceable, but they do wear out as the plastic cracks and chips.

Xeriscaping and water conservation

Xeriscaping is a topic that is cropping up more and more these days in gardening magazines and horticultural shows, as well as in the conversations of all sorts of gardeners. The word was coined in the 1980s in the United States, making this a relatively new gardening approach that is continuing to evolve and be adapted to suit various climates and terrains (the original xeriscape drought-tolerant garden was designed for gardens in the western United States). The term itself is from the Greek word for dry, *xeros*, and literally means "dry view." In practice, however, today's xeriscaping is not about creating a desert-like habitat, or vistas of brush, cacti and gravel. Nor is xeriscaping now about the exclusive use of drought-tolerant plants. Xeriscaping is about gardening with less water, and it dovetails very nicely with both low-maintenance gardening approaches and ecologically responsible gardening, or water conservation.

After an especially damp, dreary summer, gardeners are likely to bemoan the state of their tomatoes and the powdery mildew attacking their phlox instead of commenting on the reduction of their gardening workload. But not having to water your garden every time you venture out is an enormous labour saver, allowing you to spend more time enjoying the scenery rather than hosing it down. Xeriscaping is especially useful if you live in areas where nature does not provide you with a lot of moisture during the growing season—areas like northern and northwestern Ontario spring to mind. Xeriscaping also reduces maintenance because it means less pruning—plants that are not overwatered or overfertilized require less paring back. Many of the xeriscaping techniques will also help reduce weeds and therefore weeding. You may also find that xeriscaping allows you to spend less time fighting pests and disease—drought-tolerant plants often have less succulent growth and therefore tend to have fewer pests.

But even if low-maintenance gardening is not your chief concern, there are other reasons to consider employing some, if not all, of the xeriscaping techniques. Household water consumption and water supply have become pressing issues for many Ontario regions. While our country boasts the most fresh water per square kilometre in the world, water treatment for household use is an extremely costly endeavour, driven higher by our penchant for wasting vast quantities of the precious resource. In her book *The Ontario Naturalized Garden*, Lorraine Johnson notes that Canadian household water consumption goes up 50 per cent over the course of the summer, due no doubt not to any proclivity we have for doing more laundry in the summer, but to the care and feeding of our lawns and gardens.

The days when city-dwellers could crank up water consumption with no effect on expenses are quickly drawing to a close. More and more municipalities are now using water meters to charge for water consumption. And many are looking into or establishing watering restrictions. Those people who have relied on a private well no doubt have an awareness of water consumption that the rest of us are just beginning to appreciate. For them, many of the xeriscaping approaches may already be second nature.

Xeriscaping, therefore, provides a host of benefits, and as you will see, its principles are simple, straightforward and easy to accomplish. You may already be implementing many of them!

Xeriscaping guidelines

Group plants with similar water needs together

When designing your garden or adding new plants, try to group plants together not only for pleasing visual results, but also according to their moisture requirements. If all the drought-tolerant plants are in one bed, and your water-lovers in another, you can avoid overwatering the less thirsty plants and therefore conserve water and time. (If you are unsure of the water needs of a given plant you are interested in, ask a Certified Gardening Professional or CCHT at your local nursery or garden centre.)

Water deeply but less frequently

As discussed on p. 167, frequent watering is as bad for your plants as it is for your water source. Follow the watering suggestions I've outlined earlier in this chapter to save water and time and nurture hardy plants that can survive dry periods. And remember that all plants require at least a brief period of dryness between waterings.

Use low-spraying sprinklers, soaker or sprinkler hoses or in-ground systems

Water the soil, not the atmosphere, by using low-spraying or dripping watering devices that get the moisture to the soil as directly as possible. Avoid systems that spray water where it is not needed or allow water to puddle or run off. Any device that emits large droplets (usually formed by a lower-pressure system) will result in less evaporation, so avoid sprinklers and sprinkler systems that require high water pressure to operate correctly.

Match the shape of your flower beds and your water distribution

When you are creating beds for your flowers, trees and shrubs, try to use shapes that correspond with the area covered by your water distribution system. Of course, you can change your irrigation system to cover the shapes of your beds (soaker hoses and "bleeding" hoses, for example, are useful for getting into corners where sprinklers can't reach). If your beds extend out to the edge of the spray of your in-ground sprinklers, or you have used soaker and sprinkler hoses to cover only the soil in which your plants are growing, you won't be watering walkways, driveways, ground-covers and grass that don't need the moisture. And if you are designing an all-new garden, you may want to do a little juggling between the two approaches until you get a design that suits your vision and is nicely matched with its water distribution patterns.

Mulch

Mulching is one of the indispensable tenets of xeriscaping. Mulching around plants and overexposed soil reduces water evaporation from the soil and therefore reduces the watering requirements of your garden.

To conserve water, match the shape of your garden beds and your water distribution system.

Soaker and sprinkler hoses can be laid in patterns to match almost any bed shape.

Drip irrigation systems are suitable to plantings laid out in rows.

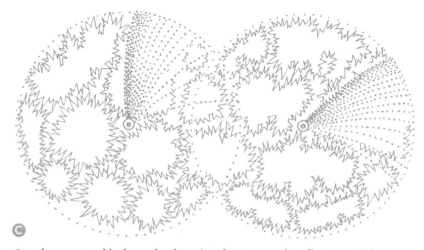

Circular or curved beds can be shaped so that in-ground oscillating sprinklers water the plants but spray no further.

A generous layer of organic mulch adds organic material to the soil, increasing quick-draining soil's ability to retain moisture. See Mulch, Mulch, Mulch, p. 185, for more details.

Improve the soil

With gardening, it's always about the soil, isn't it? The most water-efficient garden is one with rich, fertile soil that drains adequately, but not too quickly. See Soil, p. 127, for ways to increase fertility, friability, aeration and drainage. Pay particular attention to amending soil if you have very sandy soil that does not retain moisture.

Slow water flow on slopes

Slopes are naturally difficult to keep adequately watered and can create run-off and plenty of wasted water. There are a number of ways to make sure you don't lose water and to keep plantings on slopes in good shape. You may want to use drought-tolerant plants on the high points of a slope, with moisture-needing plants at the bottom where water will drain. You can also create circular depressions around plantings at any point on the slope so that water gathers naturally around the root zone (in fact, I recommend that you always do this when planting). On large slopes, shallow horizontal or angled ditches can be created at intervals along the slope to collect water and slow drainage. You can also design these ditches or swales to direct water to plantings. Alternatively, terraces can be constructed to grade the angle of the slope and slow drainage (with drought-tolerant shrubs, plants and groundcovers near the top).

Mulching or planting drought-tolerant groundcovers on a slope will slow water run-off and reduce soil erosion. Soil amendment on the slope or aeration of a lawn-covered slope will increase the soil's ability to absorb water and reduce run-off.

Create water barriers for your moisture-loving plants

If you have plants in your garden that require quite a lot of water and your garden is not particularly water-retentive, you could create water barriers that help keep water in the soil. Layered newspaper, and even plastic sheeting for bog gardens, can be used to line beds. Dig down 30 to 45 cm (12 to 18 inches), cover the base of the bed with your barrier material (it can extend up the sides, stopping about 15 cm/6 inches from the surface, if you like), and fill the bed with rich, humusy soil (you may have to amend your existing soil with compost or well-rotted manure or use a triple-mix soil to replace it altogether).

Reduce the use of raised beds

If you have soggy soil, raised beds are an ideal way to improve drainage because water evaporates from the sides of a bed as well as from the top. For the same reasons, in gardens without drainage problems, they are natural water hogs. In a xeriscaped garden, raised beds should be only slightly (10 to 15 cm/4 to 6 inches) above the rest of the ground to reduce evaporation. If your soil is well draining to start with but you want raised beds for landscaping purposes, amend soil to a depth of 45 cm (18 inches) to improve water retention.

Create windbreaks

Planting shelter belts is a long-established prairie practice. These lines of trees and shrubs break the flow of wind as it crosses open areas, reducing evaporation, wind damage to plants and crops and soil erosion on the leeward side of the plantings. You can use this principle in the wind-exposed areas of your own garden to reduce moisture lost to the drying effects of wind. You can plant an attractive line or cluster of trees, shrubs or hedges to break the path of the wind, or erect a fence or vine-covered trellis to interrupt wind flow. Windbreaks can also provide shade that slows evaporation and the drying effect of the sun. Keep in mind that the protection lies on the leeward side of the prevailing winds, so you will have to study the wind patterns in your yard carefully before you design the windbreak. And remember that solid obstacles to wind flow only force the wind over and down the wall, creating potentially damaging eddies and drafts on the other side of the wall.

Collect rainwater

How many times have you been out watering your lawn or water-loving flowers only days after a heavy shower that sent water flowing down the street into the storm sewers? In the future don't let that rainwater go down the drain. Rain barrels can be used to collect water from the eaves troughs of roofs. A variety of catchment barrels are now available from garden centres, and newer models offer various ways to drain or direct the water that is collected to your garden and to keep overflow away from your house foundation. If you create or fashion your own rain barrel, make sure that it has a well-sealed lid to prevent mosquitoes from breeding in it. Some municipalities now offer rain barrels for a small fee.

RULE OF THUMB
I have an old-fashioned wooden rain barrel at one end of our house. I find it very handy for dipping a watering can into as needs be. The open top, however, is an invitation to mosquitoes to lay eggs, which soon hatch. Solution? One inexpensive goldfish—they have a voracious appetite for mosquito larvae!

You can purchase plastic adapters to attach to the bottom of downspouts so that water can be directed to lawns or nearby beds. You might also consider stone or brick troughs that direct water from the downspouts to other areas as part of your garden design.

You will also want to make sure that roof downspouts are not leading directly into the city sewer systems (this can be quite common in some of the older neighbourhoods of Ontario cities). If your rainspout disappears into the ground, have it redirected to empty on your lawn or near your flower beds. If you don't want to do this yourself (it can be a big job), roofing or eaves trough companies can do it for you and some municipalities (the city of Toronto, for example) have programs that arrange and pay for the service.

Water catchment can also include designing your garden so that flower beds and plantings are located near the base of natural slopes or run-off patterns. When adding patios, driveways and paths to your garden design, construct them so they have a slight slope that directs rainwater towards your lawn and garden.

Consider having less lawn

Before I state the case for eliminating some of your lawn, let me be frank about my own feelings about this time-honoured institution. A few years back I read a gardening column that completely dismissed the whole idea of a "lawn." The writer said he thought that lawns were essentially boring and without visual appeal and he was stumped by the lawn's continued appeal to the population. I don't agree! As far as I'm concerned, all you have to do is kick off your shoes and walk barefoot across the soft turf of a freshly mown lawn to rediscover its appeal. And where else could your children practise somersaults, play tag or roll around with such abandon? What's more, a lush green lawn is often the most ideal "background" (or foreground) for your garden design—a visually appealing bridge between flower beds, trees and shrubs. And lawns do act as a "growing mulch," retaining soil moisture and keeping the surface air cooler (through transpiration and evaporation) than it would be with paving stones, concrete, stone mulch or other material that catches and retains heat. And grass is a groundcover unparalleled at withstanding foot traffic! A lush green lawn also reduces dust and air pollution and can prevent soil erosion and run-off. Quite frankly, I say that the garden-variety Ontario lawn is the most sophisticated living groundcover known to humankind.

That being said, many homeowners may very well be maintaining a lawn out of habit rather than enjoyment and might do well to ask if the lawn is really worth all the weeding, mowing, fertilizing—and water—to keep it.

Lawns consume a lot of water if they are kept green and lush through a summer drought. And while it is a perfectly sound gardening practice to let lawns go dormant in the heat of the summer, most folks aren't keen on the look of brown dry turf in front of their homes. Of that 50 per cent increase in summer water consumption noted earlier, much if not most will be spent on keeping our lawns green, making lawns, generally speaking, our landscape's thirstiest component. Xeriscape enthusiasts suggest that we homeowners look at our use and enjoyment of our lawn.

Do you actually *use* the lawn, or would hard surfaces such as a patio or a layer of bark mulch be just as useful? Could some or all of the lawn be replaced by drought-tolerant groundcovers, flowers, shrubs or ornamental grasses? There may be all sorts of corners where you not only don't use the grass, but can't keep it growing well. If you have a mature maple in your yard, for example, I recommend that you stop fighting the roots in your attempts to grow a lawn in that area. Try a 6- to 8-cm (2 1/2- to 3-inch) layer of cedar mulch instead. Or perhaps your lawn is suffering in a shady corner. Something else might flourish in those conditions. Are there areas that could be replaced with drought-tolerant grass types (see Gardening at the Cottage, p. 76), instead of tender Kentucky bluegrass?

If you do decide to maintain a modified area of lawn, design this area with your watering system in mind. A shape (most often round, oval or square) that coincides with the spray pattern of your sprinkler will waste the least amount of water.

Choose drought-tolerant plants

You might be surprised to learn how many wonderfully attractive and versatile annuals, perennials, shrubs and grasses are actually drought-tolerant. Many, because they have less succulent growth, are also pest and disease resistant. Drought-tolerant plants are also ideal for sandy soil, areas with high elevation, southern or western exposures, hotspots in the gardens (see Microclimates, p. 54), on slopes, in open or windy spots, near mature trees that absorb a lot of soil moisture and in very sunny spots.

RULE OF THUMB: HARD LANDSCAPING VS. SOFT
Here is some industry lingo that sometimes throws the lay-gardener. "Hard landscaping" refers to all material used to produce a landscape that does not grow. "Soft landscaping" refers to plant material and soil.

I am a proponent of using plant material when it can do the job. That's why a lawn will always have a place in my landscape. There is a place, of course, for a wooden deck or an interlocking brick patio. Bear in mind, however, that none of these produce oxygen, attract wildlife or cool your yard down on a hot summer day. I rest my case in favour of soft landscaping.

Drought-tolerant plants

PERENNIALS

Bearded iris (Iris)
Beardtongue (*Penstemon fruticosus*)
Black-eyed Susan (*Rudbeckia hirta*)
Blanket flower (*Gaillardia* × *grandiflora*)
Broad-leaved stonecrop (*Sedum* varieties)
Butterfly weed (*Asclepias tuberosa*)
Carpet bugleweed (*Ajuga reptans*)
Common yarrow (*Achillea millefolium*)
Coral bells (*Heuchera*)
Crown vetch (*Coronilla varia*) (can be invasive)
Cushion spurge (*Euphorbia polychroma*)
Daylily (*Hemerocallis*)
Desert evening primrose (*Oenothera*,
  all varieties)
Dwarf bellflower (*Campanula cochleariifolia*)
Evening primrose (*Oenothera fruticosa*)
False sunflower (*Heliopsis helianthoides*)
Flowering spurge (*Euphorbia corollata*)
Giant hyssop (*Agastache foeniculum*)
Goldenrod (*Solidago*)

Goutweed, bishop's weed (*Aegopodium*)
  (can be invasive)
Lady's mantle (*Alchemilla*) (can be invasive)
Lance-leaved coreopsis (*Coreopsis lanceolata*)
Lily of the valley (*Convallaria*)
Mother-of-thyme (*Thymus serpyllum*)
Oriental poppy (*Papaver orientale*)
Peony (*Paeonia*)
Perennial alyssum, basket-of-gold
  (*Aurinia saxatilis*)
Perennial or cranesbill geranium (*Geranium*)
Purple coneflower (*Echinacea purpurea*)
Sagebrush, mugwort (*Artemisia*)
Snow-in-summer (*Cerastium tomentosum*)
  (can be invasive)
Sweet woodruff (*Galium odoratum*)
White gasplant (*Dictamnus albus*)
Wild bergamot (*Monarda fistulosa*)
Wild lupine (*Lupinus perennis*)
Yellow coneflower (*Ratibida pinnata*)

BULBS

Tulip (*Tulipa*)

TREES AND SHRUBS

Bur oak (*Quercus macrocarpa*)
Chokecherry (*Prunus virginiana*)
Common juniper (*Juniperus communis*)
Cotoneaster (*Cotoneaster*)
Elder (*Sambucus*)
Hawthorn (*Crataegus*)
Lilac (*Syringa*)

Nanny berry (*Viburnum lentago*)
Oregon grape (*Mahonia aquifolium*)
Pine (*Pinus*)
Rugosa rose (*Rosa rugosa*)
Sand cherry (*Prunus besseyi*)
Spruce (*Picea*)

ORNAMENTAL GRASSES

Big bluestem (*Andropogon gerardii*)
Indian grass (*Sorghastrum nutans*)
Switch grass (*Panicum virgatum*)

RULE OF THUMB

Try xeriscaping techniques if you
- live in an area with only moderate or low
  levels of rainfall
- want to make gardening low-maintenance
- want to conserve water in order to minimize
  strains on a private well, or to respond to
  municipal water restrictions or environmental
  concerns

Low-maintenance gardening

Low-maintenance gardening is a terrific approach for those who love the look of a beautiful home garden but don't have the time or inclination to do much gardening, as well as for those who would rather spend more time admiring their garden than toiling in it. With four children and a busy schedule, I find myself enthusiastically embracing a low-maintenance approach to gardening. By using the following ideas, I confine most of my gardening "work" to the early spring and the fall. During the heat of July and August, I can relax with a draft beer and a book, or take a leisurely stroll through the garden to dead-head a few flowers, rather than fight weeds and disease or water and prune. Here are the keys to creating a low-maintenance garden (many of these topics are covered in greater depth in other chapters of this book, and you will notice that xeriscaping and low-maintenance have a lot in common!).

Soil improvement
The more organic material your soil has, the less watering you will have to do (rich soils retain moisture), the more nutrients your plants will enjoy (less or no fertilizing for you to do) and the more likely your plants will be able to resist disease. See Soil, p. 127 for more information about improving your soil.

Mulching
Laying organic or inorganic material on your beds and under your trees and shrubbery will reduce weeds and therefore weeding, and retain soil moisture, meaning that you will spend less time watering your plants. What's more, organic mulches increase the humus in your soil, helping out with soil improvement (without any extra effort on your part!). See, Mulch, Mulch, Mulch, p. 185, for more details.

Xeriscaping
By choosing plants with low water needs or that are drought-tolerant and employing a few other xeriscaping techniques, you can reduce your watering and maintenance routine even further. See p. 174 for more information about xeriscaping.

The shade garden
The shade garden has two distinct advantages over the sunny garden: it doesn't dry out as fast and it isn't so popular with weeds! Consider planting your garden on the north or east sides of your house or in areas of shade. See In Sun and Shade, p. 3, for more tips on creating a beautiful shade garden.

In-ground watering systems, soaker or drip hoses
Most of these systems save time as well as water. Check out the discussion of different types of systems on p. 171.

Spring preparation
There is a lot you can do in the early spring to reduce your garden workload later on.

- If you have fruit trees, flowering shrubs, shade trees and roses, consider treating them with at least two applications of dormant oil spray (an environmentally friendly combination of lime sulphur and dormant oil) to kill off overwintering diseases and insects. This will help you avoid using pesticides or working with time-consuming organic treatments of disease and pests later in the season.

- Remove as many weeds as you can while they are small and relatively easy to dislodge. May and the first two weeks of June is an ideal time in most of Ontario to do this. You'll save a lot of midsummer work!

- Mulch early in the spring before weeds become established.

- Spray fruit trees in June and early July. If you don't want to use synthetic pesticides, ask a Canadian Certified Horticultural Technician at your local garden centre for organic treatments for pests and diseases.

- Prune evergreens and early-flowering shrubs in May and early June. The soft new growth is far easier to cut through than the tough wood that will have grown by the summer.

Mulch, Mulch, Mulch

While visiting Victoria, B.C., a couple of years ago, I was invited to a wonderful garden belonging to Phoebe Noble. Phoebe is famous for her perennial geraniums—she even has one named after her. I was enjoying a guided tour of Phoebe's garden paradise when we came across an astonishing vegetable garden right in the middle of this two-acre Eden. Phoebe explained that this was her daughter Sandy's domain. Sandy's dad had passed away 12 years before and had left her with the responsibility of rototilling the veggie garden. Which she did. Once …

By the second spring Sandy was determined to try a different approach. She brought in bales of straw with which she covered the soil, and then planted directly in the straw and let nature take care of the rest. As I walked through this beautiful, weed-free vegetable garden, Sandy explained how she simply added a loose 30- to 40-cm (12- to 16-inch) layer of this inexpensive and readily available mulch every four to six weeks all summer long. By now, my curiosity had got the best of me. "How deep *is* this soil?" I asked. "I don't know. I never dig in it—I just plant in the mulch," said Sandy. "But here's a shovel. You can dig," she added. And I did. I plunged the shovel to the very top of the blade. Then I bent down and pushed my arm, almost up to my elbow, into the richest, darkest, most friable soil I have seen in a long time. Years and years of mulching with a clean, organic product had paid off for the Nobles. Mother Nature did the work and the gardeners picked the bounty of vegetables!

When people ask me the secret to successful gardening I like to adapt that old real estate saying about "location." I say that the secret to a greener thumb lies in the three "m's" of gardening: mulch, mulch and mulch. I am simplifying, of course, but mulching is so useful, so beneficial and serves so many different purposes that it is hard not to make it my number one rule of thumb. (My first rule, in fact, is that 90 per cent of gardening success is rooted in proper ground preparation, and mulch is a major part of that preparation.)

To list the many benefits of mulch, it:

✤ can, if organic, improve the nutrient content of the soil

✤ reduces weeding dramatically

✤ reduces water evaporation and the need to water

✤ protects the soil from temperature fluctuations

✤ can increase or decrease soil temperature (depending on the type of mulch used)

✤ can prevent soil compaction

✤ can reduce soil erosion, especially on slopes

✤ keeps dirt off the leaves of plants and veggies and can therefore suppress and control disease

✤ makes moving through your garden (especially the vegetable patch) easier—no muddy walkways

Increases the nutrient content of the soil

As you have read in the chapter on soil, organic material is a godsend for the garden. Using an organic mulch, especially one that breaks down relatively quickly (over a single season, for example), adds fresh organic material to your soil. As the mulch breaks down, earthworms will draw the humus down into the soil, aerating the soil as they go and producing castings that release nutrients and increase microbial activity in the soil. The organic material itself also aids aeration and water percolation and adds (depending on the type you choose) vital nutrients like nitrogen, phosphorus and potassium, and some trace elements. Organic mulches can also tie up nitrogen for a time (see Troubleshooting Mulches, p. 190), but they can free up potassium for plants. A good deal of potassium in the soil attaches itself to soil particles, where plant roots cannot take it up. With a decaying organic mulch, there is increased microbial activity, which makes potassium more readily available to plant roots.

Reduces weeding

As long as the mulch itself is weed free (be careful of weed-filled hay, manure or plant material that has not been fully composted), it can prevent weed seeds from taking root. If the mulch is deep enough, it can also suppress the growth of many of the weed seeds that may already exist in your soil. Some, however, may be able to tough it out and break through despite the lack of sunshine, but their number is sure to be fewer, and they will be relatively easy to remove from mulch-covered soil.

Reduces the need to water

Watering is not only time-consuming—it can also be wasteful (see Watering and Xeriscaping, p. 165). Any gardening technique that reduces the need to water yet keeps your plants well hydrated is worth the effort. Reducing water evaporation from the soil by applying mulch is one of the easier ways to cut down watering. Studies have shown that mulching reduces evaporation from the soil by 10 to 50 percent. Evaporation can be particularly high in hot, dry and windy conditions, but in all gardens, evaporation can be a problem. For example, did you know that morning dew is not only, as commonly believed, condensed moisture from the atmosphere that settles on the grass? It is also water that has condensed from the air pockets in the soil (drawn up from the subsoil by capillary action). Mulch keeps this condensation in the soil, rather than having it evaporate. Many organic mulches will absorb the moisture, or dew, that condenses out of the atmosphere as well, so that it doesn't evaporate as soon as the sun is out.

If too much water or rain is a problem, mulches can also help. Not only will they improve poorly draining soil over time, but you can plant right in some organic mulches, rather than in the soil, so that your plants don't have wet feet. If an overabundance of precipitation is a problem, you can also mound the mulch around the plant so that water tends to run away from the plant, rather than settle around the root area.

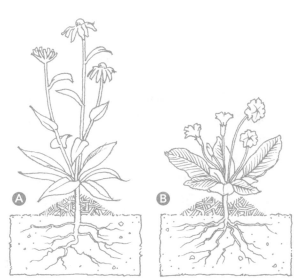

A

If your soil is waterlogged or there has been too much precipitation, you can mound mulch around the base of the plant so water tends to run away from it.

B

If you want to keep water near the root zone of a plant, mulch can be mounded, leaving a well around the stalk or base of the plant.

Moderates soil temperature

"Insulating" the garden with mulch is one technique that is very often overlooked, even by experienced gardeners, yet it can be a real lifesaver for your plants—particularly your perennials. A layer of mulch on top of the soil moderates its temperature, keeping the soil cooler on hot days and warmer on cool days. This action means that shifts in soil temperature are slowed down. In the fall and winter, this prevents soil from freezing quickly and putting plant roots into shock. (Gradual freezing lets roots acclimatize.) It also prevents freeze and thaw cycles, where the frozen ground thaws and absorbs moisture from melted snow or rain that then freezes if a cold period occurs again quickly. The refrozen ground is now filled with ice crystals, which cause the ground to heave, forcing plants out of the soil or exposing roots.

As spring rolls around, most mulch will delay the warming of the ground. This may sound counterproductive, but it can save plants from moving out of dormancy just as one last late spring freeze hits. In summer, mulch can keep the ground cooler (by as much as 6°C/40°F), preventing the sun's hot rays from heating up the surface. This is particularly useful in very sunny, hot spots in the garden where extremely warm soil temperatures can damage the roots of some plants (in particular, shallow-rooted plants or newly planted ones). Alternatively, dark organic mulches and black plastic can warm the soil up if needed. In the spring this may give plants a quicker start, and in the summer it may benefit vegetables and plants, particularly those in cool spots in the garden.

RULE OF THUMB:
TIMING IS EVERYTHING
In the vegetable garden I like to mulch my tomatoes, peppers and potatoes after the crop is put in—around mid-June. This helps to retain heat in the soil and valuable late spring moisture.

Prevents compaction and erosion

A few years ago I was out walking in a Toronto neighbourhood after what had been an extraordinarily heavy rainfall. Passing by houses whose front yards were sloped towards the street, I noticed that there were a number of yards that had been turned into front gardens. The sidewalk and street in front of one of these homes was awash in shredded bark mulch that had obviously been swept from the yard during the deluge. Collecting that mulch and replacing it would require some work, but better to lose a bit of mulch than a lot of precious topsoil, I thought. As if to prove my point, ahead of me, a few houses down the street, was a portion of sidewalk covered in dark rich earth. Looking up, I saw what appeared to be a massive garden renovation. Unfortunately what I was looking at was a front yard that had lost of good deal of soil, and along with it a number of its once beautiful plants, to the heavy rain.

Mulching can control soil erosion by slowing water run-off during heavy watering or rain. It is especially useful on sloping beds or yards. It will also, of course, protect your fine, light topsoil from blowing away in heavy wind storms as well.

But mulching serves another purpose on rainy days. Soil left exposed can be compacted by heavy rain. When it dries, this tough, compacted surface can prevent rain from the next shower from penetrating the soil. Mulching prevents compaction so that rain penetrates the soil.

Mulching can also keep the soil friable by adding organic material, and friable soil readily absorbs water.

Can reduce insect damage and disease

Mulch can also have a role in disease prevention in your garden. A layer of mulch between your plants and the soil can prevent disease spores on the soil from splashing up onto plants during a heavy rainfall. If dry mulches such as straw are placed under vegetables such as lettuce, they can prevent rot by keeping the leaves off the moist soil. (If, however, there are signs of rotting at the crown of the plant, the mulch can be pulled away to allow the soil to dry and to improve air circulation around the base of the plant.)

Mulch can also be used to combat some insects. Aluminum-coated kraft paper (available at building supply stores) or aluminum foil, laid around the base of plants, is often recommended as a way to combat aphids. The light shining off the foil makes them lose their sense of direction and they don't land on the plants nearby. And reducing aphids can also reduce viral diseases spread by aphids. As well, a deep mulch of straw or leaves (15 cm/6 inches or more) can suppress Colorado potato beetles by making it difficult for them to get out from the soil after overwintering.

Troubleshooting mulches

Despite my own enthusiasm for mulching, I have to admit that the practice has its detractors, and there is no doubt that like any gardening approach, it can have its drawbacks or complications. Here are some things to watch out for when using mulch and some solutions to potential problems.

Attractiveness

Personally, I don't much care for the look of straw in an ornamental garden. But if you have access to a quantity of good, clean straw, why turn it down? You can always top-dress organic mulches that you find less than beautiful with a mulch that you find more attractive. I like the look of cedar bark mulch and use it to disguise straw or any other mulch that looks messy or unpleasing to me.

Animals and rodents

As I mentioned earlier, mulches do act as insulation in your garden, and small furry creatures can be attracted to this warm blanket in the depths of winter. To prevent mice and other rodents from gnawing tree trunks, keep organic mulches away from the base of trees. Also, use tightly knit mulches like finely shredded bark mulch and spread it only 6 to 8 cm (2 1/2 to 3 inches) thick. Keep a ready-to-use bottle of taste and smell repellent (available at most garden centres) on hand to deter rodents.

Slugs and insects

While local earthworms will cheer on your yearly application of organic mulch, unfortunately so will slugs. Slugs, as well as a host of other insects both good and bad for the garden, like the insulation and the protection from the sun that a mulch provides. If slugs or snails become a problem, treat for them rather than abandoning the benefits of mulch. There are many ways to depopulate slugs. Saucers of beer recessed in the ground will attract the slugs and drown them (the saucers must be emptied and replenished regularly). Wood ash and diatomaceous earth around the base of plants also discourages slugs and snails, although diatomaceous earth is effective only when dry and must be reapplied if it becomes damp. Overturned grapefruit halves (which have had most of their pulp removed) will attract slugs; they crawl under the little dome for protection from the sun only to succumb to the acid from the fruit. Commercial metaldehyde-based slug bait is also available, but be careful using it if animals or pets come through your property. A new slug bait, Safers Slug and Snail Bait, recently put on the market, is safe for use around children and pets. It is environmentally friendly and effective. And of course, for the unsqueamish, there is always the pick and stomp approach to getting rid of slugs.

Air exchange

A lack of air exchange is only really a problem if you mulch too deeply or use plastic. Follow the guidelines under Types of Mulches, p. 193, for depth for individual mulches and move your mulch around occasionally if you notice that it is getting compacted or is becoming dense. You will need to cut holes in black plastic for water, but if air exchange is also a concern, you may need to remove the plastic or turn it back for a period. If damping off is a problem in your garden, keep mulch away from the base of young, tender plants.

RULE OF THUMB: DON'T USE WOOD CHIPS, CHUNKS OR SAWDUST AS A MULCH

Raw wood by-products are often available and inexpensive. This makes them tempting for Ontario gardeners to use as a mulch. What's more, the parks and recreation departments in many municipalities use this stuff, obtained from shredded-up Christmas trees and other wood that is collected, like mulch. So, why shouldn't you use raw wood mulch?

Wood and all its by-products draw nitrogen from the soil as they decompose. Nitrogen is in greater demand by your garden plants than any other element. The result of low-nitrogen levels in the soil? Yellowing leaves, weaker plants and possibly disease and insect infestation. Parks and municipalities nonetheless use raw wood as mulch because the dip in nitrogen levels has negligible effects on mature trees and shrubs. Perennials, annuals, vegetables and all tender transplants (all staples of the home garden) are extremely susceptible to low nitrogen levels.

But if you have access to wood chips, don't refuse them! They make excellent foot paths. Spread them 10 to 15 cm (4 to 6 inches) thick for a cushiony, weed-free path.

Water penetration

Most organic mulches will let water penetrate nicely, with the exception of matted leaves or dry, crusted peat moss. Remove matted leaves and put them in your compost bin (shredded leaves will decompose faster than whole leaves and are less likely to mat if used as a winter mulch). Inorganic mulches like stone chips and landscape fabrics also allow water to percolate down to the soil. Black plastic is, however, an obvious exception. With plastic, you will have to make sure that there are breaks around the area of the plant to allow water in.

Nitrogen availability

Light-coloured organic mulches such as wood chips or straw will absorb nitrogen from the soil at the beginning. For this reason, I don't recommend using raw wood by-products (see p. 191) for most gardens. But I need to point out that light-coloured mulches are only renting the nitrogen, not buying it. Eventually, when they start to decompose, the nitrogen is released back into the soil where the plants can get at it. My friend Sandy Noble's use of straw demonstrates this nicely. The straw decomposes quickly and her continued applications of it do not rob the soil of nitrogen, as there is plenty of decomposing straw beneath the new, giving up nitrogen to the soil. If you do want to introduce light-coloured mulches to your garden, I recommend supplementing the nitrogen in your soil initially or restricting their use to well-established trees, shrubs and hard plants. Keep in mind that the thinner the wood shavings, the more nitrogen they can soak up, so if you've got wood shavings rather than chips, you may want to mix them with some other kind of mulch to retard this action.

RULE OF THUMB: ORGANIC VS. PERMANENT MULCHES
Many gardeners are tempted to use stone chips or gravel as a mulch. These types of permanent mulches can look nice, but I never recommend them (other than for some types of rock gardens). Stones tend to sink into the soil, so you will be fishing them out of your beds, and breaking fingernails while you do, each time you amend the soil or plant anything new. And although they suppress weeds, they don't add anything beneficial to the soil. I always say, go organic!

Adding soil amendments

Some people don't like the idea of mulching their flower beds because they think they will not be able to get at the soil to amend it after they have mulched. It is important to remember that if you are using organic mulches, they are amending your soil as they break down, so adding compost, manure and so on to your soil, while still a good idea, may be less pressing. In the spring and fall when you do amend, rake aside the mulch, add the amendment and then replace the mulch. Don't worry if you don't get all the mulch—organic mulches can be dug into the soil with the compost. In fact, if you're using an organic mulch, you can leave it in place and apply new soil or amendments such as manure to the top of the mulch every two or three years. And when you are adding a new plant to the garden, rake aside the mulch, dig the hole, amend the soil and then replace the mulch. It is a little bit more time-consuming than working in unmulched beds, but the small amount of extra effort it takes to amend your mulched beds will more than pay for itself with reduced watering and weeding.

Types of mulches

Sawdust

I don't recommend using sawdust as a mulch. Not only does it leach nitrogen initially, it tends to overheat (a fire hazard!) and looks unappealing. If you have sawdust, compost it with generous layers of leaves (five parts to one, for example).

Bark: Chunks and chips/shredded or fibre

Unless you have a woodlot or know someone who does, you will likely be purchasing this in a garden centre. That may mean an additional gardening expense, but as a mulch, bark can be very attractive, and you will probably find it well worth the few dollars. Here are a few interesting points about bark mulch:

- Bark doesn't include the heartwood of the tree.
- Bark decomposes slowly (can take up to four years to decompose, although some shredded barks may break down more quickly).
- Redwoods are rot resistant so they are not as good a source of humus as some other barks.
- Earthworms do not seem to favour redwood products.
- Pine decomposes quickly.
- Cedar (see page 195).

Chunks (2 to 8 cm/1/2 to 3 inches) and chips (4 to 6 cm/
1 1/2 to 2 1/2 inches)

- Use chunks or chips around well-established trees and shrubs.
- Chunks or chips may wash away on slopes or get moved off beds. (Be careful when mowing a lawn near beds covered in bark chunks!)
- They absorb water.
- They harbour insects.

Shredded or fibre (2 to 5 cm/3/4 to 2 inches)

❀ Shredded or fibre mulch decomposes more quickly than chunks, therefore, not as much nitrogen leaching.

❀ It knits together when dry.

❀ It creates a great erosion-resistant soil barrier.

❀ It smothers weeds effectively.

Wood chips (8 to 10 cm/3 to 4 inches)

Wood chips obtained from garden centres do not come from pressure-treated wood, but if you've collected them from a home renovation or construction site, or from a sawmill, make sure they are untreated wood, as chemicals can leach from treated wood into the soil. And remember that the thinner the wood chips or shavings, the more nitrogen they will absorb from the soil.

❀ Light-coloured chips will leach nitrogen from soil, and soft woods (pine, cedar, spruce) absorb far more nitrogen from the soil than hardwoods. *Use only under and around well-established plants, shrubs and trees.*

❀ Wood chips lose their colour faster than bark chips and may look unattractive after a while. You can top up, but make sure you aren't mulching too deeply (you may want to remove some of the old ones first).

❀ Organically dyed wood chips in shades of red, brown and even blue are now available. They can be attractive accents for the garden (although blue on the ground can be a little unnatural looking), but they have the same nitrogen consumption as the undyed wood.

❀ Wood chips will absorb water.

❀ Earthworms do not favour redwood products.

❀ If you buy wood chips (either packaged or from a sawmill) and you notice an odour of rotten eggs, ammonia or vinegar, don't use them. The chips have gone "sour" or anaerobic and are producing substances such as methanol, acetic acid and ammonia that will harm the plants (vs. aerobic decomposition). Spread the chips out and let them dry. Turn them regularly to let the air get at them before using.

Cedar mulch (6 to 10 cm/2 1/2 to 4 inches)

❋ Cedar mulch is shredded or ground cedar bark. It may contain some cedar wood chips.

❋ It has an attractive rusty red appearance.

❋ When wet, it has a lovely scent.

❋ Cedar mulch decomposes quickly, so needs to be replaced or replenished, but won't tie the nitrogen up for long.

❋ It can be expensive.

Pine needles (8 to 15 cm/3 to 6 inches)

If you have a lot of pine trees on your property or have a cottage, these won't be hard to collect!

❋ Pine needles won't wash away on slopes.

❋ They can be worked into soil if you want extra acidity, although it will take two or three years for pine needles to have a significant effect on the pH of the soil. Won't affect the pH if left on top, but can rob nitrogen as they decompose.

❋ They can be attractive and have a pleasant smell.

❋ They may control fungal diseases to a degree.

❋ Earthworms do not seem to like pine needles.

❋ Pine needles are a great mulch for rhododendrons, azaleas and boxwood.

Evergreen boughs

If you have boughs from pruning your evergreens or from your Christmas tree or Christmas decorating, don't throw them out! They can be beautiful and very useful as a winter mulch for your garden.

❋ They are most useful as a winter mulch, laid over newly planted or fragile perennials. Snow that gathers on top of the boughs will insulate your plant, and the boughs will prevent ice and snow compaction from damaging the plant.

❋ Evergreen boughs will also protect heathers, azaleas and rhododendrons from burning in the winter sun.

Cocoa hulls (4 to 5 cm/1 1/2 to 2 inches)

One of my friends recently mulched her front garden with these small, dark shells to find her garden suddenly drawing the interest of a number of neighbourhood children. One afternoon, after a light shower, an excited little boy passed her yard and announced to his mother, "See, mum, it's the chocolate lawn!"

Cocoa hulls do often give off the aroma of chocolate, especially when wet, and their dark colour is reminiscent of the candy. Some people like this and others find it a bit off-putting, but either way the odour is short-lived (it disappears in two or three weeks) and cocoa hulls make a fine organic mulch.

* Cocoa hulls are an attractive dark brown colour.

* They have a chocolaty aroma.

* They decompose quickly (over one to two seasons depending on contact with water) so add nutrients to soil and don't tie up nitrogen, but need replacing more often than some other mulches.

* Hulls are dark so they absorb heat and warm up the soil quickly.

* They retain moisture so can get slimy or develop moulds. This is unsightly but not harmful and can be disguised by turning the mouldy layer under. (I move my cocoa mulch around with a hoe or cultivator every few weeks to help minimize mould build-up.)

* They can wash away on inclines.

Coffee grounds (2.5 cm/1 inch)

While some people like to use coffee grounds as a light mulch (you may know gardeners who like to sprinkle them around their roses or rhododendrons), I feel they are best added to your compost bin. Apparently, some coffee shops will give the grounds away to interested parties for their composters or for use as mulch (some give them only to municipal composting or community garden groups).

* Coffee grounds add acidity to soil.

* Acidity discourages some soil-borne insects and fungi.

* Coffee grounds are not particularly attractive.

* They will compact and dry out (may prevent water penetration). Never apply more than 2.5-cm (1-inch) layers.

* They smell good—depending on your taste!

Compost (2 to 5 cm/3/4 to 2 inches)

While most people tend to think of compost as a soil amendment that works nicely under other mulches, partially decomposed compost can be used as a mulch itself. As it is already decomposed, its organic material will work its way into the soil, improving both the nutrient content and composition of your soil. Mulching benefits such as weed reduction and moisture retention, however, aren't really achieved with compost. (Composted manure has the same drawbacks when used as a mulch.) Given that good compost is hard to come by (backyard composters never seem to make enough) and well-rotted manure can be expensive, I recommend that you keep these for soil amendment and top-dress your beds with another sort of organic mulch.

❀ Compost adds organic matter to the soil.

Corncobs and cornstalks (4 to 6 cm/1 1/2 to 2 1/2 inches)

If you have access to corncobs or cornstalks, they make a fine mulch for your vegetable bed, but are a little unattractive for the flower bed.

❀ Corncobs and cornstalks should be ground or shredded first.

❀ They retain moisture.

❀ They are good at inhibiting weed growth.

❀ Over time, corncobs and cornstalks may heat up, so keep them away from stalks and leaves of young or tender plants. Only apply in layers no greater than 6 cm (2 1/2 inches) thick.

Grass clippings (4 to 5 cm/1 1/2 to 2 inches)

As long as your grass isn't extremely long when you cut it, grass clippings are best left *on the grass*, where their moisture returns to the soil and they decompose to help feed the yard. But if you have a lot of clippings you can use them as a mulch, as long as your lawn hasn't been treated with a herbicide in the last three months. If your grass harbours a lot of weeds, I recommend that you throw the clippings in the composter rather than risk introducing weed seeds to other parts of your garden.

❀ Grass clippings decompose quickly, so they won't last long.

❀ They can get slimy quite rapidly (let them dry out before piling them deeply around plants).

❀ They work nicely around vegetables.

❀ They may contain weed seeds.

* As they break down, grass clippings draw nitrogen from the soil.

* Apply grass clippings in a layer 4 to 5 cm (1 1/2 to 2 inches) thick. Any deeper and they may heat up.

Straw (15 to 20 cm/6 to 8 inches)

While straw is ideal for the vegetable garden, I find it unattractive on flower beds. It is inexpensive, however, so you may want to use it in the flower garden and camouflage it with a couple of centimetres (an inch) of more attractive mulch spread on top. Also, make sure that your straw is seed free before using.

* Straw will draw nitrogen from soil during decomposition.

* It's inexpensive.

* Straw is wonderful for vegetable beds—it keeps leaves dry and away from damp soil.

* It's good under fruit trees and shrubs.

* It can be a fire hazard.

* Straw may contain weed seeds.

* It's my favourite mulch for tomatoes, peppers and potatoes.

* It's the best mulch for strawberries (which is how they got their name!).

Leaves (10 to 15 cm/4 to 6 inches)

Many garden experts decry the common habit of raking leaves and then bagging them for the garbage. Personally, I rather like it when my neighbours do this. In the autumn evenings, I can often be spotting skulking back from my neighbours' sidewalks, bags of freshly collected leaves in my arms. Leaves may mat and become soggy, reducing air and water circulation, so they work better if chopped or shredded if you are using them for spring mulch. You can also use dry whole leaves for a winter mulch, but in rainy weather remove them if they become matted. You can also mix them with other mulches to improve the consistency. Many people swear by oak leaves (which they keep separate) as a bug-inhibiting mulch. Grubs, cutworms and slugs are repelled by the bitterness of the oak leaves.

* Leaves are inexpensive and readily available.

* They provide NPK as well as boron, cobalt and magnesium.

* If not shredded, leaves may become matted.

Leaf mould (6 to 8 cm/2 1/2 to 3 inches)

Leaf mould is produced when leaves have rotted to the point that they no longer look like leaves (only the veins are left). It is an excellent source of humus that adds nutrients to the soil quickly.

* It takes six months to a year for leaves to rot and turn into leaf mould that can be used as mulch.

* Leaf mould may harbour insects.

* It is a very good weed suppressor.

* Spread it on topsoil and work in as an amendment at the end of the season.

* Leaf mould fosters the propagation of earthworms.

Newsprint (2 to 4 cm/3/4 to 1 1/2 inches unshredded/ 4 to 8 cm/1 1/2 to 3 inches shredded)

Newsprint and newspaper are often used on vegetable beds, but they can also be used on flower beds and top-dressed with other organic mulch. You can shred the paper or tear it into strips or lay it in sheets (particularly with vegetable beds; with sheets, be sure to moisten the newspaper before laying it down, or water it thoroughly afterward). Make sure you wet both the soil before laying newsprint and the newsprint itself after applying or it may blow away.

* Newsprint is inexpensive and readily available.

* It's rather unattractive if not covered with other mulch.

* All newspapers now use vegetable dye inks, so they are safe for use in the garden.

Paper pulp

It is unlikely that you will find a source for it, but if you do, paper pulp can be used as a mulch. You may have noticed that some garden products on the market use pulp already. For example, Weall & Cullen sells a lawn "repair" product that is a mix of paper pulp, grass seeds and nutrients. The pulp is a handy vehicle in which to dispense the other ingredients, and it acts as a lightweight mulch—it keeps the seeds from blowing away or being eaten by birds, it keeps them moist

RULE OF THUMB
There are a number of easy ways to chop leaves for mulch. You can run them through a shredder, if you have such a thing, or you can run over a pile with a lawn mower. If you have a power mower with a leaf catcher, this task is much easier, as the shredded leaves are collected in the catcher as you go. Make sure that your mower is set at its highest setting, and keep in mind that dry leaves shred most easily. You can also fill up a large garbage can two-thirds full of leaves and then use a power weed trimmer to shred the leaves in the can (but wear safety or sunglasses to protect your eyes from any leaves that fly upward). And if your leaves are very dry, you can fill a large plastic bag quite loosely and then stomp or walk on the bag until the leaves are crushed (this last method does not always give uniform results).

(once it has been watered) and it protects them from the sun until they germinate. It then decomposes and adds organic matter to the soil.

❋ Paper pulp does not rob the soil of nitrogen.

❋ It decomposes quickly.

❋ It's inexpensive and readily available.

Peat moss

Peat moss is not an ideal mulch because it is so dry and extremely absorbent (it acts like a sponge and doesn't allow water to penetrate). Conversely, if it crusts over on top, it may absorb very little water and allow even less to penetrate the soil. It can, however, be mixed with sawdust, wood chips and soil to serve as a mulch. It must be moistened before using.

❋ Peat moss is acidic—it is useful for acid-loving plants when mixed equally with pine needles.

Green mulches

Green mulches, also known as green manure, are often used in vegetable gardening. They are cover crops such as ryegrass, winter barley or white clover that are sown after the harvest is finished and allowed to stay in the ground over the winter. They act like a green coat for the soil, preventing erosion from water and wind, and suppressing weed growth. In the spring they are ploughed under, giving the soil a boost of nitrogen (legumes are especially good for nitrogen fixing in the soil, even before they are dug under) and other nutrients.

Living mulches or groundcovers as mulches

While not generally listed under mulches in most books, groundcovers do serve many of the same mulching functions. They keep soil covered to prevent soil erosion, moisture loss and weeds. They generally, however, don't provide much insulation, and of course, while they certainly look attractive under trees and shrubs, you don't want them competing with less hardy perennials. Some groundcovers don't like to be walked on, so may not be appropriate as a "mulch."

Geotextiles

Geotextiles are new gardening tools made of synthetic fibres. Landscape fabric is one of the most popular and useful new materials, but there are also devices like polypropylene, polyester and plastic composite mats that can be used at the base of shrubs and trees as a mulching material.

* Landscape fabric is spun polyester that allows water to penetrate soil and air to get to soil.

* Landscape fabric and other geotextiles block light that weed seeds need to germinate and grow.

* Polyester landscape fabric lasts over five years under soil.

* Geotextiles can prevent soil erosion, especially on slopes.

* Landscape fabric can be top-dressed with 0.5 to 1 cm (1/8 to 3/8 inch) of other mulch, making it more attractive and preventing the fabric from breaking down in the sunlight.

* Landscape fabric can be difficult to move to make soil amendments or for annual or vegetable planting, so you may want to use it only around "permanent" plants, such as trees or shrubs, that will not be moved around much and where you will not be amending the soil on a regular basis.

* Plastic and recycled rubber composite mats are generally small and easy to remove.

Clay chunks

These red clay chunks can be quite pretty around the base of trees and shrubs and along pathways. They can be expensive, but as you will not be replacing them regularly, they can be cost effective. If, however, you decide to remove them, they can be hard to get rid of, as they seem to be able to travel great distances!

* Clay chunks do not break down, and therefore do not need replacing on regular basis.

* They can work their way into the soil, and will be hard on hands, if you are digging. Use where you will not be tilling or digging in the soil—for example, around established trees and shrubs.

* Weeds can grow between stones, *unless you use landscape fabric underneath them.*

* Clay chunks will not be blown around and are less likely to be washed away in heavy rain than some other mulches, but can travel onto lawns and so on. Check surrounding grass carefully before mowing.

Stone chips

Like clay chunks, these can be very attractive around shrubs and trees, or interspersed between paving stones and so on, but they have some of the same drawbacks.

* Stone chips do not break down and can work their way into the soil, where they will be hard on hands when digging. Use where you will not be tilling or digging in the soil, for example, around established shrubs and trees.

* Weeds can grow between stones, unless you use landscape fabric underneath them.

* Limestone chips will raise the pH of the soil, so avoid using them around acid-loving plants; most other stone will not leach or change soil chemistry.

* Stone absorbs heat and will heat up ground underneath.

* Stone chips will not be blown around and are less likely to be washed away in heavy rain than some other mulches, but can travel onto lawns and so on. Check surrounding grass carefully before mowing.

* They can be expensive initially, but do not need replenishing like organic mulch, so may be economical in the long run.

Black plastic

While not particularly attractive, black plastic can be very useful as a vegetable garden mulch. Prepare the soil and lay sheets of plastic over the rows, anchoring at the edges (you can use soil or rocks). Make X-shaped slits where you want to plant the seedlings. Alternatively, you can lay strips of plastic between the rows.

* Black plastic will heat up the soil. Use it for heat-loving vegetables such as tomatoes, peppers, cucumbers, squash, corn, eggplant.

* Because it blocks the sun, weed seeds in the soil cannot germinate.

* Plastic prevents air-borne seeds from taking root.

* It prevents evaporation.

* Water will not penetrate unless plastic is slit or punctured.

* It will inhibit air circulation—check plants for crown rot or damping off.

* Plastic usually lasts only one season.

Clear plastic

Clear plastic can be used in the same way as black plastic. Since it allows the sun to penetrate, however, it can warm up the soil faster, at least initially, giving plants an early start. It is therefore especially useful in northern climates.

❋ Clear plastic warms up the soil.

❋ It prevents evaporation.

❋ Water will not penetrate unless plastic is slit or punctured.

❋ It will inhibit air circulation—check plants for crown rot or damping off.

❋ Plastic usually lasts only one season.

❋ Weeds can grow under it if weather is mild (in very hot weather, however, weeds under clear plastic will be killed by the excessive heat).

Applying mulches

Winter mulch

❋ Apply winter mulch after the first hard frost—if applied too early it keeps the ground warm and doesn't allow plants to go into necessary dormancy; especially useful around woody plants whose stiff roots may get heaved out of the ground with freeze-thaw action.

❋ Snow can act as a winter mulch. Shovel dry snow (making sure it hasn't been contaminated with road salt) onto your flower beds. It will insulate the beds to prevent freeze-thaw and winter kill.

Summer mulch

Apply summer mulches after soil has warmed (in most of Ontario, this is early to mid-June).

❋ Before mulching, weed thoroughly (seeds already in the soil can push up through mulch); water soil if it is dry.

❋ Use recommended depth of mulch (see above). Too little mulch will not inhibit weeds or prevent evaporation as effectively. Too much mulch can prevent water from getting through and can prevent air circulation. Mulch that is too deep can also smother tiny seedlings.

RULE OF THUMB
Should you be worried that using something like pine needles will make your soil more acidic than you want it? Not really. It does not appear that acidic material that lies on the surface of your soil greatly changes the chemistry in the soil itself. As a matter of fact, if you want to use things like coffee grounds or pine needles to make your soil slightly more acidic, you really need to work these well into the top 4 to 6 cm (1 1/2 to 2 1/2 inches) of the soil on a regular basis to effect much change (you may not see much change for several years).

- Lay organic mulch approximately 15 cm (6 inches) back from the trunks of trees to prevent nesting rodents or insects that may lead to bark or disease damage.

- The following spring, use a rake or fine hoe to rake (with care) the mulch off the top of the beds. Add more organic matter. Put mulch back and dress with new mulch. Alternatively, you can add new soil, compost or manure on top of the organic mulch every two to three years and top with a fresh layer of organic mulch.

Mulching around fruits and vegetables

Laying a thick layer of mulch around the base of fruit trees will prevent fruit that falls to the ground from getting bruised.

- Mulch between rows after planting vegetable seeds. Once the young plants are growing well, move the mulch around the plants themselves.

When mulching vegetable beds, spread mulch between rows of new seedlings. Once the plants begin to grow, move the mulch around each of them.

Mark's 100 Favourite Plants for Ontario

Choosing *only* 100 plants to recommend was a daunting task—there are so many classic favourites and exciting new cultivars out there. So let me explain how and why I chose the plants I did.

Perennials will, of course, be the backbone of any garden. And there is a reason why herbaceous perennials are growing in popularity faster than any other category of plants. They are generally winter hardy, coming back each spring like old friends. They flower for extended periods of time (at least, most of the perennials on this list do!). Many can be cut and brought indoors for bouquets, fragrance and colour. Others are extremely attractive to butterflies and hummingbirds. As they go to seed, all fall-flowering perennials attract migrating and overwintering birds.

Perhaps the attraction of perennials is that, above all else, there are so many of them. In fact, you could devote your entire gardening career to the study of perennials and still have a few books to read on the subject.

In recent years **roses** in the garden (as opposed to the cut roses you pick up at the florist) have been given short shrift. In our new-found enthusiasm for perennials, roses seem to be falling out of favour to some degree. I believe this is so for the following reasons:

* Roses are perceived to be high maintenance: insect and disease prone and in need of winterizing.

* Roses are perceived to be less colourful than perennials, only blooming well in the early summer.

* Roses are perceived to lack fragrance.

The list of my favourite rose varieties is put together in an attempt to dispel these myths. While there are roses that are prone to all of the above, there are other roses that meet the demands of the highest standards and are not a lot of work (although all roses require a minimum of six hours of sunshine each day and thrive in rich, well-drained soil). I give you an honest and frank assessment of each variety—I hope I can entice you into the rose garden.

While Ontario loves its perennials, we can't forget about the advantages of **annuals**. After surviving our famous Ontario winters, our hearts, minds and souls are starving for something colourful. Come spring there is one sure-fire way to introduce *instant* colour and that is by planting annual flowering bedding plants—in your garden beds, patio pots, hanging baskets, window boxes. Here is your chance to go crazy, treating every corner of your yard as a canvas just waiting for another brilliant brush stroke of annual flowering colour.

"Annuals" bloom for long periods of time, many from planting time (or shortly thereafter) through early fall. It is this reputation for nonstop garden and container performance that gives them the reputation they so rightly deserve.

Not all annual flowering plants perform equally well, however, so I have compiled this list of my favourites based on garden performance. Some are old favourites that cannot be beaten; others are recent introductions that deserve a spot in your garden. Just keep in mind that all annuals, by their very nature, are hungry. Flowering for the whole summer takes a lot of energy. For this reason I recommend that all annuals be fed water-soluble 20-20-20 every ten days to two weeks from the time of planting through early fall. If you have annuals in containers, the regular application of 20-20-20 is even more critical (the limited amount of space at the root zone increases the need for fertilizer).

Proper soil preparation is also important for satisfactory results (a common theme in all of my books when I write about planting virtually anything—however, this is even more important with annuals). Heavy clay soils should be dug out and removed to 30 to 40 cm (12 to 16 inches) deep and replaced with good-quality triple mix or pure compost. Marginally acceptable soil should be amended generously with well-composted cattle manure or finished compost.

How much compost is enough? There is literally no such thing as too much. So an application of 10 to 15 cm (4 to 6 inches) of compost spread over reasonably good soil and turned in with a garden fork or rototiller would go a long way in helping you to create the garden of your dreams. Take time to study pp. 136–137, where I discuss soil preparation, before you get started on your annual flower garden.

A couple more tips that will help you grow good-looking annual flowers: when flowers finish, cut them off. This is called deadheading or pinching back and will encourage lots of late-season colour. Self-sowing annuals can be a joy and curse. I planted portulaca in my front bed one year and pulled the young seedlings out from between my patio stones for two years afterward. Certain annual plants (such as amaranthus, allysum, nicotiana and datura) are famous for this. That doesn't mean you shouldn't grow them, but you should be aware that they have this aggressive habit of reproduction.

I know that many readers will not have time for annuals. Some people believe that annuals aren't worth the time and expense because they die with the frost. I believe that experienced and novice gardeners alike can benefit greatly from an eyeful of colour any time. That the colour happens to come from a plant that finishes its life cycle in one year shouldn't diminish its worth.

My "100 favourites" list wouldn't be complete without several **flowering shrubs**—the strong, woody-stemmed plants in your garden that provide the "bones" to any landscape design. Not only will these more or less permanent features provide height, a backdrop and reliable repeat performance year after year, but they also supply colour at different times of the year.

Choose your flowering shrubs with an eye to their flowering times (and colour, of course), their winter hardiness and above all, their ultimate size (how many times have I met people who have made regrettable decisions in this regard?). Mix shrubs up with your perennials and roses; interplant them with annual flowers and you will be impressed with the character your garden takes—character of a permanent nature! And with some good planning, you'll attract birds and butterflies to your garden as well.

And, finally, **trees**. "A house is a house; a well-treed house is a home." You can quote me any time on this one. When my wife, Mary, and I saw the house we are currently living in (and have been for 14 years), we were taken by the mature trees on the property—towering red oaks over 25 m (80 feet) tall and clusters of native sugar maples in both the front and backyard. In total, 15 beautiful trees on a 20-m (75-foot) lot. We knew that with a little love this house would make a wonderful home.

This story embodies my feelings about trees. Thoughtfully chosen, well placed and nurtured through the first few years as they get established, the trees on your property are not just additions to your landscape, they are—to a great degree—your legacy.

I hope that in the following list you find many choices that become your favourites too!

Key to symbols

☀ full sun   💧 moist soil   **1** zone number

🌤 partial sun   💧 average soil

🌳 shade   💧 dry (well-drained) soil

💧 any soil condition

Perennials

Adiantum pedatum (Maidenhair Fern)

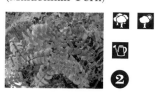

Have you noticed how ferns just "pop up" on the floor of the forest when a tree either falls down or is cut down? That tells you two important things: (a) ferns *do* love some sun (in spite of their reputation for loving the shade) and (b) they are survivors. My favourite of all winter-hardy ferns is maidenhair. It prefers good air circulation and a well-drained humusy soil and thrives all the way up to zone 2. Maidenhair fern features shiny black stems with delicate fan-shaped fronds. It has a soft, lacy appearance.
Height/spread: 30 to 60 cm (12 to 24 inches).

Agastache foeniculum 'Blue Fortune' (Anise hyssop 'Blue Fortune')

I grow this aggressive bloomer at my front door. It provides an excellent greeting to all who visit from mid-July through September. I like A. 'Blue Fortune' for its non-stop blooming and its attraction to butterflies. I might add that honeybees also like this perennial. It thrives in the sun and performs well in rich, well-drained soil.
Height/spread: 90 cm/70 cm (3 feet/28 inches).

Anemone tomentosa 'Robustissima' (Grapeleaf Anemone 'Robustissima')

This is another favourite perennial of mine for its long flowering time. A. 'Robustissima' is a highlight in the late summer and fall garden. These vigorous and hardy plants stand out in the Anemone family for their winter hardiness and their perpetual improvement from year to year. Flowers are held above the foliage on 90-cm (36-inch) stems. This plant thrives in the sun, though it's tolerant of partial shade.
Height/spread: 90 cm/120 cm (3 feet/4 feet).

Artemisia stellerana 'Silver Brocade' (Wormwood, Silver Sage 'Silver Brocade')

The addition of this plant to your garden will provide excellent permanent colour with its aromatic silver-white foliage. It's a compact plant that is well suited for containers and will remain evergreen up to zone 4. Otherwise A. 'Silver Brocade' is winter hardy to zone 2. Flowers are small and light yellow—primarily I recommend this plant for its soft fragrance and "get along with anything" silver colour. It produces a low mounding plant and blooms from August to September. Be sure to cut plants back in early spring to encourage new growth each season.
Height/spread: 15 cm/30 cm (6 inches/12 inches).

Asclepias tuberosa (Butterfly Flower)

In recent years water restrictions have been imposed during the heat of summer in our neighbourhood. This plant provides an excellent opportunity to live with a limited water supply (listen carefully, property owners in the country!) and to create a low-maintenance garden. A. tuberosa is a native plant with tremendous insect resistance, in my experience. It should be noted, however, that this is the natural food source for the monarch butterfly. With a long six-week blooming period from midsummer to early fall and attractive seed pods in the fall, this sun-lover has wide appeal.
Height/spread: 60 to 90 cm/60 cm (2 to 3 feet/2 feet).

Astilbe 'White Wings' (Astilbe 'White Wings')

If you love to cut garden flowers to bring inside, you'll love astilbe. Not only will the flowers last an extraordinary two to three weeks when cut, they also provide a wonderful show while on the plant. 'White Wings' is a compact variety that I have enjoyed in my own garden. Planted at the forefront of the perennial border, 'White Wings' is mildly fragrant; when not blooming, the fern-like foliage provides a cool addition to the garden (as all astilbes do!). All astilbes require regular watering. 'White Wings' blooms in early summer.
Height/spread: 20 cm/30 cm (8 inches/12 inches).

Astilbe × arendsii 'Flamingo' (Astilbe 'Flamingo')

I have really enjoyed putting together my astilbe collection over the last few years. A. 'Flamingo' tops my list of new favourites for its long blooming period (June through early August—unless it gets really hot, then it finishes blooming earlier). A. 'Flamingo' is a great container plant too. With pure pink plumes of fragrant flowers standing 120 cm (4 feet) tall, this astilbe will be a winner in many Ontario gardens for a long time.
Height/spread: 120 cm/60cm (4 feet/2 feet).

Athyrium niponicum 'Pictum' (Japanese Painted Fern 'Pictum')

The best-looking Japanese painted ferns I have seen have been located near water. Which is not to say that you can't plant them in the garden bed; you most certainly can! The contrasting metallic grey-green foliage is what I think makes this fern outstanding. It performs best in moist, humus-rich soil. While it is a very winter-hardy plant, I find that it performs best come spring when it has been mulched with 10 cm (4 inches) of fallen leaves in the autumn.
Height/spread: 30 to 60 cm/30 cm (12 to 24 inches/12 inches).

Campanula glomerata 'Superba' (Clustered Bellflower 'Superba')

I love *C.* 'Superba' mainly because it can be used in such a wide variety of settings. This is a versatile plant that looks great in a meadow setting, in the foreground of the perennial border or located on the outside margins of a garden pond. It's characterized by large, rich, violet-purple flowers grown in large clumps. It's an early summer–blooming perennial that grows best in partial shade with even soil moisture. In full sun, leaves may tend to scorch. It blooms from early June through July. Cut the first blossoms down when finished to encourage new ones.
Height/spread: 45 to 60 cm/ 45 to 60 cm (18 to 24 inches/ 18 to 24 inches).

Carex comans 'Frosty Curls' (Sedge 'Frosty Curls')

I like to use *C.* 'Frosty Curls' in containers in the back of our house, where we receive partial sunshine. Carex is a great plant for any sunny or partially sunny location where a touch of "exotic" is desired. This sedge variety has fine-textured arching foliage and olive-green leaves. Remove dead foliage in the spring to encourage new growth.
Height/spread: 20 to 30 cm (8 to 12 inches)/slightly wider than tall.

Ceratostigma plumbaginoides (Blue Leadwort, Plumbago)

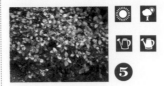

This is a slow starter in the spring but I think it is worth the wait. *C. plumbaginoides* is a great perennial for late summer and early fall colour, with its bright blue flowers and glossy green foliage. Plant plumbago in full sun for best performance. This unusual but useful ground-cover grows well in moist locations (but not overly wet ones!). It likes to be dry for the winter.
Height/spread: 20 to 30 cm/45 cm (8 to 12 inches/18 inches).

Chasmanthium latifolium (Northern Sea Oats)

I recommend this plant to anyone who wants the exotic look of ornamental grass and a low-maintenance garden. Northern sea oats is a prolific native grass that is especially suited to lightly shaded locations. The plants produce narrow leaves followed by panicles of tiny silver flowers that mature into spikelets. These interesting flower heads look like a school of small fish when caught in a gentle breeze. Northern sea oats prefers a rich, moist soil when planted in sunny spots. Prune dead foliage in the spring.
Height/spread: 75 to 90 cm/40 cm (30 to 36 inches/16 inches).

Cimicifuga ramosa 'Brunette' (Bugbane 'Brunette')

This plant is one of the highlights in my perennial border each summer. While it produces beautiful flowers slowly, just watching them develop is a lot of fun. And the deep purple, lacy foliage is an attention-getter without the flowers. Spikes of tall

fragrant pale pink flowers rise above the foliage in late summer and early fall. *C.* 'Brunette' prefers rich moist soil (as all cimicifugas do) and a partially sunny location. Once established, do not disturb the clump. Mulch around the base of the plant with pine needles or oak leaves to maintain a lower soil pH.
Height/spread: 1.5 m/2 m (5 feet/6 feet).

Coreopsis verticillata 'Moonbeam' (Threadleaf Coreopsis 'Moonbeam')

This plant was named Perennial of the Year a few years back, and for good reason. It lends itself to any sunny position in the garden where a splash of yellow is needed to "light it up." *C.* 'Moonbeam' is one of my favourites for its long blooming time, often bursting into bloom in late June and continuing to bloom well into early fall. This hardy plant tolerates winters up to zone 3. It can be late to produce new growth in the spring and may last in the garden for several years but suddenly not show up for its usual springtime performance one year, without apparent cause. Oh well, it's worth it for the colour it provides in the meantime. Prune off the first flush of finished blooms to encourage fall blossoms.
Height/spread: 30 cm/45 cm (12 inches/18 inches).

Corydalis flexuosa 'China Blue' (Fumewort 'China Blue')

I am seeing more and more of this plant in Ontario gardens and no wonder. Few "blue" flowering plants provide so much colour for such a long season (May through October). With fern-like leaves *C.* 'China Blue' lends itself nicely to the partial shade garden. Bright, hot sun will bleach out the colour of the flowers and cause the foliage to dry up prematurely. 'China Blue' performs best in a

rich, moist, well-drained soil. Mix horticultural lime into the soil in spring to enhance plant performance.
Height/spread: 20 to 30 cm/30 cm (8 to 12 inches/12 inches).

Dicentra formosa 'Luxurient' (Fern-leaf Bleeding Heart 'Luxurient')

I have lots of favourite plants, but this bleeding heart topped my list about 15 years ago and has remained there ever since. You just cannot beat *D*. 'Luxurient' for a long season of colour. 'Luxurient' offers red, heart-shaped blooms arranged on arching stems from June through September, in a semi-sunny location. The lacy, fernlike foliage adds a soft "fern dell" look to the woodland garden or perennial border. Plant in well-drained soil. If foliage turns yellow, add garden sulphur to acidify the soil and feel free to cut back to the ground in mid to late summer. Divide plants every three years to maintain vigour.
Height/spread: 30 cm/30 cm (12 inches/12 inches).

Echinacea purpurea 'Magnus' (Purple Coneflower 'Magnus')

(only this variety isn't purple— go figure!)

Another favourite perennial among the low-maintenance gardening set (you know, the people who would rather golf or sail). In fact, *E*. 'Magnus' will *stop* blooming if you fertilize it. It also does not need water, once established in the garden. Carmine-red flowers stand over a metre (yard) high above the foliage, which changes to a dramatic orange-red-yellow in fall. It's very hardy and long lived, blooms from July through September and is somewhat aggressive when grown in "ideal" conditions.
Height/spread: 120 cm/45 to 60 cm (4 feet/18 to 24 inches).

Echinacea purpurea 'Rubinstern' (Purple Coneflower 'Rubinstern')

Classified as a native plant in many publications, this cultivar is actually a hybrid of the original *Echinacea*, with the most outstanding crimson red flowers you will find on any member of the family. Blooming in midsummer, this is one tough customer that loves the sun, produces masses of blossoms in its second year and well beyond. It's one of the most powerful butterfly magnets that you can plant in the Ontario garden!
Height/spread: 50 cm/100 cm (20 inches/40 inches).

Eupatorium rugosum 'Chocolate' (Boneset, White Snakeroot 'Chocolate')

The parent of this plant (Joe Pye weed) is a native plant that was pretty much ignored by Ontario gardeners, that is until the British "discovered" it. It is now grown everywhere. I prefer *E*. 'Chocolate' to any of the eupatoriums. It features unusual bronze-purple foliage and pure white flowers from August through September. Stems are deep purple in colour, contrasting with the white umbel flowers. Plants do well in full sun and well-drained soil. They prefer cool night temperatures and are shade tolerant to a point. Too much shade will make them "stretch."
Height/spread: 90 to 120 cm/ 75 cm (3 to 4 feet/30 inches).

Gaura lindheimeri 'Siskiyou Pink' (Gaura 'Siskiyou Pink')

This aggressive bloomer is actually known to sometimes bloom itself to death (the only other plant I know of that does this is *Scabiosa* 'Butterfly Blue'). You can fix this by pruning the finished flowers off in late October. *G*. 'Siskiyou Pink' is a selection from a native plant of North America, providing blooms from June through September. Gaura require full sun to partial shade and rich, well-drained soil. In waterlogged soil, these plants will not survive. My gaura performs very well in a west-facing exposure. Mulch plants in zones 5 and 6 to ensure winter hardiness.
Height/spread: 90 to 120 cm/60 to 90 cm (3 to 4 feet/2 to 3 feet).

Hemerocallis (Daylily)

When I suggested to my wife, Mary, that we make five separate plantings of daylilies at the front of our house a couple of years ago, she was skeptical. Wouldn't it look messy? Today I think even she agrees that the summer colour is excellent (not bad, when I consider that the best design ideas for our garden are hers originally). Daylilies are reliable *perennial* plants that do come back and improve from year to year. When they grow together, you always have the option of dividing them and giving the root divisions to friends. In the meantime, very few plants in the Ontario garden provide so much low-maintenance colour for such an extended period of time. But the "extended" blooming season occurs only when you plant carefully selected varieties. There are many "old" daylily varieties that bloom for a couple of weeks and then disappear until the following season. These new ones, however, bloom for up to six weeks. All hemerocallis prefer bright sunshine and tolerate most soil conditions (except excessively wet). I like these four varieties above all:

'Happy Returns'
Gorgeous canary-yellow blossoms with an excellent growth habit. One of the few fragrant hemerocallis that blooms throughout the growing season (May to frost). Very heat-tolerant and adapts well to almost any landscape and a wide variety of soil conditions.
Height/spread: 40 cm/40 cm (16 inches/16 inches).

'Hyperion'

Fragrance is the main attraction of 'Hyperion'. It also has beautiful lemon-yellow flowers and blooms in July.
Height/spread: 100 cm/60 to 90 cm (40 inches/2 to 3 feet).

'Siloam Red Ruby'

This is a mid-season bloomer (July to heavy frost) with small rosy-red flowers outlining a green throat. The plant is short with vigorous foliage and short scapes. This Hemerocallis is a repeat bloomer with the flowers remaining open for at least 16 hours (which is unusual for daylilies!).
Height/spread: 40 cm/60 to 90 cm (16 inches/2 to 3 feet).

'Strawberry Candy'

If you could only see this gorgeous plant in full bloom when planted en masse on a sunny slope you would realize why hardy daylilies are booming in popularity. Not only is this plant hardy all the way to zone 2, it also offers the unusual bonus of a strawberry-pink flower with a rose-red eye and a golden throat that blooms repeatedly throughout the summer. Try it!
Height/spread: 60 cm/30 cm (2 feet/1 foot)

Heuchera × 'Amber Waves' (Coral Bells 'Amber Waves')

I fell in love with coral bells when my brother Peter introduced them to me at Cullen Gardens in Whitby, Ontario. Planted en masse, they just had to impress anyone passing by, but using them in my own garden, I have realized that they look great on their own. Tolerant of partial shade and great performers in full sun, coral bells are versatile. What I like about 'Amber Waves' is the unusual gold ruffled foliage that outshines the light-coloured flowers that appear in profusion in early summer. Great cut flowers too!
Height/spread: 30 cm/30 cm (12 inches/12 inches).

Hosta (Funkia, Plantain Lily)

Confession time: Hostas are one of my favourite perennial plants. Here's why: they love partial shade, but grow equally well in morning sun. They thrive in cool moisture, but don't seem to suffer through a drought. They flower; some are fragrant, others long-lasting. All attract hummingbirds and butterflies. The foliage is widely varied in appearance, so you can have a lot of them, without repeating a theme to death. And they are cool. Although filtered sun produces the best foliage colour, the greener-leafed varieties will do well in full shade and the yellower-leafed relatives in almost full sun. There is as much variance in the leaf colour as there is in the height and spread of the hosta, but all require the same TLC. Mulching with fine bark mulch will help to keep weeds to a minimum; eggshells, wood ashes and slug bait keep the slimy slugs at bay. All hostas need a drink of fertilizer now and again. Some of my favourites are the following:

Hosta 'Fragrant Bouquet'

This colourful beauty has a large bright chartreuse centre with a broad irregular band of creamy white encircling the margin of the heart-shaped leaf. The pale lilac, sweetly fragrant flowers appear in late summer and are held high above the leaves for everyone's enjoyment. 'Fragrant Bouquet' quickly forms large clumps to fill in that vacant spot in sun or part shade. As the name suggests, this hosta is very fragrant. It blooms in mid to late summer.
Height/spread: 45 cm/65 cm (18 inches/26 inches).

Hosta 'Grand Tiara'

'Grand Tiara' has golden heart-shaped leaves with a small streak of green in the centre. The tall purple flowers are a great colour addition in midsummer to this fast-growing, clump-forming hosta.
Height/spread: 35 cm/30 cm (14 inches/12 inches).

Hosta 'June'

A fantastic combination of chartreuse heart-shaped leaves with green and blue-green variegated edges. Give 'June' the spring sun to help produce this great colour combination and then more shade in the summer. *H.* 'June' reaches maturity slowly and is great for a front or mid-border location. Summer brings lavender-grey flowers for an added dash of colour. It blooms in early summer.
Height/spread: 40 cm/60 cm (16 inches/24 inches).

Hosta 'Minuteman'

'Minuteman' produces foliage that has a fresh crisp white margin around a rich green centre. This vigorous, clump-forming hosta displays a lavender, funnel-shaped flower on a leafy spike for all to see in midsummer. Growing best in partial shade and a slightly drier soil, 'Minuteman' is sure to become a favourite in the shady garden.
Height/spread: 90 cm/60 cm (3 feet/2 feet).

Iris ensata 'Variegata' (Japanese Iris 'Variegata')

This iris loves to be near water and adds colour early in the summer when most other plants are not quite ready to bloom or (as is the case of German or bearded iris) have finished their show for the season. *Iris ensata* prefers an acidic soil and can be grown in a container. Variegated Japanese iris is more prized for its outstanding 90 cm (3 foot) green and creamy yellow striped foliage than its violet-purple flower, which appears in early summer. Japanese irises have a thick, fleshy root called a rhizome that requires drier conditions once it has finished blooming to help prepare for next year's bloom. These rhizomes should be divided every three to four years and replanted just below the surface of the soil. The iris has a long history: King Louis VII adopted the flower as his Fleur-de-Louis, now known as fleur-de-lis, the official floral emblem of Quebec.
Height/spread: 90 cm/60 cm (3 feet/2 feet).

Lamium maculatum 'Pink Pewter' (Henbit 'Pink Pewter')

I love the performance of this favourite in my shade garden. The colour seems to stand out especially on dark or overcast days. 'Pink Pewter' makes a great groundcover in partial shade. It prefers a moist but well-drained, rich, high-humus soil. The silvery leaves are edged in a greenish-grey, providing a nice backdrop for the clear pink flowers. 'Pink Pewter' can be sheared lightly to encourage its spread and to help keep it compact. Divide it in spring or fall to quickly fill in areas under shrubs or in dark corners; it also combines nicely with spring-flowering bulbs. It blooms midsummer.
Height/spread: 15 to 30 cm/60 cm (6 to 12 inches/2 feet).

Lavandula 'Hidcote Blue' (Lavender 'Hidcote Blue')

One of my favourite journeys in the garden is the one that takes me past the lavender. Every time I brush past it I get a waft of that gorgeous, restful scent. Actually low-growing, woody shrubs, most lavenders are slightly drought tolerant when established. Lavenders find a home in mixed borders, cutting gardens, herb gardens and anywhere the sweet fragrance is appreciated. 'Hidcote Blue', a wonderful old favourite, has long-lasting, rich, purple-blue flower spikes in summer. It prefers a well-drained, average to humus-rich soil in full sun. Shearing lightly in the spring and after flowering will help to maintain a compact growth habit. The flowers dry well and have many uses such as sachet and potpourri. Lavenders make a great semi-formal hedge, especially bordering a rose garden! The lavender-blue flowers bloom in midsummer.

Height/spread: 30 to 40 cm/60 cm (12 to 16 inches/24 inches).

Leucanthemum × superbum 'Becky' (Shasta Daisy 'Becky')

'Becky' shasta daisy is tall, sleek and refreshingly clean. It has large, clear white flowers and glossy green leaves. This reliable winter-hardy perennial likes to be grown in average, well-drained soil in full sun. A welcome addition to any border, it blooms for several weeks in the summer, especially with some deadheading. Give this clump-forming perennial beauty good winter drainage and you'll have a winner for many years. 'Becky' can be divided every three to four years to spread its charm to friends and neighbours.
Height/spread: 90 cm/45 cm (3 feet/18 inches).

Ligularia dentata 'Othello' (Golden-Ray, Golden Groundsel 'Othello')

Ligularia grows in full sun or part shade and needs a rich, moist soil to be at its best. The large round green leaves have a purple underside for a contrast of colours. Golden-yellow spikes of daisy-like flowers are held high above the colourful leaves, painting an unforgettable picture. Give 'Othello' a place of importance in your border or near the water's edge, keeping it away from underneath trees where it must compete for water. During times of extreme heat or drought, 'Othello' will pout, but don't worry—given some water or cooler temperatures it will bounce back nicely. Dividing this long-lived, clump-forming wonder is rarely necessary. It blooms in late summer to early fall.
Height/spread: 90 to 120 cm/75 to 90 cm (3 to 4 feet/30 to 36 inches).

Monarda didyma 'Petite Delight' (Bee Balm, Oswego Tea 'Petite Delight')

'Petite Delight' bee balm is a relative of the famous mint and retains some of mint's qualities, including a faint scent in the green leaves. As its name implies, 'Petite Delight' is great for the front of a border or in pots, growing only 25 to 30 cm (10 to 12 inches) high, with clear, lavender-pink flowers in the summer. It likes to grow in a rich, moist but well-drained soil in full sun, but will also tolerate some shade. Bee balms are fast, vigorous plants forming large colonies that sometimes die out in the centre. Divide every few years, planting only the youngest and healthiest plants. Powdery mildew is sometimes a problem for bee balm, but 'Petite Delight' shows great resistance to this fungus. A wonderful plant for attracting hummingbirds and bees (an important reason for it to be one of my favourites!).
Height/spread: 25 to 30 cm/ 25 to 30 cm (10 to 12 inches/ 10 to 12 inches).

Monarda didyma 'Raspberry Wine' (Bee Balm 'Raspberry Wine')

'Raspberry Wine' bee balm is a plant that every border should have, with its strong square stems and aromatic green leaves, not to mention the elegant red-wine flowers. This bee balm prefers a rich, moist but well-drained soil in full sun or partial shade. Its bloom time is early to midsummer. This vigorous plant should be divided in the spring every few years, replanting only the youngest to keep the centres from dying out. Cut 'Raspberry Wine' back to the ground each fall and discard the foliage to help keep this winter-tolerant plant healthy. Bring 'Raspberry Wine' indoors for your added enjoyment

in bouquets. Another great plant for hummingbirds and bees!
Height/spread: 90 cm/60 cm (3 feet/2 feet).

Paeonia lactiflora 'Flame' (Peony 'Flame')

'Flame' peony is a real beauty, with its soft reddish orange flowers that mature to a hot pink with yellow stamens. This peony does best in a rich, well-drained, loamy soil in full sun but will also tolerate some shade. Flowering in early summer, it should be grown with the help of a peony ring for stability. Plant the thick fleshy roots in early fall no more than 5 cm (2 inches) below the soil and mulch for extra winter protection. Please be patient—peonies may take a few years to bloom, but they are well worth the effort! 'Flame' blooms in early summer.
Height/spread: 75 to 100 cm/ 90 cm (30 to 40 inches/36 inches).

Papaver orientale 'Brilliant' (Oriental Poppy 'Brilliant')

Come June, there is nothing like poppy flowers in the perennial garden. 'Brilliant' Oriental poppy's large, vivid, fiery scarlet petals are a great addition to the late spring or early summer flower show. It *prefers* to be grown in an average, well-drained soil in full sun. The thick, coarse, hairy foliage is unsightly and disappears after the plant finishes its bloom, so I always plant another summer-blooming perennial adjacent to it to take its place. Divide the plant in spring as the foliage appears. The seed head of Oriental poppy 'Brilliant' can provide interest and is great in dried flower arrangements.
Height/spread: 75 to 100 cm/ 60 cm (30 to 40 inches/24 inches).

Penstemon barbatus 'Prairie Dusk' (Beardtongue 'Prairie Dusk')

'Prairie Dusk' beardtongue is a North American native wildflower, with gorgeous purple, tubular flowers— great for a midsummer show of colour. 'Prairie Dusk' likes an average, well-drained soil in full sun but will also tolerate light shade. Beardtongues hate wet feet, so freely draining soil is a must! Divide this plant in the spring every few years for the best vigour. 'Prairie Dusk' makes a great cut flower, so bring it indoors for more enjoyment.
Height/spread: 60 cm/30 cm (2 feet/1 foot).

Pervoskia atriplicifolia 'Little Spire' (Russian Sage 'Little Spire')

'Little Spire' Russian sage is much like the award-winning relative 'Blue Spire', only more compact. My complaint with the traditional Russian sage is its aggressiveness, but this is not a problem with 'Little Spire'. It has blue-green foliage, and the delicate, blue fragrant flowers bloom all summer long, making it a great filler plant or used alone in masses. 'Little Spire' prefers a well-drained soil in full sun and really dislikes wet feet in the winter, but is fairly drought tolerant when established. Cut back to about 15 cm (6 inches) in the fall for all new growth the following year, producing the best summer show.
Height/spread: 60 cm/50 cm (24 inches/20 inches).

Phlox paniculata 'David' (Phlox 'David')

'David' summer phlox will add colour and excitement all summer long to any border. The tall, white, extremely fragrant flowers need a rich, evenly moist but well-drained soil for the best show. This will also help to keep powdery mildew away from this already resistant plant. Fertilize 'David' and other summer phlox in spring and early summer with 6-12-12 granular shrub food just before they bloom. Plant shorter flowering perennials in front of the taller varieties like 'David' to help mask the withering lower leaves during their summer show. Divide every three to four years to help keep the clump young and vigorous. 'David' blooms in early summer.
Height/spread: 100 cm/75 cm (40 inches/30 inches).

Pulmonaria × 'Raspberry Splash' (Lungwort 'Raspberry Splash')

This is one of my favourite perennials for the garden border—use this little beauty to brighten the early-spring shade garden. Only reaching a height of 35 cm (14 inches) and spreading to 45 cm (18 inches), 'Raspberry Splash' lungwort should hold a place of importance in the front of the border. 'Raspberry Splash' likes a rich, moist, high-humus soil in part to full shade. The raspberry-pink flower clusters are held high above the brilliant silver, sharply pointed, upwardly growing leaves to add to the colour burst. Remove the dead and tired leaves in early spring for the cleanest appear-ance. As 'Raspberry Splash' blooms in early to late spring, try combining this exciting new perennial with spring bulbs and primroses.
Height/spread: 35 cm/45 cm (14 inches/18 inches).

Rudbeckia fulgida var. *sullivantii* 'Goldsturm' (Gloriosa Daisy 'Goldsturm')

A mass display of *R.* 'Goldsturm' at the Niagara Parks school of horticulture absolutely bowled me over. It seems that many late-season gardens are exploding in *rudbeckia*, and no variety is more colourful or reliable than 'Goldsturm'. This "Black-eyed Susan," considered one of the workhorses of the summer border, produces 7.5 to 10 cm (3 to 4 inch) golden-yellow blooms for over a month (midsummer through early fall) and seed heads that remain throughout the winter. This sturdy plant performs best in moist but well-drained, average to rich soils in full sun or light shade. 'Goldsturm' rarely needs staking and combines nicely with perennial grasses and sedum 'Autumn Joy', no doubt the reason it was recently named Perennial Plant of the Year! Divide every three to four years to help keep this plant young and vigorous.
Height/spread: 60 cm/45 cm (24 inches/18 inches).

Salvia nemorosa × 'May Night' (Perennial Salvia 'May Night')

Salvia 'May Night' is an erect, clump-forming perennial with low grey-green leaves and large spikes of deep indigo-blue flowers throughout the summer. A midsummer bloomer, it was recently named Perennial Plant of the Year. Give it an average, well-drained soil in full sun or light shade and deadhead after the blooms are spent for the best seasonal performance. This plant shows good tolerance to drought. Cut back to the ground each spring and divide only if it outgrows its location. Cut the flowers of 'May Night' and bring indoors combined with other treasures of the garden for even more enjoyment.
Height/spread: 45 cm/60 cm (30 inches/24 inches).

Scabiosa columbaria 'Butterfly Blue' (Pincushion Flower 'Butterfly Blue')

Here is perhaps the most "floriferous" plant in the perennial garden. I rank it in the *top five* of my favourite perennial plants. This is another way of saying that it blooms seemingly forever (actually, from midsummer through late fall). 'Butterfly Blue' has grey-green leaves and a profusion of lacy, lavender-blue flowers, giving the best show when used in groups of three or more at the front of any border. Deadheading will prolong its display and the flowers look great in arrangements and bouquets. It likes an average, well-drained soil in full sun or light shade. Dividing this clump-forming perennial is only necessary if it's outgrowing its location.
Height/spread: 30 to 45 cm/30 cm (12 to 18 inches/12 inches).

Sedum cauticola 'Lidakense'

This hardy, drought-tolerant sedum features starry, glistening, deep pink flowers atop attractive broad blue-green leaves that have a purple blush. It's one of the best perennials for late-season colour that lasts from August to October.
Height/spread: 10 cm/30 cm (4 inches/12 inches).

Sedum × 'Autumn Joy' (Sedum, Stonecrop 'Autumn Joy')

Sedum 'Autumn Joy' may look like broccoli all summer, but watch this

perennial take over the garden in early fall and all through the winter! 'Autumn Joy' likes an average to moist but well-drained soil in full sun or light shade. The 12.5 to 15 cm (5 to 6 inch) salmon pink flowers crown the thick stems in September when most other perennials are looking rather tired. 'Autumn Joy' matures to a beautiful deep coppery red colour. The seed heads provide that extra season of interest all winter long, remaining tall and structured. This trouble-free plant rarely needs staking and can be divided every three to four years to spread the wealth to other parts of the garden. A reliable butterfly magnet!
Height/spread: 45 to 60 cm/30 to 45 cm (18 to 24 inches/12 to 18 inches).

Sidalcea × 'Brilliant' (Prairie Mallow 'Brilliant')

This is a great background plant in the perennial border. Brilliant prairie mallow produces tall racemes of carmine-red funnel-shaped flowers. 'Brilliant' looks like a miniature hollyhock. It prefers to grow in an acid, moist but well-drained soil in sun or light shade. This clump-forming perennial is narrow and upright, great for cutting for your indoor bouquets. Cut back after 'Brilliant' has finished flowering to produce a second flush of flowers. If the plants overgrow their place or start to die out in the centres, lift the clumps in the fall and replant the vigorous sections in amended soil. 'Brilliant' will bloom in mid to late summer.
Height/spread: 75 cm/30 cm (30 inches/12 inches).

Stokesia laevis 'Honeysong Purple' (Stoke's Aster 'Honeysong Purple')

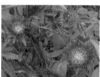

'Honeysong Purple' Stoke's aster has a brilliant, deep purple flower darkening with maturity, highlighting the contrast between the white stamens and the slightly red overtone. It will make a great addition to the front of any late-summer border. This plant does best in well-drained soil and loves full sun but will tolerate light shade. 'Honeysong Purple' makes a great cut flower for your indoor bouquets. It blooms in late summer.
Height/spread: 35 cm/35 cm (14 inches/14 inches).

Tiarella cordifolia 'Iron Butterfly' (Foamflower 'Iron Butterfly')

Foamflower is a long-blooming, low-growing perennial that really performs well in the border of the perennial garden. 'Iron Butterfly' foamflower has the largest and most divided leaves of all the foamflowers and is adorned in the centre with a dramatic black stripe, hence its name. This perennial prefers a moist, humus-rich soil in partial or full shade, but will also perform well in sun if the soil is moist. To add to this early spring show, the bottlebrush-shaped white flowers are lightly fragrant, making this plant a real gem in the front of the early spring garden. Divide 'Iron Butterfly' in the spring only if it outgrows its location. It blooms in early spring through early summer.
Height/spread: 30 cm/30 cm (12 inches/12 inches).

Roses

Hybrid teas

'Mister Lincoln' (Hybrid Tea)

'Mister Lincoln' is a time-honoured favourite hybrid tea that embodies

all the qualities of a classic hybrid tea. This is a stiff-stemmed, sturdy plant bearing dark red blooms that are great for cutting. The leathery dark green foliage is attractive on its own. 'Mister Lincoln' is disease resistant, but requires winterizing in Ontario. It blooms in late June or early summer and repeats in September.
Height/spread: 120 cm/100 cm (48 inches/40 inches).

'Peace' Hybrid Tea

In my opinion, no list of quality hybrid teas would be complete without 'Peace'. Perhaps the most popular garden rose worldwide since World War II, this exceptional plant exceeds the expectations of an experienced rose grower; so it is a "must have" for the amateur! It's a vigorous, shrubby tea rose with glossy green foliage and rounded, fully double, scented, pink-tinged yellow flowers that mature to 15 cm (6 inches) across. It blooms in early summer, repeats in fall and requires winterizing in Ontario.
Height/spread: 160 cm/100 cm (64 inches/40 inches).

Grandiflora roses
the tall show stoppers!

'Queen Elizabeth' (Grandiflora)

This is my dad's favourite rose, so I've paid close attention to this one over the years. I have observed that 'Queen Elizabeth' stands out in the background of the perennial border or rose bed. It is best known for its huge 12 cm (5 inch) soft pink blooms, dark green, leathery foliage and vigorous growth throughout the gardening season. It blooms in early summer, repeats in early fall and requires winterizing in Ontario.
Height/spread: 2 m/100 cm (6 feet/40 inches).

'Tournament of Roses' (Grandiflora)

Viewed from a distance of several metres, 'Tournament of Roses' attracts the eye every time when in bloom. Distinctive bright pink blossoms and buds provide an excellent show and a light spicy fragrance. It blooms in early summer, repeats in early fall and needs to be winterized in Ontario.
Height/spread: 160 cm/80 cm (64 inches/32 inches).

Floribunda roses
loads of colour on compact plants, best planted in a mass or as an enhancement to the perennial border.

'Impatient' (Floribunda)

Not to be confused with the annual flower impatiens, this gorgeous plant blooms and blooms—defying the notion that roses produce colour for only a couple of weeks each year. A stop-sign red with a hint of pink, 'Impatient' gets attention wherever it is planted in the sunny garden. I have grown this variety at the front of my house near the street and found it to be disease resistant and as bug-free as any rose I know. It garners more comments from generous neighbours than any other plant I have put out there. It blooms in early summer, midsummer and early fall. It requires winter protection.
Height/spread: 130 cm/100 cm (52 inches/40 inches).

Climbers
vigorous growth, lots of bloom, a grand entrance!

'Blaze' Climber

I have watched the new introductions of climbing roses come and go for over 25 years and have yet to see one variety that beats 'Blaze' (or 'Blaze Improved') for overall performance and winter hardiness. Large clusters of bright red flowers borne on strong, fast-growing plants characterize this wonderful plant. Plant one on either side of an arbour and within three years you will have a show equal to any that you have seen in a British gardening magazine. 'Blaze' blooms in early summer and repeats in early fall.
Height/spread: 3.5 to 4.5 m/100 cm (10 to 15 feet/40 inches).

'New Dawn' Climber

If you are looking for fragrance and colour, this is your climbing rose. 'New Dawn' produces more pale-pearl double-pink flowers (with a lovely light fragrance) than any variety I have seen. It blooms in early summer and repeats in early fall.
Height/spread: 3.5 m/90 to 120 cm (10 feet/3 to 4 feet).

Shrub roses
extremely winter hardy and low maintenance, and the newer varieties are defying the old notion that shrub roses bloom only once in summer. Look for these favourites!

'Bonica' Shrub Rose

'Bonica' is an outstanding rose for mass planting. The soft, double pink flowers, borne in large clusters, offer an excellent show from any distance. I have found that the secret to maximizing their incredible bloom potential is *not* to prune them, but let them go from year to year. This requires the discipline of a lazy gardener and is not recommended for the rosarian who enjoys fussing with his or her plants. No winterizing is required in zone 6, but 'Bonica' should be winterized in zone 5 and above. This rose blooms in early summer, then intermittently throughout summer with another show in early fall.
Height/spread: 90 cm/90 cm (36 inches/36 inches).

'Champlain' Explorer Rose— Canadian Introduction!

This is an outstanding winter-hardy shrub rose known for its abundant velvety red blooms and strong fragrance. Versatile too—it can be used as a free-standing shrub or as a climber. I recommend that you look over the entire selection of Explorer roses if your goal is to produce a reliable show of colour every summer, without any maintenance other than annual pruning and weeding. The blooms are at their best in early summer. No winterizing is necessary in Ontario except in zone 3 (way north!).
Height/spread: 130 cm/100 cm (52 inches/40 inches).

'Mary Rose'—David Austin

I love this plant for its disease resistance and its perseverance. I planted it in among some hostas, with only five hours of sun in the middle of summer, and still it blooms all season long. It has large, double rose-pink flowers, giving it a classic "rose look." And it's a vigorous grower that establishes itself in a year—an instant rose garden! It blooms in early summer and repeats throughout the summer.
Height/spread: 90 cm/80 cm (3 feet/32 inches).

Annuals

Ageratum (Flossflower)

This easy, fast-growing annual makes a wonderful addition to any border with its soft, brush-like flowers held high above nice green serrated leaves. The blue, pink or white flower clusters are 5 to 10 cm (2 to 4 inches) across and can hold 40 flowers or more. Flossflower is great for attracting butterflies to the front of a border or in containers. Plant this annual in well-drained soil in full sun or light shade, with good air circulation between plants. Regular applications of a balanced fertilizer throughout the season will help to encourage blooms. Regular removal of the spent blooms will help to encourage more flowers. Be careful, this plant can self-sow, leaving unwanted plants for next year. It blooms from June to the first frost.
Height/spread: 30 to 45 cm/45 to 60 cm (12 to 18 inches/18 to 24 inches).

Amaranthus (Amaranth)

Upright and bushy, this annual has multicoloured leaves, ranging from green to red, purple or sometimes bright crimson or maroon. The top coloured leaves arch out like a fountain flowing with colour. Plant amaranth in moist but well-drained, humus-rich soil in full sun. Water freely in the summer to prolong the colour show. Taller varieties may need to be staked. Amaranth often reseeds and self-sows the following year. It blooms June to September.
Height/spread: 45 to 120 cm/30 to 60 cm (18 inches to 4 feet/12 to 24 inches).

Bacopa (Bacopa)

I believe that bacopa will replace alyssum over the next few years as the most popular white (and pink!) annual border plant. Unlike alyssum, which tends to go to seed quickly in the bright sun, bacopa loves any amount of sun and tolerates a half day of shade. With its masses of single white or soft pink flowers it makes a wonderful addition to any

patio pot or hanging basket as an accent with just about any other plants. The roots must be kept cool and moist. It blooms from May 1 through to hard frost.
Height/spread: 5 cm/30 to 40 cm (2 inches/12 to 16 inches).

Begonia (Begonia—fibrous)

This is quite possibly the most versatile annual plant known. Grown both for their flower and for their colourful leaves, begonias are available in almost every colour with single and double flowers and bronze to red leaves. They make a great container plant along with their garden duties. Plant begonias in partial shade, although the bronze and red-leaved varieties will take much more sun. They like a well-drained, humus-rich soil with regular watering and fertilizing. Water when the soil becomes dry and fertilize every ten days to two weeks with 20-20-20. Begonias bloom from May to the first hard frost.
Height/spread: 15 to 60 cm/15 to 60 cm (6 to 24 inches/6 to 24 inches).

Canna × generalis (Canna Lily)

The canna lily has large gladiolus-like spikes of flowers on tall, sturdy stems with large green, bronze or variegated leaves that are tropical in appearance, like banana leaves. The flowers can be 7.5 cm (3 inches) across and come in all colours. Canna lily is great for accents, in containers or in group plantings. There are many new varieties worth looking over! Cannas should be planted in full sun and fertile soil, and watered and fertilized freely throughout the summer. Soil should be warm when planting, so be sure to wait until all threat of frost has passed. The rhizome roots need to be lifted after the frost has blackened the leaves and stored in a frost-free location for the winter.

Remove the stems and leaves, storing only the root. Deadhead regularly to encourage blooms from July to the first frost.
Height/spread: 90 to 200 cm/50 cm (3 to 6 feet/20 inches).

Cleome (Spider Flower)

This unique annual has strongly scented, ball-shaped flowers with a spidery appearance thanks to the long slender filaments that support the flowers, along with pointed seed pods that project beyond the flowers. Colours range from white to pinks and purples, and it's great for backgrounds and cutting. Grow Cleome in light, fertile, preferably sandy soil in full sun. Water and fertilize freely during the summer months. Cleome should stand freely, but may need staking in windy locations. Be warned, Cleome can seed freely and become a pest. It blooms from June to first frost.
Height/spread: 150 cm/45 cm (60 inches/18 inches).

Heliotropium (Heliotrope)

This, along with old-fashioned nicotiana, will add a romantic scent to the garden—a great "late evening mood setter" in my books. Plant this one near the porch swing (unless you have teenagers!). It is also a nice container plant and a favourite annual for the border. It adds the sweet scent of vanilla to the garden and is great for attracting butterflies. These bushy plants flower in shades of purple, lavender and white, with dense flower heads up to 10 cm (4 inches) across. Plant heliotrope in full sun and fertile, moist but well-drained soil. Deadhead to encourage flowering. Water moderately and apply 20-20-20 fertilizer every ten days to two weeks throughout the growing season. A fairly carefree annual, it does not like to be overwatered, as this may lead to problems with

whitefly and mildew. It blooms from June to September.
Height/spread: 30 to 45 cm/45 cm (12 to 18 inches/18 inches).

Impatiens (Impatiens, Busy Lizzie)

This is a continuous blooming annual in almost every colour imaginable, including bi-colours. The single or double flowers are held above the dense soft green foliage. Impatiens produce such an abundance of colour, their show is stunning, brightening up any shady location. Look for new varieties (which flower longer and tolerate more sun) like 'Canadiana' for nonstop colour all summer and 'Fiesta Double' for something compact and colourful! Plant impatiens in shade to partial shade and in fertile, moist but well-drained soil, after all threat of frost has passed. Water moderately and apply 20-20-20 fertilizer every ten days to two weeks during the growing season. Impatiens are exceptionally heavy feeders. They bloom from June to October.
Height/spread: 30 cm/45 cm (12 inches/18 inches).

Ipomoea (Sweet Potato Vine)

This annual makes a fabulous addition to any containers or baskets with its dark red, almost black, uniquely shaped foliage – or choose the bright, plugged-in colour of "lime" or the tri-coloured (white, red and green) variety. This plant will produce a purple flower, although the bloom is not the reason for its growth. Plant in well-drained, humus-rich soil in full sun or partial shade (leaf coloration is best in full sun). Water and fertilize with 20-20-20 during the summer months. Remove the tubers (which are edible) and store in a frost-free location to either eat or replant next season. Sweet Potato Vine blooms in the summer.
Height/Spread: 6 m (19 feet).

Lobelia (Lobelia)

Lobelia is a versatile, low-growing, trailing annual, great for edging, the front of a border, in containers or hanging baskets. The small tubular flowers have a unique fan-shaped lower edge, blooming in colours ranging from white, blue, and purple to pink. Hummingbirds like lobelia. It loves the sun but grows well in partial shade too! Plant in fertile, moist but well-drained soil in full sun or partial shade. To improve flowering, apply 20-20-20 fertilizer every two weeks in spring and early summer, then low nitrogen 10-60-10 every two weeks from midsummer onward. Lobelia blooms from June to October.
Height/spread: 10 to 15 cm/10 to 15 cm (4 to 6 inches/4 to 6 inches).

Nemesia (Nemesia)

Nemesia has many clusters of dainty double-lipped flowers held above the leaves for its summer show. The flowers can be red, yellow, pink, blue, purple, white or a combination of two, usually with yellow throats. It makes a nice addition to a summer border or containers. Plant in fertile, well-drained soil in partial sun for best performance (the east side of a house, out of the hot afternoon sun, is ideal). Water freely to maintain the flower show in summer and deadhead to encourage flowering. Nemesia blooms from July to September.
Height/spread: 18 to 30 cm/10 to 15 cm (7 to 12 inches/4 to 6 inches).

Nicotiana (Flowering Tobacco)

Look for the "old-fashioned" types of *nicotiana* as the new hybrids have had the fragrance bred out of them. All *nicotiana* varieties are colourful, however. Borne in profusion on erect stems, the tubular flowers can be white, red, pink, yellow or green. This is a great plant for massing or as a background plant in a mixed border. Plant in fertile, moist but well-drained soil in full sun or partial shade. Some of the taller varieties may need to be staked in open positions. *Nicotiana* blooms from June to October.
Height/spread: 1.5 m/30 cm (60 inches/12 inches).

Nigella (Love-in-a-Mist)

One of my favourite cut flowers! The showy flower of *nigella* blooms in pink, blue, purple, yellow or white, usually singly or in pairs at the top of the slender stem. The decorative, sometimes inflated seed capsules can be used in dried flower arrangements. These versatile plants can be used in a mixed, informal or annual border. Grow *nigella* in any well-drained soil in full sun. Self-seeding usually occurs, but otherwise this annual is maintenance free and blooms from July to September.
Height/spread: 50 cm/25 cm (20 inches/10 inches).

Pelargonium (Geranium)

The most popular sun-loving annual of all—and for good reason. Modern hybrid zonal geraniums are tough (i.e., wind resistant, moderately frost resistant and almost completely insect free). The ball-shaped flower cluster is borne on strong, slender stems, ranging in colours from white, red, pink and salmon to bi-colours. The green leaves can be ruffled, scalloped and sometimes bi-coloured themselves. Geraniums make a great addition to the front of a border or containers and are attractive used as massing. Look for my two favourite varieties: 'Melody' (pink) and 'Kim' (rose-red). Plant in any well-drained soil in full sun and deadhead spent geranium clusters to a node for a continued summer show. They will bloom from June until frost.
Height/spread: 30 cm/30 cm (12 inches/12 inches).

Petunia (Petunia)

There are two types of petunia most commonly grown by the home gardener: the Grandiflora, with its large, single, ruffled flowers, and the Multiflora, which has smaller but more abundant flowers. Each type blooms in a variety of colours, including bi-colours and doubles. Great for summer bedding, mixed borders and even hanging baskets with the new Surfinias (these bloom earlier and more heavily in my experience than the Wave petunias). The best bedding petunias on the market today are Songbirds ('Bluebird,' 'Cardinal,' etc.)—great for nonstop colour. Plant in any well-drained soil in full sun, with shelter from high winds. Deadhead to prolong flowering. (Note: The stems and flowers are unusually sticky.) Petunias bloom from May through to frost.
Height/spread: 45 cm/90 cm (18 inches/36 inches).

Portulaca (Moss Rose)

Here is a "heat-seeking" plant with colour that looks "plugged in." It features the strongest colours in the annual flower family (next, that is, to gerbera). This spreading red-stemmed annual grows easily, adding a burst of colour to the front of any border. The shimmering rose-like flowers are held above the succulent stems, blooming in red, yellow, orange, purple and white. Moss rose can also be used in containers and hanging planters. Plant in any well-drained, preferably sandy, loam in full sun. It can also be directly seeded to your location. Moss rose is relatively maintenance-free, but can self-seed prolifically. It blooms from June to October. **Height/spread:** 10 to 20 cm/15 cm (4 to 8 inches/6 inches).

Scaevola (Scaevola)

Scaevola is a shrubby trailing annual with clusters of fan-shaped purple-blue flowers borne on leafy stems. The continuous production of flowers provides an interesting show in hanging baskets and containers. Grow scaevola in a moderately fertile, well-drained soil in full sun or light shade. Apply a balanced fertilizer monthly and water regularly during the summer. Scaevola blooms from May to October. **Height/spread:** 50 cm/50 cm (20 inches/20 inches).

Solenostemon (Coleus)

This bushy annual is mostly grown for its vibrant leaf colours which sometimes include two or three colours on the same leaf. (Look for 'Cranberry Salad' for wonderful colour.) The colours available are sometimes enhanced by ruffled or scalloped edges. Small insignificant flowers will appear any time during the summer and should be pinched out to maintain the leaf coloration. It's the perfect addition to the late-season garden (and for cottagers returning home in late summer!). Plant coleus in early summer after threat of frost has passed, in full sun or light shade in humus-rich, moist but well-drained soil. Pinch back in the early stages to encourage bushy growth, and provide a sheltered location in a windy garden. The flowers bloom in summer, but coleus looks its best in August through early October. **Height/spread:** 90 cm/90 cm (3 feet/3 feet).

Verbena (Verbena)

This bushy, spreading annual is one of my favourite container plants for sun. It is also great for an annual border, edging or hanging baskets. During the summer, panicles of flowers sometimes 7.5 cm (3 inches) across appear in white, pink, red, yellow and purple. These flowers can be lightly scented and usually have a white eye. Plant in any well-drained soil in full sun. Water freely and apply a balanced fertilizer monthly during the summer. No other maintenance is needed! Verbena blooms from July to September. **Height/spread:** 45 cm/30 to 50 cm (18 inches/12 to 20 inches).

Zinnia (Zinnia)

Zinnias are grown for their solitary daisy-like single or double flowers. Blooming in almost every colour, they make a great addition to an annual or mixed border. Tall varieties make excellent cut flowers. Some smaller varieties can also be used in containers or window boxes. Plant in any well-drained, fertile soil in full sun. Deadheading should be done regularly to promote repeat flowering from June to frost. **Height/spread:** 60 cm/30 cm (24 inches/12 inches).

Flowering shrubs

Amelanchier canadensis (Downy Serviceberry)

A very hardy, native Ontario flowering shrub that heralds the spring

season with its star-shaped white blossoms in April. This is an aggressive plant that some people consider to grow more like a tree than a shrub. Give this plant lots of room. Berries ripen in fall and are edible (if the birds don't get to them first), and the autumn foliage is a beautiful apricot colour. **Height/spread:** 4 to 5 m/6 to 7 m (12 to 15 feet/20 to 25 feet).

Buddleia davidii (Butterfly Bush)

It is no coincidence that the landscape around the butterfly conservatory in Niagara Falls is dominated by this wonderful, fragrant, flowering shrub. Its signature blossoms of blue, red, pink, white or purple are borne on long stems (well suited to cutting!) from midsummer right through to frost. The very fragrant blossoms really do attract butterflies like no other shrub. In fact, I refer to *buddleia* as the "butterfly magnet." In zone 5, butterfly bush often freezes back to the ground but comes back from the root each spring—in fact, you should cut last year's branches back severely. Treat it as a herbaceous perennial in zone 5 and warmer zones. **Height/spread:** 1.5 to 3 m/1.5 to 3 m (5 to 10 feet/5 to 10 feet).

Hibiscus syriacus (Rose of Sharon)

Here is a flowering shrub that has come a long way since I first got into gardening over 25 years ago. It seems that the hybridizers keep coming up with improvements to this wonderful family of flowering shrubs. More than anything, you have to be impressed with the generous quantity of blooms that seem to explode from the current year's growth in midsummer and just keep coming until mid to late fall. Some of the blossoms on the new cultivars are so large that many people mistake them for the

herbaceous types of hibiscus. Look for these excellent new varieties: 'Aphrodite' with brilliant green leaves showing off the plentiful single, light pink flowers—each with a dark eye; 'White Chiffon', a long-blooming, large single white flowering plant featuring a lacy centre that creates unique anemone-like blooms; 'Minerva', an upright-growing plant with many single lavender-pink and reddish-purple-eyed blooms. Hardy to zone 5 (in a location protected from the northwest wind) and zone 6, where they tolerate northwest wind nicely.
Height/spread: 3.5 m/2 m (10 feet/6 feet).

Hydrangea macrophylla (Snowball Hydrangea)

I have been very impressed with the new varieties of hydrangea introduced over recent years. It seems that they just keep getting better. Look for *H.* 'Bouquet Rose' for beautiful violet to mauve flowers in midsummer. 'Nikko Blue' is an excellent selection if you are looking for a hardy plant (to zone 5) that produces the same snowball-shaped blue flowers that you have seen on hydrangeas in Victoria, B.C. The plants are somewhat smaller, however. *H. macrophylla* like bright sunshine but protection from dry afternoon sun (not a problem if you are irrigating during the heat of an Ontario summer) and will tolerate a half day of shade (though the more shade, the less vigorous the blooming). Prune hydrangea only after flowering and protect the shrubs during the winter by surrounding them with a burlap screen filled with leaves.
Height/spread: 1.5 m/1.5 m (5 feet/5 feet).

Itea virginica (Little Henry Sweetspire)

Gaining in popularity in recent years, this is an excellent choice of shrub if you're looking for a substitute for 'Bridal Wreath' spirea. *Itea* produces beautiful white flower spikes in early to midsummer followed by brilliant reddish-purple fall foliage. It loves the sun but tolerates half a day of shade.
Height/spread: 80 cm/50 cm (32 inches/20 inches).

Potentilla fruticosa (Potentilla, Cinquefoil)

Where sunny hotspots are concerned and where colour all summer long is demanded, the highest recommendation that I can offer in the flowering shrub department is for the potentilla. Long ago it was a favourite in Ontario home landscapes. It has withstood the test of time and at the same time been improved upon to a great degree. The distinct bright yellow, buttercup-shaped flowers have always been its signature. Now you can also choose from some excellent varieties that offer a wider selection of flower colours. Look for 'Abbotswood' white, 'Pink Beauty' pink and 'Red Ace' orange red. Each of these plants blooms in the early summer and continues to bloom all season long. 'Red Ace' grows to two-thirds of the size given below. Always plant in the sun, and prune back hard in the spring.
Height/spread: 100 cm/80 cm (40 inches/32 inches).

Spirea × *bumalda* (Spirea)

Time was, spirea was spirea. You could choose between the white cascading flowers of 'Bridal Wreath' and the flat, umbel-shaped flowers of 'Frobels'. Today in the Weall & Cullen catalogue we offer no fewer than 13 varieties, including the old standbys, and every one of them is worth a look at, for its own reasons.

If you want a flowering shrub that is very colourful and low maintenance, look for *S.* 'Goldflame', a beautiful flowering shrub that produces masses of carmine-red blooms in midsummer—and continues to bloom for three to four weeks. The golden foliage is in itself an attraction, appearing in spring with bright yellow leaves and staying that way reliably (except in the shade) all season long. Spirea prefers sun but tolerates up to three hours of shade daily. Prune back hard in the spring.
Height/spread: 130 cm/130 cm (52 inches/52 inches).

Syringa vulgaris (French Hybrid Lilac)

If you have adequate space in a sunny spot in your landscape to accommodate a mature lilac, there is little doubt in my mind that a French hybrid lilac would make a welcome addition– especially if you are looking for great mid-spring colour (when your eyes are perhaps most in need of it!) and for the unparalleled fragrance of the French hybrids. Look for my favourite varieties 'Agincourt Beauty' (named after my home "village"), with its many single, deep violet blooms and sugary fragrance. 'Katherine Havemeyer' is covered with masses of light pink blooms and glossy green foliage. Or, for something completely different, 'Sensation' has a large cluster of fragrant bicoloured purple and white blossoms. They favour a slightly alkaline soil, so an application of horticultural lime in spring is beneficial. They are tolerant of a wide range of soil conditions. (To learn more about lilacs, visit the Royal Botanical Gardens in Hamilton/Burlington during blooming time in mid-May. The largest collection of lilacs in North America is there for all to see. Bring your camera. Call 905-527-1158 or visit their Web site at www.rbg.ca for more information.)
Height/spread: 3.5 m/3.5 m (10 feet/10 feet).

Viburnum carlesii (Korean Spice Viburnum)

I put this hardy flowering shrub right at the top of my list for fragrance. Truly, nothing beats it. And the flowers seem to arrive early enough in spring to always surprise my otherwise winter-weary sense of smell. While the bloom period is generally only two to three weeks long, that, frankly, is part of the romance of this shrub. Available both as a woody shrub that branches out from the ground and as a standard "dwarf tree," Korean spice viburnum is a winner. It's a good plant for a foundation planting or in a large (half-barrel sized) container.
Height/spread: 2 m/2 m (6 feet/6 feet).

Weigela florida (Wine and Roses Weigela)

Don't let the "florida" part of the name mislead you. Weigela (sometimes called "Wiggle-ya" by the uninitiated) is one of my favourites due to its beautiful foliage, its burst of colour in mid-spring and the long—all summer long, in fact!—flowering season. This alone makes it an exceptional plant. When you consider that weigela is tolerant of most soils (though it doesn't like to sit in water, so avoid wet spots), that it is generally disease- and insect-free and that it maintains a well-groomed shape without a lot of trimming, no matter how you slice it, this is an excellent permanent addition to the shrub border. It does prefer a sunny position. Choose from the entire family of weigelas and you can't go wrong. However, I really like 'Wine and Roses' for the wonderful burgundy foliage, highlighted with rosy pink and white flowers—on the same plant.
Height/spread: 1.2 m/2.5 m (4 feet/8 feet).

Trees

Acer palmatum (Japanese Maple)

It is impossible to imagine Ontario gardeners not having the ability to choose from the many Japanese maple cultivars. Yet, just 20 years ago, most garden centres offered only a couple of named varieties. Why the change? Consumer demand has given garden retailers the incentive to expand their Japanese maple offerings; it is just one more sign that Ontario gardeners are getting much more sophisticated. Choose from Japanese maples that grow aggressively into 4- to 5-m (12- to 15-foot) high "dwarf trees," like 'Bloodgood' (zone 5) and the hardiest of the red Japanese maples, 'Atropurpureum' (zone 4). Others are more suited to the background of the perennial border or located in the foundation planting, like the deeply serrated 'Inabe Shidare' (zone 6), which holds its crimson colour well into the fall. This "collector" plant will grow to 1.9 m (6 feet) tall and equally wide. Plant Japanese maples in a location that is sheltered from northwest winds and prepare the planting hole with generous quantities of finished compost and mulch to prevent drying in the summer.
Height/spread: varies according to cultivar.

Fagus sylvatica (European Beech)

There are so many beautiful beech varieties that are well suited to the Ontario garden that I have seen some garden designers use them to dominate every quadrant of a yard. I understand the attraction. Beech trees reach maturity relatively quickly, are generally insect- and disease-free and hold their leaves later than most deciduous trees (some retain their leaves until the

following spring!). The smooth bark of beech trees is their signature, making them the most popular tree of all for lovers who want to carve their initials into some living organism. The popular 'Purple Fountain' beech grows to 4.5 to 6 m (15 to 20 feet) tall and 3.5 to 4.5 m wide (10 to 15 feet). The summer foliage is deep purple fading to a golden bronze in fall.
Height/spread: varies according to cultivar.

Ginkgo biloba 'Autumn Gold' (Maidenhair Tree or Ginkgo 'Autumn Gold')

You might want to grow a ginkgo in your yard for the story that it tells. Once thought to be extinct, one remaining specimen was "discovered" nearly 300 years ago. By 1730, it was a popular tree with garden designers all over Europe. What makes the story even more incredible is that the ginkgo is widely acknowledged as the oldest "living" tree on earth. Its ancestry goes back more than 150 million years. This is a "specimen" tree that prefers full sun and requires very little pruning. The 'Autumn Gold' is a wonderful selection if you are looking for the added interest that the colourful foliage brings to the yard. Plant only male trees, as the females produce a foul odour when in bloom.
Height/spread: 12 to 15 m/7 m (40 to 50 feet/25 feet).

Picea pungens 'Glauca' (Colorado Blue Spruce 'Glauca')

Providing that you can give this giant specimen of a tree lots of sun, it can grow just about anywhere. Hardy to zone 2, Colorado blue spruce is the perfect "Christmas tree" form (though I wouldn't recommend that you grow it for this purpose). It is symmetrical and pyramidal in form,

and it produces dense branches that are covered in blue-green to silver-blue needles. The intensity of the blue colour varies a great deal from tree to tree (they are *not* grafted, but grown from seed), so select yours personally from the garden centre.
Height/spread: 18 to 20 m/6 to 9 m (60 to 70 feet/20 to 30 feet).

Pinus strobus (White Pine)

Native to Ontario, this is our official provincial tree. That may be reason enough to grow a white pine, except that it is best suited to rural conditions, as it is not very tolerant of air pollution. You can't beat it for its soft green texture and feel, its robust growth habit and hardiness. If you wish to see your white pine mature into a relatively symmetrical shape, plant it out of prevailing westerly winds. This huge evergreen is truly a specimen that requires lots of space.
Height/spread: 20 m/6 to 9 m (70 feet/20 to 30 feet).

Pyrus calleryana 'Aristocrat' (Ornamental Pear 'Aristocrat')

'Aristocrat' is a great ornamental pear, but with a faster growing habit than 'Chanticleer'. Blessed with all the positive attributes of the best ornamental pear, 'Aristocrat' offers an abundance of white flowers in mid-spring as well.
Height/spread: 9 to 12 m/6 to 9 m (30 to 40 feet/20 to 30 feet).

Pyrus calleryana 'Chanticleer' (Ornamental Pear 'Chanticleer')

Here is a handsome tree that surpasses all others in the "formal, good looks" department. A neighbour of mine has three of these lining one side of his front yard and every time I walk by I admire them. Ornamental pears look like other fruit-bearing pears, with their glossy leaves, beautiful creamy white flowers in May and spade (as in the ace of spades) shape. This tree does not need pruning, is relatively free of diseases and pests (though fireblight can be a problem in some areas) and tolerates somewhat heavy soils. The glossy green foliage all summer long is one of its trademarks; it displays bright red foliage in the fall.
Height/spread: 6 to 9 m/3.5 to 4.5 m (20 to 30 feet/10 to 15 feet).

Quercus robur 'Fastigiata' (Pyramidal English Oak 'Fastigiata')

If you are looking for a tall, permanent tree that will fit into a small space, this may be the tree for you. I love just about any oak, but the pyramidal English oak is truly one of my favourites. It produces dark green leaves late in spring, which turn copper in fall and remain on the plant (in most cases) right through the winter. The "old" leaves drop when the new leaves are produced in spring, qualifying it as a "deciduous evergreen." It is insect and disease resistant.
Height/spread: 12 to 15 m/6 to 9 m (40 to 50 feet/20 to 30 feet).

Syringa reticulata 'Ivory Silk' (Japanese Tree Lilac 'Ivory Silk')

This is a very popular "dwarf" flowering tree throughout much of North America and for some very good reasons. Its compact, oval form lends itself to many sites where space is limited. 'Ivory Silk' has large clusters of creamy white flowers in late spring (after French hybrid lilacs have finished blossoming). I have always been impressed by the length of the blossoming period—often more than three weeks! With bright green, glossy foliage throughout the season, the only thing this tree doesn't seem to have going for it is fragrance. 'Ivory Silk' was developed by Ontario's own Sheridan Nurseries and prefers sun.
Height/spread: 6 to 9 m/6 to 9 m (20 to 30 feet/20 to 30 feet).

Tsuga canadensis (Canadian Hemlock)

This is another native plant that will mature into a giant—although this beauty lends itself to pruning and tolerates substantial shade. I have seen native hemlock grown as a screen (not a hedge) that provides excellent privacy. Plant young trees that are no more than 2 m (6 feet) high, as the larger specimens do not transplant well. Hemlock has a graceful pyramidal form with short, soft needles.
Height/spread: 18 to 20 m/4 to 6 m (60 to 70 feet/12 to 20 feet).

Appendix I

Ontario Zone Map

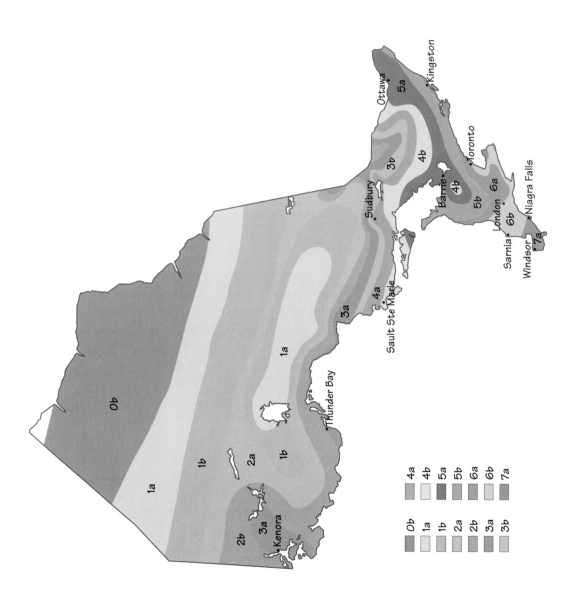

Appendix II

Frost-Free Days and Annual Precipitation for Ontario Cities*

The cities listed below were chosen based on location in the province, population and availability of climate data. Please check the city or town closest to you.

CITY	LAST SPRING FROST	FIRST FALL FROST	AVERAGE ANNUAL RAINFALL IN MM	AVERAGE ANNUAL TOTAL PRECIPITATION IN MM**
Atikokan	June 14	Sept. 3	580.7	762.9
Bancroft	May 25	Sept. 18	709.5	905.1
Barrie	May 25	Sept. 18	n/a	n/a
Belleville	May 1	Oct. 10	701.5	852.3
Brampton	May 17	Sept. 30	n/a	n/a
Brantford	May 18	Oct. 7	740.3	854.7
Brockville	May 9	Oct. 4	773.8	978.7
Cambridge	May 10	Oct. 1	759.7	886.8
Chapleau	June 5	Sept. 6	n/a	n/a
Chatham	Apr. 30	Oct. 22	n/a	n/a
Cobourg	May 1	Oct.1	n/a	n/a
Cochrane	June 14	Aug. 28	603.9	920.1
Collingwood	May 15	Oct. 12	n/a	n/a
Cornwall	May 6	Oct. 6	753.3	962.1
Dryden	May 17	Sept. 20	516.3	685.4
Elliot Lake	May 20	Sept. 24	n/a	n/a
Fort Erie	May 4	Oct. 18	844.1	1016.5
Fort Frances	May 23	Sept. 20	580.1	729.6
Geraldton	June 17	Aug. 24	n/a	n/a
Goderich	May 9	Oct. 25	n/a	n/a
Gore Bay	May 13	Oct. 11	602.3	789.2
Grimsby	Apr. 25	Oct. 27	739.2	880.3
Haliburton	May 28	Sept. 19	730.2	983.1
Hamilton	May 4	Oct. 13	743.3	890.4
Hanover	May 24	Sept. 25	n/a	n/a
Huntsville	May 17	Oct. 3	718.2	992.9
Kapuskasing	May 10	Sept. 2	557.7	861.0
Kenora	May 17	Sept. 27	472.7	632.5
Kingston	May 1	Oct. 11	791.4	963.9
Kirkland Lake	May 30	Sept. 14	587.4	875.7
Kitchener/Waterloo	May 10	Oct. 9	768.2 (Waterloo)	928.5 (Waterloo)
Leamington	Apr. 24	Oct. 28	n/a	n/a
Lindsay	May 11	Sept. 28	666.9	855.6
London	May 10	Oct. 5	778.8	955.1
Midland	May 2	Oct. 11	712.3	1063.5
Moosonee	June 19	Aug. 29	499.8	700.1
Muskoka	May 26	Sept. 17	766.8	1054.0

CITY	LAST SPRING FROST	FIRST FALL FROST	AVERAGE ANNUAL RAINFALL IN MM	AVERAGE ANNUAL TOTAL PRECIPITATION IN MM**
New Liskeard	June 2	Sept. 10	n/a	n/a
Newmarket	May 12	Oct. 2	n/a	n/a
Niagara Falls	May 3	Oct. 23	789.4	953.1
North Bay	May 19	Sept. 24	735.8	974.2
Oakville	May 2	Oct. 12	n/a	n/a
Orangeville	May 29	Sept. 21	707.0	875.4
Orillia	May 18	Sept. 26	732.9	1005.4
Oshawa	May 1	Oct. 10	754.7	880.3
Ottawa	May 7	Oct. 2	700.5	869.5
Owen Sound	May 12	Oct. 15	748.9	1087.6
Parry Sound	May 17	Sept. 28	n/a	n/a
Petawawa	May 27	Sept. 15	611.1	813.7
Peterborough	May 20	Sept. 20	665.5	828.8
Picton	Apr. 27	Oct. 18	744.5	946.3
Port Colborne	Apr. 11	Oct. 21	825.3	993.8
Red Lake	May 23	Sept. 20	455.4	633.8
Richmond Hill	May 11	Oct. 6	689.0	847.4
Sarnia	May 6	Oct. 15	711.1	824.7
Sault Ste. Marie	May 24	Sept. 29	633.0	905.9
Smith Falls	May 5	Sept. 27	n/a	n/a
St. Catharines	Apr. 28	Oct. 18	n/a	n/a
St. Thomas	May 14	Oct. 4	n/a	n/a
Stratford	May 14	Oct. 3	796.3	1050.6
Sudbury	May 18	Sept. 24	635.8	871.8
Terrace Bay	June 9	Sept. 9	n/a	n/a
Thunder Bay	May 30	Sept. 12	546.8	703.5
Timmins	June 4	Sept. 4	580.6	873.4
Tobermory	May 14	Oct. 11	n/a	n/a
Toronto	May 8	Oct. 5	664.7	780.8
Wallaceburg	Apr. 26	Oct. 16	n/a	n/a
Wawa	June 3	Sept. 12	n/a	n/a
White River	June 19	Aug. 15	n/a	n/a
Wiarton	May 17	Oct. 6	717.1	999.5
Windsor	Apr. 26	Oct. 21	787.8	901.6
Woodstock	May 16	Oct. 2	806.5	932.0

* These statistics are from Environment Canada/Meteorological Service of Canada.

Frost-free dates were last calculated by Environment Canada in 1983. Statistics suggest that across Canada, average temperatures have been rising, giving all cities more frost-free days. Use the dates provided above as guidelines only. Precipitation rates are from the 2001 database.

**Total precipitation figures include snowfall.

Appendix III

Gardening Web Sites

If there's one thing I've discovered, it's that gardeners use the Web! My own site, www.markcullen.com, receives thousands of hits a month. I imagine that gardeners may enjoy their time on the Net the most between October and March, when they are forced out of their gardens by inclement weather. And the Web is a great resource—there is a wealth of information and opinion out there and plenty of Web guides that navigate this territory for the surfer. It's also a good place to "chat" with other gardeners, swapping ideas and sharing experiences. Here are a few of the Web sites that I have found interesting (including my own!).

www.markcullen.com

Check out my Web site, where you can join one of our many garden forums to exchange ideas with other gardeners, get updates on my public speaking engagements and radio and television schedule or shop for garden products. You can also browse my extensive gardening library to find information on plants, soil, gardening techniques and pest and disease control.

www.gardentimeonline.com   www.gardencrazy.com
www.gardenguides.com   www.gardennet.com
www.gardeninglaunchpad.com   www.plantideas.com
www.gardenersnet.com   www.Icangarden.com

These sites, many based in the United States, help surfers navigate the extraordinary quantity of information and services available on the Web. Most provide plant and gardening information and links to other gardening sites and garden centres. Many host gardening forums and seed exchanges. Some can direct you to photo galleries and virtual garden tours.

www.gardenweb.com

This general gardening site features links to plant and seed exchanges, discussion forums and the Hortiplex database. While the database doesn't give plant descriptions, it does provide links to information on and photos of specific plants provided by the United States Department of Agriculture and other data banks. It is also a great resource if you know the common name of a plant but not its botanical name, or vice versa. If you read that "heuchera" is a lovely flower, you can quickly find out that "coral bells" is what you are after!

www.garden.org

This Web site, run by the nonprofit National Gardening Association (out of the United States), features a host of articles on just about every gardening topic. It also runs the Web site kidsgardening.com, which provides resources for parents and teachers on gardening activities for children. The site offers how-to projects, a message board, a newsletter, a seed swap, a gardening dictionary and an events calendar.

www.hort.net

This Web site has an impressive photo gallery of over 2,100 images of specific plants. It also has a variety of interesting articles on plants, gardening and other horticultural issues. Interestingly, it is designed, hosted and managed by Mallorn computing—a horticultural software company.

www.hgtv.ca

If you enjoy getting gardening ideas, information and inspiration while relaxing in front of the TV, this site will guide you through the numerous wonderful gardening shows that HGTV has to offer.

www.gardeninglife.ca
www.canadiangarden.com

These Web sites of *Gardening Life* magazine and *Canadian Garden* magazine give you information about the current issues and subscriptions.

www.ontariogardener.com

This is the Web site for *Ontario Gardener* magazine where you can check out articles and find out more about the magazine.

www.wildflowermag.com

This site provides information about *Wild Flower* magazine and a generous list of links to other native plant resources.

www.usda.gov/news/garden.htm

This site, run by the United States Department of Agriculture, has a wonderful section called Home Gardening. It covers a host of topics and links you to information provided by a number of horticultural and agricultural programs at universities and colleges and to other gardening Web sites.

www.gov.on.ca/OMAFRA

This site is the Ontario Ministry of Agriculture's Web site. It is focused primarily on providing agricultural information and statistics, but if you need help identifying pests or finding solutions to pest problems, it has a section that provides descriptions and photos of diseases of various fruits and vegetables, with suggestions for prevention and treatment.

www.mnr.gov.on.ca/MNR/nhic/nhic.html

This Ontario Ministry of Natural Resources, Natural Heritage Information Centre site has information about rare and endangered Ontario native plants.

www.ene.gov.on.ca

The Ontario Ministry of the Environment Web site has a fact sheet available about chemical-free gardening and a list of other government publications available on the Web on topics such as pesticide use, composting and grass clippings.

www.interlog.com/~rooftop

This is the site of the Rooftop Garden Resource Group, which was formed to encourage and support rooftop gardening in Toronto. The site offers information about and photos of rooftop gardens (including rooftop vegetable gardens) and invites questions from any interested rooftop gardener.

www.rbg.ca

The Web site of the Royal Botanical Gardens in Hamilton has information about the gardens and their public lectures and other programs, as well as information about native orchids of Canada and rare Ontario plants, among other topics.

www.evergreen.ca

Evergreen is a national charitable foundation that works towards bringing nature and communities together by creating greener schools, communities and homes. The Web site has information about grants and resources for and locations of community naturalization and greening projects, as well as a resource list of native plant nurseries.

www.goc.com

Canadian Organic Growers operates this useful site, which provides information, discussion forums, event updates, newsletters and publications and links to the sites of other organic-gardening organizations.

www.ontarionature.org

This Web site of the Federation of Ontario Naturalists features articles and information about conservation and restoration efforts in Ontario. It also offers an "Ask the Naturalist" service, where you can post your question to a naturalist. The Nature Network provides newsletters and information on the seven ecological regions of Ontario. The Conservation tab features a section on "natural invaders"—invasive species to avoid planting.

www.nanps.org

The Web site of the North American Native Plant Society features articles, plant information, photos, a seed exchange and a list of native plant sources.

www.pfaf.org

Plants for a Future is a British environmental group focusing on plant uses (medicinal, culinary, etc.). They have a database of over 7,000 plants with detailed information and descriptions.

www.organicallyspeaking.net

This United States–based e-newsletter provides a wealth of information about organic gardening and environmental issues. It also offers a selection of publications on various organic-gardening topics and links to other sites.

www.wildflowerfarm.com

This wonderfully helpful Web site is provided by the folks at Wildflower Farm outside the village of Schomberg, Ontario. It provides lists of their plant inventory, as well as information about wildflower and meadow gardening.

www.sweetgrassgardens.com

North America's first native-owned and -operated native plant nursery is "diligently working to preserve, restore and maintain the pre-European plant species indigenous to North America." The Web site provides lists of plants available from the nursery and information about the nursery, including directions and a map.

www.shareagfoundation.org

Visit this Web site to find out more about this charitable organization that assists impoverished communities in developing countries by helping them establish agricultural projects.

Photo Credits

Colour Insert

Colour insert photographs located between page 112 and page 113 © Andrew Leyerle.

The following people and organizations kindly allowed their gardens to be photographed for the colour insert. They are, in order of photo appearance:

Wayne Gibson, Toronto, Ontario
The Growth Group, Toronto, Ontario
Brenda Simmons and Peter Chisholm, 6 Oneida Avenue, Algonquin Island, Toronto, Ontario
Mark Cullen, Toronto, Ontario
Dianne Dietrich, Toronto, Ontario
Dianne Dietrich, Toronto, Ontario
Inga Wood, Coldwater, Ontario
Dianne Dietrich, Toronto, Ontario
Malle and Peter Nagy, East Toronto, Ontario
Linda Keary and Stephen Moreland, Orillia, Ontario
Inga Wood, Coldwater, Ontario
Inga Wood, Coldwater, Ontario
Brenda Simmons and Peter Chisholm, 6 Oneida Avenue, Algonquin Island, Toronto, Ontario
Jim French, Stoney Lake, Ontario
Yvonne Cunningham, 959 Book Road West, Ancaster, Ontario
www.wildflowerfarm.com. 868-GRO-WILD
Dianne Dietrich, Toronto, Ontario
Barbara and Michael Edgecombe, Lake Muskoka, Ontario
Mary Lou, owner of the popular Toronto Beaches clothing store, Hello May Lou
Barbara and Michael Edgecombe, Lake Muskoka, Ontario
Walt and Marlene Bulas, West Street North, Orillia, Ontario
David Lee and Peggy Karfilis, 822 Palmerston Avenue, Toronto, Ontario
Linda Shaw, Ancaster, Ontario
Jim French, Stoney Lake, Ontario

Mark's 100 Favourite Plants for Ontario

Photos in Mark's 100 Favourite Plants for Ontario, pp. 209–223, courtesy of Weall & Cullen Garden Centres, with the exception of the following:

p. 209 *Anemone tomentosa* 'Robustissima' and *Astilbe* 'White Wings': Artplus Group
p. 210 *Campanula glomerata* 'Superba,' *Ceratostigma plumbaginoides*, and *Corydalis flexuosa* 'China Blue': Walter's Gardens Inc.
p. 211 *Echinacea purpurea* 'Rubinstern' and *Eupatorium rugosum* 'Chocolate': Walter's Gardens Inc.
p. 212 *Heuchera* x 'Amber Waves': Walter's Gardens Inc.
p. 213 *Leucanthemum x superbum* 'Becky,' *Monarda didyma* 'Petite Delight,' and *Monarda didyma* 'Raspberry Wine': Walter's Gardens Inc.
p. 215 *Salvia nemorosa* x 'May Night': Walter's Gardens Inc.

Index

A

acid-loving plants, 135
air exchange, 191
air pollution, 55
alkaline-loving plants, 135
All Seasons Gardener (Cullen),
    61, 64
alpine plants, 57
Alpine strawberries, 93
amaranth (*Amaranthus*), 217
animals. *See* wildlife
anise hyssop 'Blue Fortune'
    (*A. foeniculum* 'Blue
    Fortune'), 209
annuals
    bloom time, 16
    cold-tolerant, 58–59
    container gardening, 33
    fall blooms, 16
    favourites, 206–207, 217–220
    half-hardy, 58–59
    hardy, 59
    in northern gardens, 59–60
    perennials as, 60
    pinching back, 151
    plant height and scale, 35–36
    planting, 148–151
    shade, 10
    spring/early blooming, 16
    super-hardy, 58
antidessiccant, 62
arid areas, 55
arugula, 93, 103
asparagus, 87, 115–116
astilbe 'Flamingo' (A. x arendsii
    'Flamingo'), 209
astilbe 'White Wings' (A. 'White
    Wings'), 209

B

baby's breath (*G. elegans*), 59
bachelor's button (*C. cyanus*), 59
bacopa (*Bacopa*), 217–218
bark, 193
Bartholomew, Mel, 87, 88
basil, 93, 120

beans, snap. *See* snap beans
bearberry cotoneaster, 58
beardtongue 'Prairie Dusk'
    (*P. barbatus* 'Prairie
    Dusk'), 214
bed preparation, 161–163
bedding plants. *See* annuals
bee balm 'Petite Delight'
    (*M. didyma* 'Petite
    Delight'), 213
bee balm 'Raspberry Wine'
    (*M. didyma* 'Raspberry
    Wine'), 213–214
beet (*B. vulgaris*), 101, 103
begonia, fibrous (*Begonia*), 218
Belgian chicory, 105
"Benefits of Growing Native
    Plants," 46
big bluestem (*A. gerardii*), 50
big gardens, 24–28
birch (*Betula*), 158
black-eyed Susan (*R. fulgida*),
    43, 50
black plastic, 202
bloodmeal, 78, 139, 157
bloom time, 14–16
blue leadwort (*C. plum
    baginoides*), 210
blueberries (*Vaccinium*), 116
bog gardens, 73–74
bog plants, 74
bok choy, 110
bonemeal, 139
boneset 'Chocolate'
    (*E. rugosum* 'Chocolate'), 211
borders, 25–27
boron, 133
bottle gentian (*G. andrewsii*), 50
boxwood, 62
broccoli, 96, 101, 104
Brussels sprouts, 101
bugbane 'Brunette' (*C. ramosa*
    'Brunette'), 210
bulbs
    bloodmeal, 78
    foliage, 157
    hardy, 58
    naturalization, 156

overwintering, 156
planting, 154–156
predators, 157
wildlife protection, 78
busy Lizzie. *See* impatiens
    (*Impatiens*)
butterfly bush (*B. davidii*), 220
butterfly flower (*A. tuberosa*), 209
butterfly weed (*A. tuberosa*), 50

C

cabbage, 93, 99, 101, 110
calcium, 131, 132
California poppy
    (*E. californica*), 59
Canada anemone
    (*A. canadensis*), 50
Canada bluegrass (*P.
    compressa*), 76
Canada lily (*L. canadense*), 50
Canadian Certified
    Horticultural Technician
    (CCHT), 148
Canadian hemlock
    (*T. canadensis*), 223
Canadian Landscape and
    Nursery Certification
    Program, 148
Canadian Nursery Trades
    Association, 148
Canadian Shield, 67
canna lily (*C. x generalis*), 218
canoe birch (*B. papyrifera*),
    13, 67
cardinal flower (*L. cardinalis*), 50
carrot (*D. carota sativa*), 93,
    96, 101, 104
catchment basins, 169
cauliflower, 101
cedar mulch, 195
chewings fescue (*F. rubra var.
    commutata*), 76
chicory (*Cichorium*), 105
Chinese parsley, 122
chives, 93, 120–121
chlorine, 133
cilantro, 121